W9-BQZ-335

UNFAIR COMPETITION

UNFAIR COMPETITION
The Profits of Nonprofits

James T. Bennett
Thomas J. DiLorenzo

HAMILTON PRESS
Lanham • New York • London

Copyright © 1989 by

James T. Bennett and Thomas J. DiLorenzo

Hamilton Press

4720 Boston Way
Lanham, MD 20706

3 Henrietta Street
London WC2E 8LU England

Printed in the United States of America

British Cataloging in Publication Information Available

Library of Congress Cataloging-in-Publication Data

Bennett, James T.
Unfair competition : the profits of nonprofits / James T. Bennett, Thomas J. DiLorenzo
p. cm.
Includes bibliographies and index.
1. Corporations, Nonprofit—United States. 2. Government business
enterprises—United States. 3. Competition, Unfair—United States.
1. DiLorenzo, Thomas J. II. Title
HD2769.2.U6B46   1989
338.6'048'0973—dc 19   88–23600 CIP
ISBN 0–8191–7180–8 (alk. paper)
ISBN 0–8191–7181–6 (pbk. : alk. paper)

All Hamilton Press are produced on acid-free paper.
The paper used in this publication meets the minimum requirements of American
National Standard for Information Sciences—Permanence of Paper for Printed Library
Materials, ANSI Z39.48–1984.

Hamilton Press

Contents

Tables

Preface

To all appearances, government is doing everything possible to promote the development and expansion of the small business sector in the United States. At the federal level, for example, the Small Business Administration (SBA) acts as "advocate" for small businesses, and the White House has sponsored conferences on small business problems. Many state governments have established agencies that are similar to the SBA, and their governors have also sponsored conferences to enhance an understanding of the concerns of entrepreneurs and to promote statewide economic development. At the local level, chambers of commerce and business and professional organizations are widely perceived as closely tied to government officials who are attuned to and concerned about small business issues.

But appearances can be deceiving. While politicians publicly praise the contributions small businesses have made to economic progress, government is competing unfairly with small firms, both directly as a producer and a provider of services and indirectly by granting tax exemptions and giving taxpayer subsidies to profit-making "nonprofit" organizations. Not infrequently, the competition from government enterprises and tax-exempt nonprofit organizations is so intense and so biased that many private firms are driven from the marketplace; others struggle to survive. Competition from the commercial nonprofit sector also discourages the formation of new firms, which would provide employment and stimulate economic growth.

Commercial nonprofit competition with small businesses is endemic and expanding rapidly. Local governments, for example, are providing large numbers of health and recreation facilities (e.g., health clubs, skating rinks, swimming pools); lending video cassettes through public libraries; and operating parking lots and garages, refuse collection, health services, and ambulance services. State employees build and repair roads, maintain and repair vehicles, prepare and serve food, clean buildings, and engage in a wide range of social and educational services in direct competition with private firms. The federal government operates hundreds of printing plants, maintains and repairs vehicles and ships, sells subsidized clothing and food to military personnel, and engages in myriad activities that are properly the province of the private sector.

Private firms are at a decided disadvantage in this competition. Nonprofit enterprises pay no taxes and borrow at preferred rates of interest because state and local governments and their affiliated entities are tax exempt. Nonprofits often receive low-interest, federally guaranteed loans and are not required to post performance bonds. They are generally exempt from the regulations that impose enormous costs on private firms through compliance and paperwork. Unlike private businesses, they often pay no rent on the buildings they occupy, and they frequently receive direct subsidies from taxpayers. Unsatisfied customers find it difficult, if not impossible, to obtain legal redress because nonprofit entities are often protected from litigation. Even on the occasions when a suit can be brought against a nonprofit, the plaintiff faces a process that is often prohibitively expensive. The decisive advantages enjoyed by commercial nonprofit enterprises enable them to charge much lower prices and user fees than private firms, many of which lose their competitive edge and find it difficult to survive.

Small business is a critical part of the national economy. In recent years, it has been responsible for most of the new jobs created, as traditional "smoke stack" industries have declined. Consequently, public policies that discourage the formation of new small businesses and threaten existing ones adversely affect economic growth and development. Furthermore, even though theoretically many nonprofit firms provide benefits to lower-income and other disadvantaged individuals, in reality their clientele is frequently the affluent. Many of the nation's YMCAs, for example, are located in affluent neighborhoods and serve a wealthy constituency. The same is true for hundreds of public park and recreation districts that are located in the country's wealthiest suburbs. The less affluent lose out in this arrangement. Not only are they denied access to these "nonprofit" facilities, but they also have to pay for them through their taxes. The system is inequitable as well as inefficient.

When commercial, nonprofit enterprises displace small businesses, resources are allocated more by the whims of political authorities—those who direct government enterprises and grant advantages to "nonprofit" firms—and less by consumers. A private business that does not tailor its product to meet consumers' tastes will not long survive, but taxpayer subsidies may permit commercial nonprofit enterprises to thrive regardless of the quality of their services.

The nature and consequences of nonprofit competition with small private firms is crucial to economic growth and development, yet it is neither fully understood nor appreciated by policy makers, members of the media, or the general public. An in-depth analysis of these issues is urgently needed; this book is a step toward filling this void.

Many individuals have encouraged and assisted us in this research. Allen D. Greif introduced us to the topic and its significance and provided both information and inspiration. Others who have aided our work include Joseph O'Neil, Kenton Pattie, Wayne Smith, and John McCarthy. Stacey Tomlins and John Blundell of the Institute for Humane Studies at George Mason University were especially helpful at the early stages of this project. Ken Chilton and Murray Weidenbaum of the Center for the Study of American Business at Washington University in St. Louis provided many useful comments and insights. We are indebted to Murray Weidenbaum for granting DiLorenzo a John M. Olin visiting professorship at the Center during the year in which this book was written; the scholarly atmosphere there greatly facilitated this research. Marianne Keddington edited the manuscript, and research assistance was provided by Thomas Crandall, Daniel Craig, Donna Cole, Richard Cook, Jane Cashett, Joe O'Dwyer, and Todd Howard.

We are also most grateful to the John M. Olin Foundation, the J.M. Foundation, the Earhart Foundation, and the Sarah Scaife Foundation. These organizations have long and patiently supported our research efforts. We, of course, take full responsibility for any errors.

I.

Unfair Competition: Issues and Implications

A sense of "fairness" or "equity" is instilled in everyone at an early age. It is difficult to discuss fairness in purely abstract terms, but an essential element is that equals should be treated alike. Fairness requires that the same rules and regulations govern all individuals, organizations, and groups that are engaged in the same activities. The notion of equal opportunity can be applied to every social, political, and economic situation. In the American system of justice, the Fourteenth Amendment to the Constitution has explicitly mandated equal opportunity, guaranteeing to every member of society "the equal protection of the laws."

This book investigates unfair competition. When two types of organizations engaged in identical commercial activities are treated differently under the law, there is unfair competition. This condition is particularly evident in nonprofit organizations that operate under different rules and regulations than private, profit-seeking firms. Government has granted nonprofits special privileges that give them significant advantages in the marketplace. They are exempt from federal, state, and local taxation and from many regulations; they receive preferential postal rates and other subsidies; and they often have preference in obtaining government grants and contracts. These exemptions and privileges reduce the production costs for nonprofits and give them an edge over their private competitors.

Unfair competition by nonprofits is not a new phenomenon. As early as 1874 the Metropolitan Museum of Art in New York City retained a professional to photograph items in its collections so that

1

the prints could be sold to the public; the museum established its first sales shop in 1908.[1] This foray into commercial activity appeared to be harmless at the time and elicited little comment. For decades, no one was concerned about the commercial activities of nonprofits. First of all, the nonprofit sector was small; second, the commercial activities of nonprofits was limited in scope; and third, as long as taxes were low and there were few regulations, the privileges enjoyed by nonprofits did not give them a decisive advantage over for-profits. Unfair competition did not appear as a public policy issue until the late 1940s, when Mueller Macaroni was donated to New York University and became a tax-exempt, nonprofit entity. In 1950, Congress passed the Unrelated Business Income tax, which in some cases required nonprofits to pay federal taxes on income obtained from activities unrelated to the reason they received tax exemption.

During the 1960s and 1970s, Great Society programs encouraged the rapid expansion of the nonprofit sector. Many of these programs were to be carried out through a public-private sector partnership in which the public sector funded programs carried out by nonprofit organizations. At the same time, regulatory legislation proliferated at all government levels, greatly increasing compliance costs for private firms; nonprofits were frequently exempted from these regulations. During the late 1970s, budget exigencies began to reduce public sector support of nonprofits; in response, these organizations, now far more numerous, turned more to commercial activities as an alternative source of revenue.

Because of their special privileges, nonprofits can aggressively compete with for-profits. For-profits have been penalized even further to the extent that they (along with taxpayers generally) have borne the cost of the subsidies in the form of higher taxes and postal rates. In many cases, existing profit-seeking firms have been driven from the market or have suffered economic losses, and new firms have been discouraged from entering markets in which nonprofits operate. Small firms have been particularly affected.[2] And because small firms are the primary sources of both new jobs and innovations in the U.S. economy, unfair competition from nonprofits has slowed economic growth and technical change and has reduced economic opportunities.[3] Moreover, nonprofit organizations are much less efficient than for-profit firms in producing goods and services. The controls on their managers and competitive pressures from the marketplace are so much weaker than they are for profit-seeking firms that when nonprofits replace for-profits productivity declines and more resources must be used to produce the same quantity of goods and services. Unfair competition has far-reaching, negative consequences.

Nonprofit organizations have existed for a long time in this country, and most of them perform socially useful services. Although many believe that nonprofits are charities devoted to aiding the poor, the hungry, the unemployed, and the less fortunate in society, only about 10 percent of all nonprofits have charitable objectives. The vast majority are religious, educational, research, and scientific organizations or unions and business associations. We are not concerned in this book with nonprofit status *per se* or with the special privileges granted to these organizations. Our concern is the *abuse* of nonprofit status by commercial "nonprofit" businesses. We have found that the rationales used to justify nonprofit status generally cannot be applied to the *commercial* activities of nonprofits.

Furthermore, the issue is not competition *per se*, but unfair competition. Whenever a nonprofit produces goods and services in competition with for-profits, simple equity demands that the nonprofit be subject to the same tax laws, pay the same postal rates, and be governed by the same regulations as its profit-seeking counterparts. In short, if a nonprofit wants to operate a commercial enterprise, it should set up a for-profit subsidiary.

Our study is presented in seven chapters. Chapter 2 notes the distinguishing characteristics of commercial nonprofit organizations, specifies the special privileges that permit them to engage in unfair competition, and attempts to gauge the size and scope of the commercial nonprofit sector. At best, information on nonprofits and their business activities are fragmentary and incomplete; data have not been systematically collected for this sector of the economy, despite its growing size and importance. The evidence indicates, however, that roughly 1.2 million nonprofits currently operate in the U.S., constituting about 5 percent of all private organizations. Nonprofits employ millions of workers, produce close to 10 percent of the nation's output, and had expenditures approaching a quarter of a trillion dollars in 1985. Employment and output of the nonprofit sector is growing more rapidly than the economy as a whole. Public enterprises also enjoy special privileges in the marketplace and produce goods and services in competition with for-profit firms. Thus, the public sector also engages in unfair competition. Hundreds of thousands of public employees are currently engaged in commercial activities at all levels of government.

The three primary rationales for nonprofit organizations (thin markets, market failure, and public goods) are examined in chapter 2 to show that they cannot be applied to the commercial activities of nonprofit organizations. The Unrelated Business Income tax, passed more than three decades ago to eliminate unfair competition, is vague and court interpretations of its provisions have been whimsical, if not contradictory. Enforcement has been lax, and the law has become riddled with exceptions. There is evidence of widespread concern about unfair competition in the small business community. At least forty-two state legislatures have responded by passing resolutions regarding unfair competition and its adverse effects on small firms.

In chapter 3, attention is given to the incentive structures within nonprofit organizations, how these incentives differ from those faced by owners and managers of for-profit firms, and how incentives affect nonprofit operations. Directors and managers of nonprofits have much greater discretion in their actions and are much less accountable to those they serve than are directors and managers of for-profits. We have found that the term "nonprofit" is deceiving; many nonprofit organizations are highly profitable, and although these profits cannot be directly distributed to individuals associated with the organization, there are perfectly legal (and some illegal) means whereby the profits of nonprofits can benefit those who oversee and are engaged in their operations. In fact, one of the major reasons that some charitable organizations have moved toward more commercial activities is that charity is not profitable. The incentive structure of nonprofits indicates that these organizations will not produce goods and services at lowest cost, so that nonprofits are far less efficient than their for-profit counterparts. In addition to their direct governmental subsidies and their exemptions from taxation and regulation, nonprofits enjoy a "halo" effect arising from the widely accepted belief that nonprofits have charitable intentions, whereas for-profits are dominated by the profit motive and greed. But there is evidence that consumers and taxpayers are better served by for-profit entities that do not receive hidden subsidies and that are monitored and controlled by market forces.

Chapters 4, 5, and 6 deal with unfair competition in several industries. Chapter 4 reviews unfair competition in the hospital and medical care industries, where unfair competition has been so severe that the for-profit hospital has almost become a historical curiosity. The hospital industry holds particular interest because a legislative privilege has allowed nonprofit hospitals to legally purchase prescription drugs at prices far below those charged to others. As a result, a diversion market has been created that threatens the integrity of all pharmaceuticals used in the U.S. Nonprofit hospitals have attempted to justify their special status by claiming that they serve the poor who otherwise would not receive treatment. Studies have shown, however, that for-profits have given as much, if not more, assistance to the poor, and many nonprofits have shirked their obligations to the poor. Furthermore, there are cases of directors, managers, and professionals at nonprofit hospitals enriching themselves through self-dealing arrangements. Unfair competition in medical care is pervasive and out of control.

Unfair competition in the physical fitness industry is reviewed in detail in chapter 5. For decades, the YMCA/YWCA has been an important American institution, but in recent years this nonprofit organization has changed dramatically. It has largely abandoned its emphasis on programs for young people and concentrated instead on serving urban professionals in lavish health clubs that compete with private, profit-seeking facilities. In several cases, courts have revoked the tax-exempt status of YMCAs because they no longer serve their charitable roles. Local governments are also actively engaged in the physical fitness industry through the construction and operation of public facilities.

Chapter 6 is concerned with unfair competition in audiovisual services and computer software. More and more, colleges and universities are actively competing with for-profits in the production, sale, and distribution of audiovisual materials and have used their privileged position as nonprofits to undercut the prices of their for-profit counterparts. The largest unfair competitor in this industry is the federal government, which distributes thousands of films of every description through its National Audiovisual Center. The educational software market is dominated by the Minnesota Educational Computing Corporation, a nonprofit arm of the state that develops, markets, and licenses computer programs nationwide.

These three chapters reveal only the tip of the iceberg of unfair competition by private nonprofit organizations. Unfortunately, there is no way to determine how many small firms have suffered losses or have been driven from the market by nonprofit competition, nor is there a count of the number of firms that were never established because unfair competition discouraged entrants. It is even possible that a business could be harmed by unfair competition and the owners and managers might not be aware of it. The evidence from these chapters shows dramatically that nonprofits are actively engaged in commercial activities and that small firms are adversely affected.

Chapter 7 is devoted to the commercial activities of government. The public sector routinely carries on thousands of commercial activities that displace private, taxpaying firms. A vast and growing literature on private versus public production of goods and services has consistently shown that the public sector is a far less efficient producer than the private sector. So extensive and convincing is the evidence that the "Bureaucratic Rule of Two" has been proposed: When a service once produced by the private sector is produced by the public sector, the unit cost of production roughly doubles. Privatization initiatives in the U.S., Europe, the Far East, and even in some communist countries are based on the realization that private firms are far superior to the public sector as producers. Because the incentives of managers in the public sector are very similar to those in nonprofits, the public sector is an integral part of the problem of unfair competition.

The final chapter addresses the question "What should be done about unfair competition?" The only way to eliminate unfair competition and its negative effects for the economy is to make nonprofits and for-profits compete under the same rules. The issue is not competition, but *unfair* competition. The simplest solution, then, is to require nonprofits to form for-profit subsidiaries when they engage in commercial activities. This would place both types of organizations on a "level playing field"; fairness and equity considerations cannot be satisfied by anything less.

In this book, we have only scratched the surface of this timely and important topic. Far too little is currently known about the nonprofit sector in general and even less is known about unfair competition and its effects on the economy. When facts are not available, the vacuum is too often filled with myth and speculation. Public policy should not be based on misconceptions or misunderstandings—the issues are too vital to the nation's economic future. We hope that this research will serve as a catalyst encouraging others to further investigate the nonprofit sector and unfair competition.

Notes to Chapter 1

1. Edward Skloot, "Should Not-For-Profits Go Into Business?" *Harvard Business Review* (January/February 1983), p. 20.

2. "Unfair Competition by Nonprofit Organizations With Small Business: An Issue for the 1980s," 3d ed. (Washington, D.C.: U.S. Small Business Administration, 1984).

3. See David L. Birch, "Who Creates Jobs?" *The Public Interest* (Fall 1981): 3–14, and Steven Solomon, *Small Business USA: The Role of Small Companies in Sparking America's Economic Transformation* (New York: Crown Publishers, 1986).

II.

The Dimensions of the Commercial Nonprofit Sector

Nonprofit entities have "been a feature of Anglo-American law for nearly a millenium,"[1] but concern about unfair competition has only recently surfaced. In response to growing complaints about unfair competition arising from the special privileges accorded nonprofit organizations, the U.S. Small Business Administration has identified unfair competition as "an issue for the 1980s."[2] The justification for the preferential treatment given to nonprofits is rarely stated explicitly, but it rests on some vague and poorly developed notions of "thin markets," "market failure," and "public goods." Even though the rationales for nonprofit privileges may be applicable to their charitable functions, it does not follow that the same rationales can be used to justify their commerical activities. In 1950, Congress attempted to deal with unfair competition by requiring nonprofits to pay taxes on their "unrelated business income," but the current concern about unfair competition indicates that this approach has not been effective in eliminating unfair competition. The special privileges of nonprofits go far beyond exemption from federal taxation.

The Privileges of Nonprofits

The most important privilege given to nonprofit organizations is their tax-exempt status, which covers federal, state, and local income taxes; sales taxes; and property taxes. Nonprofits also receive special treatment from the federal government regarding unemployment

9

insurance, minimum wages, securities regulation, bankruptcy, anti-trust restrictions, and copyright and enjoy exemptions from a host of onerous state and local laws and regulations regarding franchises, inspections, bonds, and so forth.[3] The Federal Trade Commission, a consumer watchdog agency empowered to prevent "persons, part-nerships and corporations" from employing unfair methods of com-petition or engaging in unfair or deceptive acts or practices, has no jurisdiction over most nonprofits.[4] The Federal Trade Commission Act narrowly defines a "corporation" as a for-profit entity or a trade association representing for-profit entities, so that most nonprofits are outside the Commission's jurisdiction.[5]

In addition to the special privileges that nonprofits enjoy, public policy sometimes forces for-profit firms to subsidize their nonprofit competitors. For example, government contracts are often reserved for nonprofit organizations whose operations are subsidized by tax revenues collected from the private firms with which they compete. Moreover, private firms are urged to contribute to charity fund drives, such as the United Way, which subsidize the operations of many nonprofits engaged in commercial ventures.[6]

Even employees of nonprofits are treated differently under federal tax law than their counterparts in the private sector. For example, private-sector employees may contribute as much as $7,500 per year tax free to a retirement account, but employees of nonprofits may shelter up to $9,500 per year.[7] Prior to the 1985 reform of the social security program, employees of nonprofits did not have to be part of the social security system.[8] Because tax laws provide nonprofit em-ployees with generous benefit allowances, nonprofit employers can pay them lower wages and still offer a total benefit package that equals that available in the private sector. In this way, public policies lower the wage costs of nonprofits. These costs may also be lower for nonprofits than for comparable for-profits because of the number of volunteer workers used. Nonprofit organizations are often regarded as charitable organizations, and millions of public-spirited individuals contribute time and effort to them, including participating in their commercial activities.

Nonprofits also receive preferential postal rates from the govern-ment, which permits them to mail promotional material at bulk rates far below those paid by private firms.[9] In early 1987, nonprofit organizations paid 8.5 cents postage on each ounce of bulk mail; profit-seeking firms would have been charged 12.5 cents per ounce for the identical mailing, that is, 47 percent more. Direct mail advertising is an important way to reach consumers, and nonprofits in competition with private firms have a significant advantage in this area. For example, The Smithsonian Institution mails a glossy catalog several times each year promoting a wide variety of products. The 32–page spring 1987 issue of the catalog measures approximately 9.5 by 7 inches and weighs 2.13 ounces. Because of its nonprofit status, the museum can mail 100,000 copies of the catalog for approximately $18,165; a for-profit firm would pay about $26,713 for an identical mailing, or $8,538 more.

The effect of these special privileges is that governmental policy not only reduces the costs of nonprofit organizations, but it also raises the costs of doing business for their for-profit competitors. Profit-seeking firms must pay higher taxes and postal rates to offset the subsidies accorded nonprofits. Thus, because of this preferential treatment, competition between nonprofits and for-profits is inherently unfair.

The Size of the Commercial Nonprofit Sector

The most accurate statement that can be made about the nonprofit segment of the economy is that information about it is fragmentary and incomplete. There is not even consensus on an appropriate term to describe nonprofits; suggestions include "third," "independent," and "voluntary" sector. In recent years, three groups have begun large-scale studies on nonprofits: Yale University's Institution for Social and Policy Studies began a Program on Nonprofit Organizations in 1978; the Independent Sector, itself a nonprofit coalition of more than 600 corporate, foundation, and voluntary organizations, began in 1984 a biennial series of statistical profiles of the "independent sector"; and in June 1982 The Urban Institute launched a multiyear project to examine the scope and operations of the nonprofit sector. Each of these efforts differs in approach and emphasis and, although each makes important contributions to the understanding of nonprofits, much remains to be done. As stated in a brochure describing Yale's program, "The size and scope of America's nonprofit . . . sector is a distinguishing characteristic of our social order. Yet for a long time the third sector has been the least well understood aspect of our national life."[10]

While there may not be a consensus on terminology, there is agreement about the essential distinguishing characteristic of all nonprofits: "A nonprofit organization is, in essence, an organization that is barred from distributing its net earnings, if any, to individuals who exercise control over it, such as members, officers, directors, or trustees."[11] A nonprofit can be (and often is) a profitable enterprise in that its revenue or income exceeds its expenses, but its net earnings must be retained and used to finance the organization's facilities and the services the organization was formed to provide. In contrast to a private for-profit firm, which seeks to earn profits for distribution to its owners, a nonprofit is prohibited from *directly* distributing profits to anyone associated with the organization. This constraint has important economic implications, for it has a significant impact on the incentives of managers and directors of nonprofit organizations (see chapter 3).

Like most private, profit-seeking firms, nonprofits are typically corporations granted charters by a state or the District of Columbia. Some states grant nonprofit charters only to organizations formed for specified purposes; other states permit nonprofits to engage in any legal activity. Nonprofits are not necessarily charitable organizations. Charities are widely regarded as organizations that assist the poor, the handicapped, and the less fortunate in society, but "only about 10% of charities do that. Many organizations, declared to be charities by the IRS, serve the wealthy and middle class, operate institutions such as Harvard University or the Music Center of Los Angeles County or exist to promote public awareness of issues. Charities exist that favor both more and less defense spending, for example."[12] Research by the Urban Institute reveals that private nonprofit organizations tended to treat the "more deserving" poor, if they helped the poor at all, while the most difficult hardship cases were left to government organizations: "Indeed, [the Urban Institute] survey of 3400 human service organizations revealed that the poor comprised the majority of the clients of only about 30 percent of the agencies, and that for half of the agencies, the poor constituted less than 10 percent of the clientele."[13]

In a research study for the Yale University program on nonprofits, Henry Hansmann attempted to categorize nonprofits by source of income and type of control. Donative nonprofits, such as the Red Cross and the Salvation Army, receive most of their income from grants or donations and commercial nonprofits, such as hospitals, nursing homes, and labor unions, obtain most of their income from payments received for the provision of services. Hansmann distinguished "mutual nonprofits," which are controlled by their patrons (e.g., country clubs) from "entrepreneurial nonprofits," which are largely free from the control of their patrons and usually have a self-perpetuating board of directors.[14] There is enormous diversity among nonprofits in terms of control and revenue sources, and Hansmann's categories do not capture the implications of this diversity for unfair competition. For example, a "donative nonprofit" can engage in unfair competition just as easily as a "commercial nonprofit" can. As an illustration, when Humane Society clinics offer spaying and neutering at lower prices than are charged by veterinarians in private practice, they are engaged in a commercial activity. In a similar way, many churches sell Christmas trees to their members and to the general public. Examples are legion. Hansmann recognized that "the distinction between commercial and donative nonprofits is simply one of degree, rather than a difference in kind. . . . There is thus a strong commercial element in donative nonprofits; they are, in effect, engaged in the sale of services."[15] A strong argument can be made, then, that all nonprofits are potentially commercial nonprofits.

The three research programs on the nonprofit sector have excluded the public sector and focused exclusively on private organizations. But there is no question that units of government have the critical structural feature of all nonprofit organizations. Surpluses are not directly distributed to elected officials or to public employees; in the public sector, compensation is determined by either civil service regulations or by legislative action. In addition, the incentives of public sector managers are similar to those of managers in private nonprofits, and public sector firms enjoy most of the special privileges (especially tax exemptions) that benefit nonprofits. In analyzing unfair competition, "public nonprofits" must be taken into account, for government at all levels competes directly with private firms. The public sector will be treated explicitly as a unique source of unfair competition.

The Private Nonprofit Sector. A nongovernmental organization is designated a nonprofit when it is established for purposes that the federal tax code recognizes as exempt from taxation.[16] Thus, the nonprofit designation is an artificial construct resulting from the political process of federal taxation. According to the statistical profiles developed by Independent Sector, at least 1.2 million nonprofit organizations operated in the U.S. in 1984, but only 838,319 are reported in Table 2.1.[17] This large discrepancy in the number of organizations highlights the problem of obtaining accurate data on nonprofits. There are thousands of organizations that operate as

TABLE 2.1

Number of Active Entities on IRS Master File of Tax-Exempt Organizations

(Fiscal year ending September 30)

Tax Code Number	Type of tax-exempt organization	1977	1982	1984	1985
501(c)(1)	Corporations organized under an act of Congress	1,072	24	24	24
501(c)(2)	Title-holding companies	5,223	5,522	5,679	5,758
501(c)(3)	Religious, charitable, etc.	276,455	322,826	352,884	366,071
501(c)(4)	Social welfare	129,496	131,578	130,344	131,250
501(c)(5)	Labor, agricultural organizations	87,656	86,322	76,753	75,632
501(c)(6)	Business leagues	44,100	51,065	53,303	54,217
501(c)(7)	Social and recreational clubs	50,031	54,036	55,666	57,343
501(c)(8)	Fraternal beneficiary societies	141,138	116,549	92,431	94,435
501(c)(9)	Voluntary employees' societies	6,486	8,703	10,145	10,668
501(c)(10)	Domestic fraternal beneficiary societies	12,410	18,570	16,116	15,924
501(c)(11)	Teachers' retirement fund	13	13	11	11
501(c)(12)	Benevolent life insurance associations	4,801	5,071	5,200	5,244
501(c)(13)	Cemetery companies	5,264	6,290	6,845	7,239
501(c)(14)	Credit unions	5,074	6,074	6,053	6,032
501(c)(15)	Mutual insurance companies	1,450	1,073	998	967
501(c)(16)	Corporations to finance crop operation	31	22	19	18
501(c)(17)	Supplemental unemployment benefit trusts	800	784	747	726
501(c)(18)	Employee-funded pension trusts	4	3	3	3
501(c)(19)	War veterans' organizations	14,305	28,851	22,100	23,062
501(c)(20)	Legal services organizations	—	90	140	167
501(c)(21)	Black lung trusts	—	9	14	15
501(d)	Religious and apostolic organizations	63	68	81	82
501(e)	Cooperative hospital service organizations	—	106	90	82
501(f)	Cooperative service organizations of operating educational organizations				
521	Farmers' cooperatives	3,794	2,791	2,673	2,542
	TOTAL	789,666	841,440	838,319	857,512

Source: Virginia Ann Hodgkinson and Murray S. Weitzman, *Dimensions of the Independent Sector: A Statistical Profile* 2d ed. (Washington, D.C.: Independent Sector, 1986), p. 17.

charities and are not required to apply for tax-exempt status, as long as annual revenues are under $5,000. Religious organizations are also tax-exempt and are not required to report to the IRS or to apply for a tax exemption. When a church or religious group requests a ruling, blanket coverage is automatically granted for all of its units, including social welfare organizations and schools. Some nonprofits file omnibus tax forms that apply to many separate entities. The Boy Scouts, for example, can file one tax return to cover hundreds of separately incorporated Boy Scout councils.[18]

Other discrepancies are equally apparent. Between 1977 and 1982, the number of organizations exempt under Section 501(c)(1) of the Internal Revenue Code plummeted from 1,072 to only 24 in 1982 (see Table 2.1). The nonprofits that retained the exemption are corporations organized under an act of Congress and are considered instrumentalities of the United States. They include the Commodity Credit Corporation, the Federal Crop Insurance Corporation, the Federal Deposit Insurance Corporation, and the Federal Home Loan Banks. There has been no explanation for the elimination of more than 1,000 501(c)(1) federal entities from the file of active tax-exempt organizations, but evidently, some recategorization occurred. It is also interesting that in a report to Rep. Daniel Rostenkowski (D-Ill.), chairman of the House Committee on Ways and Means, the General Accounting Office indicated that 44 organizations were in category 501(c)(1) of the IRS master file for fiscal year 1983.[19] Clearly, there are serious weaknesses in these data. Although it is apparent that the number of nonprofit organizations is larger than that reported by the IRS, it is impossible to determine how many entities have been omitted. All nonprofits with more than $25,000 in annual revenue must file tax returns (Form 990) containing detailed information on revenues and expenditures, but this information is not entered into IRS computers. Because of the prohibitive cost of manual tabulation, therefore, this source of information is lost.[20]

Despite the shortcomings in the data, it is clear that there is a large number of nonprofit organizations and that the number has been growing. Independent Sector limits its definition of the "independent sector" to entities exempted from taxation under sections 501(c)(3) and 501(c)(4), the educational, scientific, religious, and other charitable organizations as well as private foundations (which dispense grants), community, civic, and social welfare organizations.

Not all nonprofits are equal, at least from the perspective of the federal tax code.[21] Organizations exempted under Section 501(c)(3) may receive contributions that are tax-deductible for the donor; non-profits classified under other sections of 501(c) generally cannot receive tax-deductible contributions. When adjustments are made for the number of churches and religious organizations, Independent Sector has estimated that 821,000 nonprofits are exempted under 501(c)(3) and 501(c)(4) alone.[22] Roughly one out of every twenty organizations in the United States, therefore, is a nonprofit.

Independent Sector has also attempted to determine the significance of the 501(c)(3) and (4) categories to the national economy. For the period 1977 to 1982, the independent sector

- Increased its employment at an annual rate of 3.7 percent, a much faster rate than the annual rate of growth for all nonagricultural employees (2.0 percent).
- Increased its share of total employment in the economy from 8.6 percent (8.8 million) to 9.7 percent (11.0 million). These figures include volunteer time, the equivalent of 3.3 million employees in 1977 and 4.7 million employees in 1984.
- Increased its share of total income from employment from 6.7 percent ($75.9 billion) to 7.5 percent ($139.2 billion). These figures also include the imputed value of volunteer time.
- Grew faster than other sectors in the national economy. The independent sector increased its share of national income from 5.2 percent ($84.4 billion) to 5.8 percent ($155.8 billion). This trend did not continue after 1982, however, for between 1982 and 1984, this sector's share of national income declined to 5.6 percent ($176.3 billion). Again, the imputed value of volunteer time is included in these estimates.[23]

The independent sector, then, has been growing rapidly, generates substantial employment and income, uses the services of millions of volunteers, and constitutes a significant force in the economy. The growth has not been evenly distributed across types of organizations, however:

The major growth from 1977 to 1982 was in health services, up 59 percent, and social services, up 99 percent. During this period, employment in arts and cultural organizations increased 75 percent, but from a much smaller base. But employment at colleges and universities; religious organizations; and civic, social, and fraternal organizations increased at a slower rate than all employment in nonagricultural jobs.[24]

Data obtained from the *Survey of Current Business* published by the Bureau of the Census reveal that private nonprofit organizations make substantial expenditures each year. In 1985, all nonprofits spent $238.7 billion, compared with $83.6 billion in 1975. After adjusting for inflation, nonprofits spent $88 billion in constant 1972 dollars in 1985, a 31 percent increase over the $67.6 billion (in 1972 dollars) spent in 1975. In 1985, nonprofits expended $1,000 for every person in the United States.

From data drawn from the National Income Accounts, which include all nonprofits, Hansmann concluded:

> The data suggest that the nonprofit sector accounted for roughly 2.8% of national income in 1974. More dramatic than the absolute size of the sector has been its growth. It has more than doubled as a percentage of national income since 1929, when the figure was 1.2%. Furthermore, the growth of the sector has been particularly rapid in recent years: the share of national income it represents increased by roughly 33% in the period 1960–1974. The growth of the sector in absolute terms, of course, has been even more dramatic.
>
> Because nonprofits are concentrated in the labor-intensive service industries, the share of total direct employment accounted for by nonprofits is even larger than its contribution to GNP, amounting to 5.9% in 1973.[25]

Unlike the Independent Sector estimates, Hansmann's include all categories of 501(c) organizations, but the National Income Accounts make no provision for the value of services donated by volunteers.

Even though there are major differences in the approaches taken by Independent Sector and by Hansmann, they both confirm that the nonprofit sector is large, rapidly growing, an important source of employment, and a significant part of the national economy.[26] There is no evidence that these trends have slowed. In early 1987, *Newsweek* reported that

> tax-exempt institutions are one of the fastest-growing segments of the economy, with annual revenues of more that $300 billion— or about 8 percent of the gross national product. They're big employers too; in the Northeast, the 100 largest nonprofit firms employ more people than the region's 100 leading industrial companies, reports *New England Business* magazine.[27]

The research conducted by The Urban Institute has yet another emphasis and approach. The Urban Institute's principal goal was to assess the relationship between government and the private nonprofit sector, and analysts used case studies rather than aggregate statistics. They intensively studied the activities of nonprofits in one large, one medium-sized, and one small metropolitan area plus one rural county in each of the four major Census Bureau regions of the U.S. The findings were revealing. For example, in 1982 1,200 nonprofits were operating in Pittsburgh with expenditures of approximately $2 billion, a sum that exceeded the combined budgets of the city of Pittsburgh and Allegheny County.[28] This is not atypical: "In Atlanta, nonprofit expenditures are four times larger than the city budget, and in San Francisco, they are two times larger."[29] Thus, nonprofit service organizations (excluding religious congregations and agencies serving members, e.g., labor unions, and business and professional groups) often swamp local governments in terms of budget size and numbers. By any standard of comparison, the nonprofit sector is immense. The Urban Institute estimated that nonprofit service organizations employed five times as many workers as the auto industry and accounted for one of every five service workers in the economy.[30]

The Urban Institute study also found that most nonprofit organizations were established quite recently: "two out of every three agencies in existence as of 1982 were formed since 1960."[31] This expansion coincides with the growth of governmental expenditures in the social services field that occurred with the Great Society initiatives of the Johnson administration. Although many people believe that private philanthropy supports nonprofits, The Urban Institute reported that

> federal support to the nonprofit sector alone amounted to $40.4 billion in 1980. This represented about 36 percent of total federal spending in these fields. State and local government own-source revenues would likewise add another $8–10 billion to this total. By comparison, private contributions to these same kinds of organizations in 1980 totalled approximately $25.5 billion, or about 40 percent less than the federal contribution and about 50 percent less than the overall government contribution. These findings thus confirm the central conclusion of the Filer Commission that government is a more important source of revenue to nonprofit services providers (exclusive of churches) than all of private giving combined.[32]

Taxpayers' funds have financed the rapid growth of the nonprofit sector over the past 25 years, "stimulating the birth of new nonprofit institutions to help carry out Great Society goals."[33] Changes in governmental spending priorities have also provided the stimulus for the commercial activities of nonprofits:

. . . the arrangements that have been forged between nonprofit organizations and government have been exposed to serious strains over the past several years because of the budget reductions that began in the late 1970s and accelerated with the Reagan Administration's budget-cutting efforts in the early 1980s. . . . Federal spending in areas of concern to nonprofit organizations dropped by 9 percent in inflation-adjusted dollars between 1980 and 1984. For nonprofit organizations other than hospitals, this drop translated into a loss of $4.5 billion, or 27 percent of their federal support. Social service, community development, and education organizations were particularly hard hit by these changes.

·   ·   ·   ·   ·   ·   ·   ·

To cope with these cuts, nonprofit organizations have turned to other sources of funds. In general they have managed to offset most of the government cutbacks in the process. However, the major source of net income has not been private charity but service fees and charges. In other words, forced by budget cuts to become less governmental, nonprofit agencies have responded not by becoming more charitable, but *by becoming more commercial* (emphasis added).[34]

The adoption of commercial activities by nonprofits came swiftly and has been widely viewed as an alternative to reductions in governmental funding. There is evidence, however, that the move by nonprofits to "enterprise activities" began well before the late 1970s and prior to cuts in social program budgets. In 1983, James C. Crimmins and Mary Kiel reported research findings on profitmaking activities of nonprofits in *Enterprise in the Nonprofit Sector*. Their conclusions, based on responses to a questionnaire sent to 501(c)(3) organizations, indicated that a large number of nonprofits had begun commercial enterprises to generate "enterprise revenue" since 1970: "Sixty-nine percent of the organizations we surveyed have given birth to new enterprise within the past twelve years. Sixty percent generate some of their revenues from enterprise activities."[35] The survey also indicated that "very small organizations (budget size under $100,000) do not rely on enterprise revenues. . . . Of the sample with budgets over $10 million, all have some amount of enterprise."[36] Commercial activities are not usually initiated by small nonprofits, but by larger, more established organizations. The evidence also indicates that nonprofits have been highly successful. Crimmins and Keil reported that "for our total sample, *average budget growth* from 1976 to 1981 was 139 percent, and 64 percent experienced *real* budget growth (in excess of inflation). For organizations that saw enterprise revenues become a more significant share of their income, the budgets grew on average over 200 percent."[37]

The Scope of Commercial Nonprofit Enterprise. Nonprofits offer a formidable array of activities in which they can compete with profit-seeking firms, ranging from the performing arts to youth activities. The list of IRS activity codes (see Appendix Table A2.1), however, does not begin to capture the wide range of commercial activities routinely undertaken by nonprofits. For example, many professional organizations, such as the American Economic Association and the American Statistical Association, offer their members life, excess medical, disability, and other forms of insurance at attractive rates. College and university bookstores sell computers, clothing, and drug-store and gift items. In competition with local hotels and motels, institutions of higher education have begun to rent dorm rooms to the public for special events during the summer. Alumni associations offer tours to their members at discount prices.

Among the more aggressive nonprofits are museums, which market merchandise, arrange travel tours, publish books and magazines, and produce audiovisual materials for sale to the public. The Smithsonian Institution, which calls itself the "nation's attic," publishes *Smithsonian*, a glossy, monthly publication that carries advertising directed at higher income groups. The magazine also advertises domestic and foreign "study tours" sponsored by the Smithsonian. Domestic tours for 1987 feature trips to Florida, Arizona, Texas, New York, New England, Utah, and Chicago, plus tours of the Lewis and Clark Trail and steamboat travel on the Mississippi River. Foreign tours are conducted in New Zealand, Mexico, Costa Rica, the South Pacific, Australia, Japan, Guatemala, Wales, Malaysia, Borneo, France, Ireland, England, Scotland, Canada, China, Austria, and Switzerland.[38] The museum's 13 shops sell books, jewelry, decorator items, clothing, posters, toys, furniture, linens, and novelties; these items are also offered through catalogs mailed at the bulk rate for nonprofit organizations. In 1985, the Smithsonian's gift shops and mail-order catalog produced $27 million in annual sales.[39] Subscribers to *Smithsonian* become "associates" and can purchase merchandise at reduced prices and have access to special restaurant facilities. Members of the Smithsonian's Board of Regents, the principal governing body, are appointed by the President of the Senate, the Speaker of the House of Representatives, and by joint resolution of Congress. Most of the Smithsonian's operating funds come from the federal government, some from federal taxes paid by private firms that compete with the museum. The commercial activities of the Smithsonian are typical of those conducted by other museums in the nation's capital.[40]

Traditionally, business leagues or associations with nonprofit status under Section 501(c)(6) of the IRS code have obtained most of their operating revenues from membership dues, rental of mailing lists, and advertising in trade publications. Their mode of operation, however, is rapidly changing, and an industry is developing to assist these nonprofits in commercial ventures that will reduce their reliance on dues as their primary source of income. For example, *Association Marketing* is a monthly tabloid in its second year that contains "materials relating to the marketing of association services and products." Each issue features a "Non-Dues Income Idea Center."[41] The January 1987 issue contains a table listing "more than 60 different categories of nondues income, ranging from accounting services to travel services, and more than 300 ways that associations can make money."[42] Many of the suggestions involve direct competition with private commercial firms. For example, nonprofit associations are encouraged to provide accounting, financial, debt collection, and inventory control services; operate an advertising agency; publish, sell, and distribute books; arrange car rentals, tours, and travel; offer group legal services and insurance of every description; operate an employment referral agency; engage in labor negotiations; produce and sell novelties, plaques, and memorabilia; rent office space; test products; merchandise store fixtures and office equipment; conduct safety programs; print in-house and for others; establish a telephone co-op and offer cooperative purchasing of office supplies, auto leases, and "personal items"; and conduct product and consumer surveys. In the expectation that other revenue-generating ideas will surface, the table is preceded by the notation that "an updated listing will be published periodically."[43]

According to the *Washington Post*, association executives actively search for alternative sources of revenue:

> By offering additional services such as educational, marketing, or statistical programs, many associations have increased their

income. But such services are only a few of the ways associations have made more money. Among other things, groups have provided an advertising agency for members, endorsed products or services, published membership directories and buyers' guides, and invested.[44]

A survey conducted by the Greater Washington Society of Association Executives regarding "nontraditional" income sources revealed that, after the sale or rental of mailing lists and labels, "group life insurance, book publishing, and car rental or leasing were the next most popular methods. Nine of the 20 most popular benefits were insurance programs."[45]

Labor unions, which are nonprofits under section 501(c)(5) of the IRS code, are also having serious difficulties with their traditional source of income, membership dues.[46] Although unions have not yet turned to commercial ventures on a wide scale to ease their financial problems, such a course of action can be anticipated.

The objective here is not to present a comprehensive view of the commercial activities of nonprofits but merely to illustrate the diversity of nonprofit commercial activity. The point is that nonprofits have turned to enterprise activity on a large scale and, given the size and scope of the nonprofit sector, that the potential impact on small, profit-seeking firms is enormous. Nonprofits are increasingly shifting their efforts to commercial activity, spurred by a new industry that exists solely to promote business ventures for them. For example, a three-day workshop on how nonprofits should become involved in commercial activities is offered by the Grantsmanship Center, which describes itself as the nation's "oldest and largest fundraising institution." The Center's brochure asserts:

> Most nonprofits are locked into traditional fundraising approaches. If fundraising and grantsmanship get you all you need—terrific. If not, it's time to look into the hottest area of nonprofit funding—launching a business enterprise. Your nonprofit agency can start a business—and generate dollars that aren't dependent on grants or contributions. And it can do this legally, and keep its tax-exempt status.
>
> Driven by financial necessity, more and more nonprofits are launching enterprises that can generate income to sustain their regular programs. These enterprises range from shoestring businesses to multi-million dollar deals. They include thrift stores and gift stores, restaurants, periodicals and mail-order services,

housing and real estate syndication, cable television franchising, and much more.[47]

The commercialization strategy has become so successful that for some nonprofits sales of goods and services are the primary source of revenue. Fully 92 percent of total revenues in nonprofit health care delivery are provided by sales of goods and services; in scientific research, the figure is 86 percent; in housing, 61 percent; in higher education, 82 percent; and for mutual organizations (e.g., mutual insurance companies, credit unions, and clubs), 99 percent.[48] When a nonprofit finds that it can operate a successful commercial enterprise, it has strong incentives to expand the organization's entrepreneurial function. An imitation effect encourages other nonprofits to undertake similar efforts. The managers and board members of other nonprofits who may have been reluctant to start commercial ventures on principle will find it increasingly acceptable and desirable; as the practice spreads, inhibitions against it are lessened. In this way, the commercialization of the nonprofit sector will accelerate, increasing the negative effects on profit-seeking firms.

Commercial Activities of the Public Sector. Unfair competition extends far beyond the boundaries of the private nonprofit sector, for government is also extensively involved in commercial activities that compete with profit-seeking firms. Public enterprises have the essential characteristic of nonprofit organizations: No individual directly receives the profits or operating surpluses generated. Public firms also enjoy virtually all of the special privileges granted to private nonprofit organizations. Typically, they enjoy even greater competitive advantages in the marketplace than do private nonprofits. For example, government enterprises can excercise the power of eminent domain; they can borrow at interest rates considerably below those paid by small for-profit firms because of tax-exempt interest payments;[49] their operating costs are subsidized by taxes; and they are usually given monopoly status by law. Even when taxpayers choose private alternatives over a public enterprise, they must support the public firm. For example, parents who send their children to private schools must continue to pay taxes to support public schools. Thus, public provision of services is a highly effective deterrent to competition from private firms. Whenever government embarks on new commercial activities or expands existing ones, private firms are crowded out of the market or are discouraged from entering it. These "crowding out" effects are the same whether the unfair competitor is a private nonprofit or a public enterprise.

The extent of unfair competition by the public sector is enormous. In June 1981, the U.S. General Accounting Office reported that an estimated 400,000 federal employees—nearly one fourth of the federal civilian work force (excluding the postal service)—are currently operating over 11,000 commercial or industrial activities at an estimated cost of $19 billion a year.[50] Rowland R. Hughes, former director of the Bureau of the Budget, has put into perspective the federal government's involvement in private sector activities:

> The Federal government today . . . is . . . the largest electric power producer in the country, the largest insurer, the largest lender and the largest borrower, the largest landlord and the largest tenant, the largest holder of timberland, the largest owner of grain, the largest warehouse operator, the largest shipowner, and the largest truckfleet operator.[51]

The federal government is also a major retailer (through its military commissaries and post exchanges), a caterer, a laundry operator, a producer of health care services, a motor vehicle mechanic, a printer, a janitorial service, a motion picture producer, and much more.

To reverse this trend, the Reagan administration advocated "privatization"—reliance on the private sector for goods and services whenever possible—as one of its major policy initiatives, but the results have been disappointing. Between 1981 and 1987, over 100,000 federal employees were added to the Department of Defense alone, and almost all of them perform commercial work.[52] During the Reagan administration, the federal government encroached even further into activities that properly belong in the small business sector. For example, at the same time the Department of Defense was claiming that a larger military budget was essential to national security, the Trident Submarine Base at Bangor, Washington, used taxpayers' funds to purchase "a 46 passenger luxury coach. . . . [with] reclining seats, AM-FM radio and restroom [which] provide all the comforts of home to make Morale, Welfare and Recreation shopping trips and a multitude of tours available and enjoyable."[53] In January 1987, the base offered 10 ski trips lasting from one to five days. Civilians were welcomed on all trips, but at higher prices than charged to military personnel and their dependents.[54] Before the base purchased the luxury coach, morale, welfare, and recreation trips were offered through charter arrangements with private coach companies. The private operators whose taxes contributed to the Navy's bus have, in effect, subsidized their own competitor. The Bangor example is only one of many that can illustrate the extensive and growing encroachment of the federal government on the private sector at taxpayers' expense.

The public sector's crowding out of small business is prevalent at the state and local levels of government as well. Local governments operate hospitals, ambulance services, printing plants, data processing facilities, trash and debt collection, fire and security protection services, building and road maintenance, parks and recreational services, and a host of other services routinely provided by commercial firms. State governments operate similar commercial activities.[55] (See chapter 7 for a more detailed discussion of these issues and their economic implications.)

Obtaining complete and accurate information on the size and scope of the public sector is nearly impossible; published statistics are misleading and grossly underestimate public-sector employment, borrowing, debt, and expenditures. The public sector is much larger than commonly believed because many governmental activities have been moved "off-budget."[56] At the federal level, for example, the Tennessee Valley Authority, the Bonneville Power Authority, the Federal Financing Bank, and the Strategic Petroleum Reserve are off-budget entities; their income, debt, expenditures, and employment do not appear in the federal budget. There are thousands of off-budget enterprises that compete with for-profit firms at the state and local levels of government as well (see chapter 3). These organizations have legislatively mandated powers and privileges that in many cases far exceed those granted to nonprofit firms or on-budget government enterprises.

Overall, unfair competition arises from three distinct sources: nonprofits; on-budget commercial activities of government; and off-budget enterprises established by federal, state, and local governments. Each source operates under a legislatively mandated set of tax laws and regulations that provides a marked competitive advantage over private commercial firms.

The Rationales for Special Privileges

Although government has granted numerous special privileges to both nonprofit organizations and public enterprises, no law has ever explicitly stated the justification for this special treatment. On one occasion, a report of the Committee on Ways and Means dealing with with the Revenue Act of 1938 noted that

> the exemption from taxation of money or property devoted to charitable and other purposes is based upon the theory that government is compensated for the loss of revenues by its relief from financial burden which would otherwise have to be met by appropriations from public funds and by the benefits resulting from promotion of the general welfare.[57]

Aside from this very general rationale, three other primary reasons have been implicitly given to explain government's special treatment of nonprofits: thin markets, market failure, and public goods.

Thin Markets. A "thin market" is a market in which the demand for a product or service is so small that no commercial firm could make a profit selling it. Because of their subsidies which artificially lower costs, nonprofits can serve such a market. But this justification does not stand up under even casual examination in the context of unfair competition. By definition, unfair competition occurs when nonprofits compete with for-profits. If the thin market rationale were valid, for-profits would have never entered the market in the first place and unfair competition could not occur. (This point is considered in more detail in chapter 6.)

Market Failure. For markets to operate properly, information must be readily available to buyers so that they can assess the quality of services or products before making purchases. In some cases, notably health care, consumers may find it difficult to judge the quality of services or whether or not the services are needed at all. Most patients have no idea what tests and diagnostic procedures are essential or the efficacy of treatments and drugs, so they trust their physicians and hospitals to provide the care that is needed. Under such circumstances, it is argued, for-profit firms have an incentive to maximize profits by reducing the quality of care and by providing unnecessary tests and treatments at excessive prices. A nonprofit organization, however, which theoretically does not earn profits, should have no incentive to provide inferior or redundant care at excessive prices. Using this logic, nonprofit status assures the public of high quality services at reasonable prices.

This rationale has a certain intuitive appeal, but there is no evidence that the quality of care at nonprofit hospitals is superior to that provided by for-profits, or proprietaries:

When proprietaries have been compared with nonprofit hospitals of similar size, offering comparable services, no obvious quality differences have been shown to exist. One study, for example, found that when similar size hospitals are compared, there is little difference between the percentage of proprietary and non-proprietary hospitals that are accredited.

There is no evidence to indicate that proprietary hospitals are inferior in quality. In fact, some proprietary hospitals were created in order to improve the quality of care offered to the public.[58]

Comparing the pricing policies of for-profit and nonprofit hospitals is more complicated. Studies that have analyzed average cost per patient day have found that proprietary hospitals are more expensive than either nonproprietary or government facilities. Ralph Berry sampled 6,000 short-term general hospitals and adjusted for differences among hospitals in size, quality of services, scope of services offered, input costs, and other factors affecting efficiency. He found that the average cost per patient day was $47.29 at for-profit hospitals, $43.68 at nonproprietaries, and $43.60 at government hospitals.[59] But these cost statistics are misleading, because the relevant comparison is total cost per *stay*, not average cost per day. Patients who pay $50 per day and stay for three days are worse off financially than patients who pay $100 per day and stay only one day. Hospitals have an incentive to lengthen the time patients stay because it keeps occupancy rates high and the cost of care drops dramatically once a patient is recovering. Although it has been argued that early discharge is actually better for the patient's health,[60] there is ample evidence that patients are kept in the hospital far longer than necessary.[61] Many practitioners believe that length of stay is the most critical indicator of a hospital's efficiency,[62] and nonprofit hospitals generally keep patients longer than proprietaries. When length of stay was factored in to the analysis, the average total cost of medical care at proprietary hospitals ($324.56) was lower than at nonprofit hospitals ($338.71) or at government hospitals ($327.87).[63]

There is little empirical evidence that nonprofits provide higher quality care or services at lower cost than for-profit hospitals do. Even though informational problems may contribute to market failure in the health care field, there is no evidence that tax exemptions and other privileges given to nonprofit hospitals correct this problem (see chapter 3). The market failure rationale for subsidizing nonprofits, at least in this instance, cannot withstand close examination.

Public Goods. The most common rationale offered for giving special privileges to nonprofits is that they provide "public goods" that commercial firms would not produce. Public goods differ from private goods in a number of respects. A "pure" public good has the following characteristics: (1) additional users do not deprive others of the good; (2) increasing numbers of users can be accommodated at little or no additional cost; (3) it is difficult or prohibitively costly to charge people for the good on the basis of use; and (4) it cannot be produced or sold very easily in small units. Consider a museum as an example of a public good. When one person views an exhibit, the content of the exhibit for the next patron is not altered; once the expense of arranging an exhibit has been incurred, the costs do not vary with the number of visitors; fees are not based on time spent in the museum (although some charge flat entrance fees); and museums tend to have extensive collections.

It is widely accepted that society benefits from the preservation and dissemination of our cultural and artistic heritage and history through the educational function provided by museums. There is the presumption that everyone in society is better off because museums exist. Some museums are operated by the government and are supported by tax dollars; others are operated by nonprofit organizations and are financed by individual contributions and corporate and foundation grants. Tax exemptions lower the cost of these organizations, and tax-deductibile contributions encourage donors to finance them. Most museums would find it difficult, if not impossible, to survive if they had to operate as for-profit private firms.[64]

Unless they received government subsidies, for-profit firms do not produce pure public goods because of the free rider problem. As Hansmann explained:

> If a public good is to be provided at the optimal level, and in the most efficient fashion, each individual should contribute toward its production a sum equal to the value he places upon it. However, individuals have an incentive to contribute little or nothing toward the cost of producing such a good for two reasons: first, the individual's contribution is likely to be so small in proportion to the total that it will not appreciably affect the amount of the good that is provided, and second, the individual will in any case be able to enjoy the amounts of the good that are financed by the contributions of others. Thus, there is little relationship between the size of an individual's contribution and

the amount of the good that he enjoys. Assuming all individuals follow this logic and become "free riders," then little or none of the good will be supplied, even though collective demand for the good is in fact quite high. Thus, economists generally have concluded that the private market is an inefficient means of providing public goods, and have looked to alternatives such as public financing as a better approach.[65]

Because of the free rider problem, public goods must be financed by taxation, which requires those who enjoy the benefits to pay the cost, or special incentives must be given to private nonprofits. When public goods are involved, there is a role for nonprofits and their special privileges can be justified.

The corporate community has never objected to nonprofit organizations providing public goods or to the special privileges that permit them to do so at reduced cost. In fact, corporate philanthropy has generously supported every conceivable type of nonprofit activity that benefits the public, including art museums, theaters, symphony orchestras, public television, educational institutions, and the more traditional charities such as the United Way, the Salvation Army, and CARE. Unfair competition does not arise in markets for pure public goods because a commercial market for these goods and services does not exist.

The public goods rationale does not hold up when private nonprofits and public enterprises compete with for-profit firms that produce similar goods and services. For example, economists agree that one of the quintessential public goods is national defense. Aircraft (e.g., bombers, fighters, and reconnaissance planes) is a critical component of the country's defense capability, but just because national defense is a public good does not mean that public enterprises or private nonprofits should produce aircraft for the Department of Defense. For-profit companies already manufacture commercial and private aircraft, using technologies and production methods that are so similar that entry into the market for defense airframes by nonprofits constitutes unfair competition. The public goods nature of national defense requires governmental *finance* but not *production* by public enterprise or by private nonprofits.

Few goods or services are "pure" public goods. It is easy to identify a public good: whenever a product or service is produced by a for-profit firm, the public good rationale for nonprofit production does not apply. Whenever possible, private firms should be used to produce public goods; the incentive structure in private organizations encourages efficiency and results in minimum costs of production (see chapters 3 and 7).

In sum, in the context of unfair competition, the three rationales used to justify the special privileges enjoyed by nonprofit and public enterprises cannot withstand close scrutiny.

Some Legal and Taxing Issues

When a nonprofit organization engages in commercial activities and competes with a for-profit firm, the principle of "horizontal equity" in taxation, which requires that equals be treated equally, is violated. At issue is the basic question of fairness.

Under the Internal Revenue Code, organizations that are exempted from taxation under Section 501(c)(3) can engage in virtually unlimited commercial activities; the code makes the critical distinction that exempt status is based on the *primary purpose* of the organization, not on its activities. The only requirement for the retention of tax-exempt status is that the surpluses generated by the business activities be used for tax-exempt purposes.

Although unfair competition has existed for decades, it was not until the late 1940s that it surfaced as a public policy issue. In 1948, a group of alumni donated the Meuller Macaroni Company to New York University's law school. As an educational institution, NYU enjoyed nonprofit status and persuaded a court that the company should also be tax-exempt on the grounds that the company's profits were to be used to support the university's educational mission. By a simple change in ownership, a private commercial firm was made into a charity. There was some concern in the private sector that "If something is not done . . ., the macaroni monopoly will be in the hands of the universities."[66]

In response to complaints of unfair competition by Mueller's competitors, Congress amended the Internal Revenue Code in 1950. No effort was made to constrain or eliminate commercial activities by nonprofits; rather, Congress attempted to tax the "unrelated business income" (UBI) of tax-exempt organizations:

> The income subject to the tax is the gross income from an unrelated trade or business regularly carried on by the organization. Three criteria must be satisfied in order for the income to

be subject to the tax. First, the income must be income from a trade or business, that is, "any activity carried on for the production of income from the sale of goods or performance of services." Second, the trade or business must be regularly carried on. Finally, the trade or business must be an unrelated trade or business. A business of an exempt organization is considered unrelated if it is "not substantially related (aside from the need of such organization for income or funds or the use it makes of the profits derived) to the exercise or performance by such organization of its charitable, educational, or other purpose or function constituting the basis for its exemption. . . ."[67]

The purpose of the UBI tax was to reduce unfair competition by nonprofits: "The problem at which the tax on unrelated business income is directed is primarily that of unfair competition";[68] "the unrelated business income tax was intended to eliminate the conduct of unrelated businesses by exempt organizations as a source of unfair competition with private enterprise."[69] But UBI tax revenues have been so small that they have done little to rectify the problem of unfair competition. Total collections were $24.97 million in fiscal year 1977, $27.47 million in 1978, $24.97 million in 1979, $27.92 million in 1980, and $34.31 million in 1981.[70] More recent estimates show UBI revenues of approximately $50 million in fiscal year 1984, $80 million in 1985, and $153 million in 1986.[71] Over a period of six fiscal years, "the total tax collected was less than .05% of corporate income tax collections."[72]

There are several reasons why the UBI tax has not been effective at stemming or eliminating unfair competition. First, the UBI tax does nothing to reduce the inequities in postage rates or to eliminate the regulatory and other legislative advantages enjoyed by nonprofits. Second, there is widespread noncompliance and substantial tax loss due to nonreporting. A 1985 General Accounting Office study found that the

IRS does not have sufficient information on UBI tax noncompliance to fully understand the nature and magnitude of UBI noncompliance and develop profiles of high noncompliant tax-exempt organizations engaging in UBI activity. Without such information, IRS' current selection system cannot routinely focus on high noncompliant tax-exempt UBI organizations. These are organizations which regularly do not properly report UBI earnings or pay UBI tax due. Because IRS data show increasing UBI activity, high estimates of tax loss due to UBI nonreporting, and low yield from most of IRS' current UBI examinations, IRS may want to focus more on UBI organizations with a high potential for being noncompliant in addition to assuring that exempt organizations are operating in accordance with their exempt purposes.[73]

As of November 1983, approximately 23,000 nonprofits filed UBI returns; the IRS examined 2,186 of the returns in fiscal year 1982 and 2,127 in fiscal year 1983—roughly 9 percent. The IRS examinations resulted in additional taxes of $14,142,930 collected in fiscal year 1982 and $10,371,402 in fiscal year 1983.[74]

Third, the original law exempted "businesses carried on largely by volunteers, businesses conducted primarily for the convenience of members, students, patients and others, and businesses which consist of the sale of donated merchandise."[75] Then, the Tax Reform Act of 1976 "expressly excepted from the ambit of the tax the conduct of certain entertainment at fairs and expositions, the conduct of convention and trade shows by certain exempt organizations, and the performance of certain services for small hospitals. In 1978, Congress enacted an exception for certain bingo games. . . ."[76] In addition, income from all research performed by colleges, universities, or hospitals is exempt from UBI.

Finally, neither the courts nor the IRS apply a consistent standard in determining whether a commercial activity is "substantially related" to the primary purpose under which the organization was granted tax-exempt status. For example, a zoo sold jewelry with animal motifs, a commercial activity that the IRS ruled was taxable; stuffed animals sold by the zoo were tax-exempt.[77] A nonprofit hospital in a small Texas community operated an in-house pharmacy that sold products to hospital patients, private patients of doctors on the hospital staff, and the general public. In *Hi-Plains Hospital* v. *United States*, the court ruled that sales to private patients of staff doctors were tax exempt but that sales to the general public were taxable. The court reasoned that the hospital was in need of physicians to provide health care and that the convenience of a pharmacy for the doctors' patients made it easier to keep doctors on the staff. Thus, the sale of pharmaceuticals to private patients of staff doctors helped the hospital perform its tax-exempt function of providing hospital care. A dissenting judge opined that pharmacy sales to nonhospital patients had little to do with the organization's primary mission and noted that the purpose and intent of UBI taxes was to prevent "unfair competition" with for-profits. He concluded that

> by hair-splitting, judge-determined distinctions with regard to generically similar facts, profit-making activities conducted by charitable institutions separate from their tax-exempt purpose will be permitted to enjoy a competitive advantage over tax-paying businesses attempting to afford the same service, contrary to the Congressional intent made manifest by the legislative history and statutory provisions requiring taxation of such profit-making subsidiary operations.[78]

The convoluted nature of the distinction between taxable and tax-exempt income from commercial activities by nonprofits is evident in numerous IRS rulings and court cases.[79] One researcher who studied the exceptions to the UBI concluded that "exempt organizations should be encouraged to take advantage of the exceptions to minimize their tax liability."[80] As evidenced by the small amounts collected under the UBI tax, nonprofits have taken this suggestion to heart. Administrative and judicial interpretation of what is "significantly related" to the purposes for which nonprofit organizations were established has been vague, confusing, and contradictory; IRS enforcement and audit of the UBI tax law has been sporadic; and the compliance by nonprofit organizations in filing Form 990–T and in reporting the full amount of unrelated business income has been half-hearted. The only reasonable conclusion is that the UBI tax has been ineffective in achieving its goal of reducing unfair competition.

In theory, steps have also been taken to reduce unfair competition by public enterprises that compete with private firms. At the federal level, Office of Management and Budget (OMB) Circular A–76 states that, whenever possible, the federal government will rely on the private sector to produce goods and services. But loopholes and exceptions in the OMB directive and less than vigorous enforcement have limited its effectiveness. Some states have procurement policies modeled on Circular A–76, but after more than two decades of experience with A–76 at the federal level there is no reason to believe that the state versions have produced results that are dramatically different.[81]

The Intensity of Unfair Competition

Currently, more than 1.2 million private nonprofits employ millions of workers and volunteers and produce about 10 percent of gross national product. This sector is growing rapidly, and the future portends more commercial activity by private nonprofits as traditional sources of income dry up. Reductions in government spending, waning corporate support for nonprofits, and a marked decline in the formation of private foundations will encourage nonprofits to engage in new or expand existing commercial activities.[82]

In an effort to obtain information on the current level of nonprofit competition, the U.S. General Accounting Office (GAO) sent a questionnaire to 1,738 randomly selected firms in six industries that had voiced concern about this issue.[83] The GAO study found that nonprofits compete in all six industries (see Table 2.2) but that the intensity of competition varies across industries. For example, 90 percent of the respondents in the racquet sports and 84 percent of the respondents in the research and testing industry reported at least one nonprofit competitor, but more than half of the travel agents (55 percent) and tour operators (57 percent) reported no nonprofit competitors.[84] More agreement was found in responses to a question about whether competition from tax-exempt organizations had increased or decreased between 1980 and 1985. At least 90 percent of respondents in all six industries indicated that nonprofit competition was the same or greater in 1985 as in 1980, and more than half reported that competition was more intense in 1985 than in 1980.[85] The sources of nonprofit competition mentioned most frequently include public and private colleges and universities, state and local governments, religious organizations, business and professional organizations, hospitals, research organizations, YMCAs and YWCAs, recreation or fitness clubs, and humane or animal welfare organizations.

The GAO based its analysis on a survey questionnaire because "data do not exist to quantify the nature, extent, and impact of competition between these two communities [nonprofit and for-profit sectors]."[86] But there are serious weaknesses in a questionnaire approach. First, the questionnaire was sent only to *existing* firms; no effort was made to contact firms that had been driven out of business by unfair competition. Second, an important effect of nonprofit competition is that it discourages the formation of new firms, and it is impossible to survey (or count) entities that were never established. Finally, a case can be made that managers of for-profit firms might not realize the damage caused by unfair competition. Suppose that a for-profit operates in a rapidly growing market where sales double each year; the for-profit's annual growth rate would be 100 percent.

TABLE 2.2
Number of Perceived Tax-Exempt Competitors by Businesses Within Selected Industries[a]

Industry	Projected respondents	No competitors number	%	One competitor number	%	More than one competitor number	%	Top three types of tax-exempt competitors[b] Organizations	Percentage of respondents
Audio-visual	356	128	36	25	7	203	57	University or college—public	63
								Government—state or local	52
								University or college—private	43
Racquet sports	462	47	10	89	19	326	71	YM/YWCA or YM/YWHA	85
								Recreation/health/sports/fitness club	65
								Hospital	41
Research and Testing	215	34	16	4	2	177	82	University or college—public	79
								Government—state or local	60
								Research organization	56
Tour	28	16	57	1	6	11	39	Religious organizations	60
								University or college—public	56
								Business or professional association	55
Travel agent	7,349	4,016	55	472	6	2,861	39	Religious organizations	67
								University or college—public	63
								Social/fraternal organization	60
Veterinarian	18,444	7,191	39	3,733	20	7,520	41	Humane or animal welfare organization	60
								Government—state or local	24
								University or college—public	15

Source: U.S. General Accounting Office, *Competition Between Taxable Businesses and Tax-Exempt Organizations* (GAO/GGD-87-40BR) (Washington, D.C.: GAO, 1987), p. 31.
[a]Percentages have been rounded to the nearest whole number.
[b]Types of tax-exempt organizations perceived to compete to a moderate, great, or very great extent with questionnaire respondents over the past six years (1980–1985).

If a nonprofit enters the market and takes, say, half of the new business, the for-profit firm experiences a growth rate of only 50 percent. Under these circumstances, the manager of the for-profit might respond that nonprofit competition was unimportant. Only if the for-profit manager knew the amount of business lost would the full effect of the harm caused by unfair competition be known. Moreover, if other for-profits entered the market, it would be difficult to ascertain to what extent the lower growth rate was due to unfair competition and to what extent it could be traced to new for-profit competitors.

Little is known about the extent of unfair competition in various industries, its impact on existing firms, and its effects on the formation of new businesses. Despite its shortcomings, the GAO survey dramatically reveals the need for in-depth analyses of the problem. But to understand more fully the nature and impact of unfair competition so that correctives can be developed, it is first necessary to understand how nonprofit organizations are managed and to obtain a more complete picture of the effects on small business.

Notes to Chapter 2

1. Henry B. Hansmann, "The Role of Nonprofit Enterprise," *Yale Law Journal* (April 1980), p. 884.

2. "Unfair Competition By Nonprofit Organizations with Small Business: An Issue for the 1980s," 3rd ed. (Washington, D.C.: Small Business Administration, 1984).

3. 26 U.S.C. Sec. 410(a)(8)(B) (1976); 29 U.S.C. Sec. 203(r) (1976); 29 C.F.R. Sec. 779.214 (1982); 15 U.S.C. Sec. 77c(a)(4) (1982); 11 U.S.C. Sec. 303(a) (1982); *Marjorie Webster Junior College* v. *Middle States Association of Colleges and Secondary Schools*, 432 F.2d 650 (D.C. Cir. 1970), *cert. denied*, 400 U.S. 965 (1970); 17 U.S.C. Secs. 110,111(a)(4), 112(b), 118(d)(3) (1976).

4. 15 U.S.C. Sec. 45 (1982). Associations representing private, for-profit corporations are tax-exempt themselves under Section 501(c)(6) of the Internal Revenue Code.

5. 15 U.S.C. Sec. 44 (1982).

6. Janice C. Simpson, "United Way Turns to Small Businesses As Support Wanes at Some Big Firms," *Wall Street Journal*, January 8, 1987.

7. See Sec. 401(k) and Sec. 403(b) of the federal tax code.

8. 42 U.S.C. Sec. 410(a)(8)(B) (1976).

9. 39 U.S.C. Sec. 3626 (1976).

10. *Program on Nonprofit Organizations* (New Haven, CT: Yale University Institution for Social and Policy Studies, n.d.).

11. Hansmann, "Role of Nonprofit Enterprise." IRS *Income Tax Regulations* dealing with exempt organizations state in Section 1.501(c)(3)–1.(b)(2) that "an organization is not operated exclusively for one or more exempt purposes if its net earnings enure in whole or in part to the benefit of private shareholders or individuals."

12. David Johnston, "IRS Seeks to Impose Curbs on Lobbying by Charities," *Los Angeles Times*, January 1, 1987.

13. Lester M. Salamon, *Partners in Public Service: Toward a Theory of Government-Nonprofit Relations* (Washington, D.C.: The Urban Institute, 1985), p. 44.

14. Hansmann, "Role of Nonprofit Enterprise," pp. 840–43.

15. Ibid., pp. 872–73.

16. Most nonprofit organizations are covered by various subsections of section 501(c) of the Internal Revenue Code; farmers' cooperatives, however, are governed by regulations in Section 521.

17. Virginia Ann Hodgkinson and Murray S. Weitzman, *Dimensions of the Independent Sector: A Statistical Profile*, 2d. ed. (Washington, D.C.: Independent Sector, 1986), p. 11.

18. Ibid.

19. U.S. General Accounting Office, *Statistical Data on Tax-Exempt Organizations Earning Unrelated Business Income (GAO/GGD–85–43)* (Washington, D.C.: GAO, 1985), p. 4.

20. The IRS does prepare a "standard abstract" of the data on Form 990 for public use, but the activity code system used makes it nearly impossible to determine accurately whether the organizations are service providers, fund-raisers, or grant makers, and many organizations are miscoded. For a fuller treatment of these and other problems with IRS data, see Salamon, "Partners in Public Service," pp. 16–17, n. 16.

21. Exemption from federal taxation of income can be rescinded. Prior to 1951, mutual savings banks and savings and loan associations were exempt from federal income taxes. These organizations helped wage-earners and farmers and provided services for lower-income workers, a market that commercial banks disdained (the market was too "thin" for commercial entry). When mutual savings banks and savings and loans became important in the economy and no longer served a special market, the tax-exemption was withdrawn. See John Copeland and Gabriel Rudney, "Business Income of Nonprofits and Competitive Advantage—II," *Tax Notes* (December 29, 1986), pp. 1228–29. It is interesting that credit unions, which serve the same functions as banks, still retain their tax exemption. Some other "mutuals," such as the American Automobile Association and insurance companies, also pay taxes, even though they have 501(c) status under the Internal Revenue Code; these organizations are called "not-for-profits" and, because they do not enjoy the special privileges of nonprofits, they do not engage in unfair competition.

22. Adding the 338,224 churches and religious organizations produces the 1.2 million total number of nonprofits for 1985.

23. Hodgkinson and Weitzman, *Dimensions of the Independent Sector*, p. 3. For additional data on nonprofit employment and earnings, see Denis Johnston and Gabriel Rudney, "Characteristics of Workers in Nonprofit Organizations," *Monthly Labor Review* (July 1987): 28–33.

24. Ibid., p. 12.

25. Hansmann, "Role of Nonprofit Enterprise," pp. 835–36, n. 1.

26. Lester Salamon refers to two other estimates of the size of the nonprofit sector that produce similar results. See Salamon, "Partners in Public Service," p. 16, n. 16.

27. Erik Calonius, Sue Hutchinson, Vicki Quade, and Brad Risinger, "There's Big Money in the 'Nonprofits': Charity Begins at Home," *Newsweek*, January 5, 1987.

28. Lester Salamon, "The Invisible Partnership: Government and the Nonprofit Sector," *Bell Atlantic Quarterly* (Autumn 1984), p. 2.

29. Lester M. Salamon, "Nonprofits: The Results Are Coming In," *Foundation News* (July/August 1984), p. 17.

30. Ibid.

31. Ibid.

32. Salamon, "Partners in Public Service," pp. 9–10.

33. Salamon, "The Invisible Partnership," p. 5.

34. Ibid., pp. 5–7.

35. James C. Crimmins and Mary Keil, *Enterprise in the Nonprofit Sector* (Washington, D.C.: Partners for Livable Places, 1983), p. 14.

36. Ibid., p. 132.

37. Ibid., p. 131.

38. *Smithsonian* (January 1987), pp. 138–39.

39. D'Vera Cohn and Barbara Vobejda, "Arts, Education Groups Now Making Millions," *Washington Post*, November 24, 1985.

40. See Jim Sweeny, "Museum Shops the Place to Perfect the Art of Giving," *Fairfax* (VA) *Journal*, December 4, 1986; Howard S. Abramson, "Geographic Travels Tax-Free: Nonprofit Status Gives Magazine Competitive Edge," *Washington Post*, March 8, 1987.

41. *Association Marketing*, January 1987, pp. 2, 7.

42. "Associations Searching for New Ways to Generate Money," *Washington Post* (Business Supplement), February 2, 1987.

43. "Non-Dues Income Sources," *Association Marketing*, January 1987, pp. 3–4.

44. "Associations Searching for New Ways to Generate Money."

45. Ibid.

46. Leo Troy, "The Rise and Fall of American Trade Unions: The Labor Movement from FDR to RR," in *Unions in Transition: Entering the Second Century*, ed. Seymour Martin Lipset (San Francisco: Institute for Contemporary Studies, 1986), pp. 75–109.

47. As cited in Small Business Administration, "Unfair Competition," p. 10.

48. Ibid., p. 9.

49. Interest payments on bonds issued by state and local governments for public purposes are exempt from federal income taxes; interest payments on federal debt are exempt from state and local income taxes. The 1986 tax reform act makes interest payments on state and local government debt that is used for private purposes (such as industrial development bonds) subject to federal income tax.

50. U.S. General Accounting Office, *Civil Servants and Contract Employees: Who Should Do What for the Federal Government?* (FPCD–81–43) (Washington, D.C.: GAO, June 19, 1981).

51. Quoted in testimony of James S. Hostetler in U.S. Congress, Senate, Committee on Small Business, *Government Competition with Small Business. Hearings Before the Subcommittee on Advocacy and the Future of Small Business of the Senate Committee on Small Business*, 97th Cong., 1st sess., 1981, p. 23.

52. See *Capitol Comment* (Washington, D.C.: Citizens for a Sound Economy, October 16, 1985).

53. "Bus Supports Recreation Trips," *The Trident Tides* (Bangor, WA), December 12, 1986, p. 5. Apparently, the Navy is having difficulty counting the number of seats on its luxury coach. The number of seats is given as 46 in *Trident Tides*, but is reported as 44 in *Up Scope* ("The MWR Newsletter for Subase Bangor, Jackson Park & Keyport"), January 1987, p. 1.

54. "Outdoor Recreation," *Up Scope*, January 1987, pp. 10, 12.

55. There is a large and growing literature dealing with public-sector competition with private firms. For example, see James T. Bennett and Manuel H. Johnson, *Better Government at Half the Price: Private Production of Public Services* (Ottawa, IL: Caroline House Publishers, 1981); Stuart M. Butler, *Privatizing Federal Spending: A Strategy to Eliminate the Deficit* (New York: Universe Books, 1985); E.S. Savas, *Privatizing the Public Sector* (Chatham, NJ: Chatham House, 1982); Madsen Pirie, *Dismantling the State: The Theory and Practice of Privatization* (Dallas: National Center for Policy Analysis, 1985).

56. A detailed review of the off-budget sector is given in James T. Bennett and Thomas J. DiLorenzo, *Underground Government: The Off-Budget Public Sector* (Washington, D.C.: The Cato Institute, 1985).

57. Quoted in John Copeland and Gabriel Rudney, "Business Income of Nonprofits and Competitive Advantage," *Tax Notes* (November 24, 1986), p. 749.

58. John C. Goodman, *The Regulation of Medical Care: Is the Price Too High?* (Washington, D.C.: Cato Institute, 1980), p. 54.

59. Ibid., p. 56.

60. Paul T. Lahti, "Early Post Operative Discharge of Patients from the Hospital," *Surgery* (March 1968): 410–15.

61. Victor Fuchs, *Who Shall Live?* (New York: Basic Books, 1974), p. 98.

62. Ibid.

63. Goodman, *Regulation of Medical Care*, Table 4.2, p. 56.

64. There are exceptions. A for-profit Elvis Presley "museum" which, *inter alia*, displays the singer's clothing, Cadillac convertible, and other memorabilia, operates on an admission fee basis in the Potomac Mills Mall in Woodbridge, Virginia. The long-term financial viability of this enterprise remains to be seen.
65. Hansmann, "Role of Nonprofit Enterprise," pp. 348–49.
66. Susan Rose-Ackerman, "Unfair Competition and Corporate Income Taxation," *Stanford Law Review* (May 1982), p. 1017. At the time, New York University "also owned a leather company, a piston ring factory, and a chinaware manufacturing operation. Other colleges and universities owned enterprises manufacturing automobile parts, cotton gins, and food products, and operated an airport, a street railway, a hydroelectric plant, and a radio station" (n. 2).
67. Carla A. Neely, "Exceptions to the Term 'Unrelated Trade or Business' Under Section 513(a)," *Journal of Air Law and Commerce* (1985), pp. 837–38.
68. Senate Report No. 2375, 81st Cong., 2d. Sess., 1950, pp. 28–29.
69. Neely, "Exceptions," p. 839.
70. Rose-Ackerman, "Unfair Competition," pp. 1017–18, n. 4.
71. Robert L. Hill, "What's Fair Is Fair," *Oregon Business* (August 1986), p. 23; Mark Thompson, "New Tax Law Changes: Problems for Nonprofit Groups," *Baltimore Daily Record*, October 11, 1986; Laura Saunders, "Profits? Who, me?" *Forbes*, March 23, 1987, p. 106.
72. Rose-Ackerman, "Unfair Competition," p. 1017, n. 4.
73. U.S. General Accounting Office, *Statistical Data on Tax-Exempt Organizations Earning Unrelated Business Income*, Report to the House Ways and Means Subcommittee on Oversight, March 29, 1985, GAO/GGD–85–43, p. ii.
74. William J. Anderson, Director, U.S. General Accounting Office, to Daniel Rostenkowski, Chairman, Committee on Ways and Means, House of Representatives, March 29, 1985 (B–217690), pp. 5, 7.
75. Neely, "Exceptions," p. 839.
76. Ibid., pp. 840–41.
77. Small Business Administration, "Unfair Competition", p. 29, n. 61.
78. 670 F. 2d 528 (5th Cir. 1982), p. 535.
79. See Neely, "Exceptions."
80. Ibid., p. 864.
81. See, for example, U.S. Small Business Administration, Office of the Chief Council for Advocacy, *Government Competition: A Threat to Small Business, Report of the SBA Advocacy Task Group on Government Competition with Small Business* (Washington, D.C.: U.S. SBA, March 1980) and Senate Committee on Small Business, *Government Competition with Small Business*.
82. Simpson, "United Way"; "New Investigations of Private Philanthropy," Program on Nonprofit Organizations, Institute for Social and Policy Studies, Yale University (Fall, 1985), p. 6. According to this source, "fewer than 30 major foundations were created in the early 1980s, the lowest number of new foundations since the depression decade of the 1930s."

83. U.S. General Accounting Office, *Competition Between Taxable Businesses and Tax-Exempt Organizations (GAO/GGD–87–40BR)* (Washington, D.C.: GAO, 1987), esp. pp. 30–36.

84. This result seems odd and is contradicted by a survey taken by the National Tour Association, Inc. (NTA), a trade association that represents tour operators. An NTA "Member Viewpoint" survey "indicated that 89 percent of the Association's tour operators are *adversely impacted* by nonprofit competition," and NTA's "Board of Directors has formally designated *unfair competition by nonprofit organizations as the association's top priority issue for 1987.*" See *Tuesday* (A Periodic Publication of the National Tour Association News Bureau), vol. 7, February 24, 1987.

85. General Accounting Office, *Competition Between Taxable Businesses*, p. 35.

86. Ibid., p. 1.

TABLE A2.1
Nonprofit Entities (Excluding Foundations) by Activity Codes, National Summary
(Year Ending December 31, 1972)

Code	Description	Code	Description
01	Arts (performing arts, fine arts, etc.)	33	Fund raising
02	Advertising	34	Garden club
03	Alumni activities	35	Gifts to charitable organizations
04	Association of employees	36	Gifts to individuals
05	Association of employers	37	Handicapped, aid to
06	Athletics	38	Health agency
07	Bookstore	39	Historical sites, historical records, preservation of, etc.
08	Business promotion		
09	Cafeteria, restaurant, snack bar, food services	40	Hobby club
10	Camp	41	Hospital nursing home, etc.
11	Cemetery or burial association	42	Housing for aged
12	Civic welfare	43	Housing (other)
13	Civil liberties or rights	44	Humanitarian activities
14	Clinic	45	Indian (tribe, cultures, etc.)
15	Commemorative organization (centennial, monument, etc.)	46	Industrial development
		47	Insurance
		48	International operations
16	Commodity exchange	49	Juvenile delinquency, combating of
17	Community deterioration, prevention of	50	Legislative activities
18	Community fund	51	Library
19	Conservation (natural resources, wildlife)	52	Loans
		53	Marketing members' products
20	Country club	54	Medical care
21	Credit reporting	55	Museum
22	Educational institution	56	Nursery
23	Educational (other)	57	Parent or parents-teachers association
24	Emergency or disaster aid fund	58	Patriotic activities
25	Employees, welfare of	59	Pensions, profit-sharing trust, etc.
26	Employment assistance, retraining, apprentice or vocational training	60	Perpetual care fund
		61	Professional advancement
		62	Public safety
27	Endowment fund	63	Publishing, radio, TV, etc.
28	Exhibitions, fairs, trade shows	64	Real estate activities
29	Farming	65	Recreation
30	Federal, state or local government agency	66	Religious institution (church, synagogue, etc.)
31	Financial services	67	Religious (other)
32	Fraternity or sorority	68	Rental of owned property

TABLE A2.1 (continued)

Code	Description	Code	Description
69	Research and development	84	Vacation plan
70	Retirement plan	85	Veterans activities
71	Royalties, receipt of	86	Volunteer firemen's
72	Scholarships		organization
73	Senior citizens or retirees	87	Voter education
74	Services to members	88	World peace, promotion of
75	Sick or death benefits to	89	YMCA, YMHA, etc.
	members	90	Youth activities
76	Social activities	91	Instrumentality of government
77	Sports activities		agency
78	Student activities	93	Nonexempt charitable trust
79	Testing	94	170(B) (A) (vi) determinations
80	Thrift shop, retail outlet, etc.	95	509(A) (2) determinations
81	Traffic or tariff bureau	96	Private schools
82	Unemployment benefits	98	Denials or failed to establish
83	Urban renewal	99	EOMF handbook (522)

Source: Burton A. Weisbrod, *The Voluntary Nonprofit Sector* (Lexington, MA: Lexington Books, 1977), pp. 43–4.

from the organization's operations, but there is evidence that this prohibition is not very well enforced. Consequently, the managers of many nonprofit organizations enrich themselves at the expense of their organizations and their patrons. They may receive excessive salaries, low-interest loans from the organization, or personal services and amenities paid for out of organization funds. In addition, businesses that are owned by the managers might receive generous contracts for goods and services, friends and relatives might be given patronage jobs, or the organization might purchase or lease real estate from its managers at inflated prices. Such abuses have been documented in numerous CNE operations, including nursing homes, hospitals, private schools, and workshops for the handicapped.[1]

CNE Boards of Directors

In contrast to private corporations where boards of directors are ultimately responsible to and elected by shareholders, board members of CNEs are usually elected or appointed by a small clique of activists in the nonprofit organization. There are no shareholders who must be satisfied. And in contrast to governmental enterprises, there are no general political interests—that is, voters—that must be satisfied. In a sense, CNE boards are responsible to no one but themselves and a small leadership cadre within the organization.

Not infrequently, board members may be involved in business activities that are directly related to those of the CNE, such as banking, real estate, legal counsel, or construction. Although blatant conflicts of interest may prevent outright financial gain by board members, they may be able to inconspicuously direct the organization's business dealings to their own business partners. This also occurs in the for-profit sector when, for example, a local businessman on a bank's board of directors wants his business partners to receive credit. In the for-profit sector, however, the bottom line of profits constrains such behavior: If inside dealings are not profitable, the bank will be penalized by lower profits and the threat of bankruptcy.

Conflicts of interest by board members are more likely to flourish in the nonprofit sector. Board members are not directly responsible to shareholders—as are corporate board members—or to voters—as are government officials, and once appointed to a term in office board members are quite secure. There is, then, considerable latitude for board members to pursue their own interests.

Managers of CNEs are responsible for the day-to-day operations of their organizations, which are supposedly carried out under policies set by the board. There is no doubt that CNE managers have considerable discretion, for part-time board members have neither the time nor the inclination to become intimately involved with details of an organization's operation. Because CNE management is critically judged by the organization's financial viability, there are pressures to avoid risky undertakings that may prove to be unprofitable; there are strong incentives to "cream the market" by engaging in only those activities that generate large amounts of revenue relative to the associated costs. This is what makes CNEs so paradoxical. They are ostensibly charitable, not profit-seeking organizations; but because truly charitable activities are not always profitable, in an accounting sense, they have redirected their organizations into commercial activities that are.

Empire-Building Incentives

There are ample incentives to encourage managers to expand the operations of CNEs and increase the cash flow. After operating expenses and debt-service charges have been paid, the excess revenue is held internally (i.e., it is not distributed to shareholders) and may be used by management for perquisites. Thus, there are strong reasons for CNE managers to be "growth oriented" and to expand their empires rapidly, even if a broad interpretation of the organization's mission is required. This kind of expansion is increasingly financed by commercial, profit-making activities that have little to do with the organization's charitable or public service purposes. There are also empire builders in the for-profit sector, but competitive markets limit such behavior there. The limits are much weaker, if they exist at all, in the nonprofit sector.

Information Problems

There is also a fundamental difference in the way information is used in the for-profit and nonprofit sectors. Both types of organizations utilize information about production and distribution techniques, marketing strategies, and so on. Typically, information relevant to the operation of the enterprise is gathered by lower-level employees and eventually is filtered up to top decision makers—the president of the company, the board of directors, or upper-level management. In all organizations there is an incentive for employees to tell their superiors the "good" news—the news they think the boss wants to hear. For instance, the company's corporate financial analyst may know that a particular investment project has costs that outweigh the benefits but may not point this out if the project is favored by the boss. Such incentives exist in both for-profit and nonprofit enterprises.[2] The effect in any organization is that information is lost or distorted before it makes its way to the top decision makers and decisions are made less efficiently. This phenomenon is likely to be even more severe in larger organizations.

In the private sector, the chickens do eventually come home to roost. The distorted information will cause profits to decline as decisions are made on the basis of misleading or incomplete information, so there are incentives to constrain such behavior. Any private business that ignores the bottom line for an extended period of time will not only forego profits but may also go out of business. Such incentives do not exist in the nonprofit sector. Because there are no profit and loss statements in that sector, informational distortions may persist.

Monopolistic Incentives

Because of their special legislative privileges, many CNEs are local monopolies—another source of inefficiency. Like governmental enterprises, many CNEs are effectively statutory monopolies established by legislative fiat. An example is a nonprofit hospital that can underprice a for-profit hospital and thereby keep it from entering the local market. Without the threat of competition, a nonprofit hospital can charge monopoly prices and has weaker incentives for implementing cost-cutting and product-improving measures. The same is true for CNEs in many other industries that exhibit what economists call motivational inefficiency or "x-inefficiency."[3]

Although CNEs engage in commercial undertakings, they are quite different from commercial firms. CNEs are much more like government enterprises in that they compete unfairly with private enterprises because of the special privileges they enjoy, such as their tax-exempt status. Despite these similarities, there are some key differences between CNEs and governmental enterprises. Perhaps the most

striking difference is that while governmental enterprises are ultimately accountable to voters, CNEs must respond to no similar
interest group. They enjoy many of the legislative privileges of
governmental enterprises but are less accountable to the public.

Every politician promises to serve the "public interest," and on
election day the voters decide whether he or she has kept those
promises. The managers and directors of CNEs also maintain that
their work serves the public interest, but, unlike public officials, they
never face an electoral judgment day. This gives them even greater
latitude than government officials have to pursue their own self
interests.

CNEs: Accountable to Whom?

Employees, managers, and directors of CNEs frequently claim that
nonprofit enterprises tend to be more "accountable" to the community than private, for-profit businesses. For instance, the National
Assembly of Voluntary and Social Welfare Organizations, a trade
association representing the interests of CNE management, recently
asserted that

> Nonprofits are more accountable to the community at large than
> are for-profit firms. The involvement of the community in non-
> profits, through board representation, volunteer commitments
> and donations, creates an "ombudsman" effect that is not pres-
> ent in for-profit firms.[4]

Such claims, however, reveal a fundamental misunderstanding of
how the free enterprise system works. Profit-seeking firms may also
place community representatives on their boards for publicity reasons. But in terms of their performance the firms *must* be accountable
to the community if they are to survive. They cannot produce inferior
goods or goods for which there is no demand if they wish to remain
competitive, regardless of who is on the board of directors. The firms
must be accountable to a large portion of the community who are
their existing or potential customers.

In contrast, nonprofit organizations are not necessarily accountable
to the community simply because two or three members of the
community are on the board of directors. These individuals are not
elected by the community and, therefore, do not necessarily represent the views of other citizens. A private business that tried to

advertise and sell its product solely on the basis that it had appointed, say, a local clergyman or government official to its board of directors would be mercilessly ridiculed. Yet, this is precisely the argument CNEs make regarding their supposedly superior public accountability.

CNEs also claim that they "lend a consistency and stability to the provision of . . . services that is not characteristic of for-profit firms, which, historically, have entered and left markets based upon their profitability."[5]

This reasoning also reveals a misunderstanding of the free enterprise system and the role of profits and losses. One of the benefits of the system is that private businesses leave markets when they are no longer profitable. This usually occurs when consumer demands shift and consumers no longer prefer to spend as much of their income on those items. When businesses leave one market and enter another, therefore, it is precisely *because* they are accountable to consumers. The markets that businesses enter are the ones where new consumer demands have arisen; the markets they leave are ones where consumer demands have withered. This makes the free enterprise system much more accountable to consumers than either the government or the nonprofit sector. In the private sector, the only way to earn profits in the long run is to be accountable to consumers. Highly publicized business failures, such as the Ford Edsel and AMC Pacer automobiles, are a testament to how consumers are the final arbiters in the free enterprise system. By contrast, governmentally subsidized nonprofit enterprises can remain in business long after there is any real need for them.

The Issue of Equity

The National Assembly of Voluntary and Social Welfare Organizations, among others, also claims that commercial nonprofit enterprises ensure a more equitable distribution of services:

> Nonprofits historically have insured that our most vulnerable populations are served. To the extent that for-profit firms supplant nonprofits . . . either needs will go unmet, government will have to do more, or new . . . structures will have to be crafted to ensure an equitable distribution of services.[6]

As a general principle this assertion is questionable. Historically, many nonprofit organizations *have* helped many of those in need of charity, but there are numerous exceptions. Many CNEs routinely claim that their services are necessary and worthy of subsidies because for-profit firms are only interested in "skimming the cream"—that is, serving only the most lucrative markets and leaving the less affluent and the underprivileged without adequate services. But consider the following description of one CNE that appeared in *Time* magazine:

> The gleaming red brick and glass building on Rhode Island Avenue in Washington [D.C.] is a temple to physical perfection, boasting steam rooms and whirlpool baths, mirrored exercise rooms and an equipment-packed Nautilus center, tanning beds and a pro shop. The most striking feature: a row of street-level windows that floods the pool area with natural light and forms a balcony from which passersby can view the lobbyists, lawyers and other upwardly mobile types who swarm the waters every morning, noon and evening. The capital's toniest private health club? Hardly. This is the . . . YMCA.[7]

The *Time* article also reported that the Washington, D.C. YMCA is no aberration: "In cities and suburbs across the country, the Y is . . . putting up gleaming facilities that rival the ritziest of private clubs."[8] Because of its nonprofit tax exemption and other special privileges, the YMCA can offer much lower rates than many private health clubs. For example, the new YMCA in downtown Los Angeles charges $390 per year; its nearest competitor, the Los Angeles Athletic Club, charges $960 in annual fees.[9] In the name of helping the underprivileged, the YMCA is profiting by building glamorous health clubs for the affluent. There are other examples, in later chapters, of how many CNEs may in theory promote a more "equitable" distribution of services but in practice serve a narrow, privileged clientele.

The Effect of Incentives on Performance

Because the incentives in CNEs are similar to those of governmental enterprises, the performance of their managers can be expected to be roughly similar. This implies that, like governmental enterprises, CNEs are likely to provide goods and services at a higher cost than equivalent goods and services provided by private, competitive businesses. The evidence that governmental enterprises provide goods and services at a much higher cost than private competitive firms is so overwhelming that a "bureaucratic rule of two" has been proposed: Government provision of goods and services is likely to approximately double the unit cost of production.[10]

The bureaucratic rule of two may apply to CNEs as well. There is reason to suspect, however, that CNEs may be even *less* efficient than most governmental enterprises, given that they operate without both market and electoral constraints. There are numerous examples of how the lack of an electoral (or shareholder) constraint affects the performance of nonprofit organizations.[11] These examples are provided by the activities of government off-budget enterprises (OBEs) that have been formed at the federal, state, and local levels of government.[12]

OBEs have been established in the U.S. primarily to bypass the wishes of the electorate whenever the voters express a demand for fiscal restraint. OBEs are "public corporations" created by politicians and given far more latitude and discretion than regular on-budget governmental enterprises. Their spending and borrowing does not appear on the budget documents of the governmental jurisdictions that created them, which shields them from public scrutiny. Because they are off budget, they need not go through highly-publicized budget hearings. They finance much of their operations without direct voter approval by selling revenue bonds, which usually do not require a referendum. They are managed by political appointees, not elected officials. OBEs enjoy all the tax and regulatory privileges that other governmental enterprises do, which gives them an advantage over private-sector competitors. But they are likely to be even more detached from taxpayer scrutiny than on-budget governmental enterprises because of the fact that they are off the books. The experiences of New York State under Governor Nelson Rockefeller illustrates the OBE phenomenon.

When Nelson Rockefeller became governor of New York in 1959 he announced an aggressive program of governmental activity. To finance his plans, Rockefeller raised taxes during his first five years in office about twice as fast as during the preceding four years, which generated much taxpayer discontent. Consequently, taxpayers began to oppose his spending plans by rejecting bond referenda. Rockefeller bypassed taxpayer opposition by simply financing them through OBEs. For example, in the late 1950s when voters rejected a $100 million housing bond issue for the third time, the governor created the off-budget Housing Finance Authority. In 1961, voters rejected a $500 million higher-education bond issue for the fourth time; Rocke-feller responded by creating the off-budget State University Construc-tion Fund. In 1965, the voters rejected, for the fifth time, a housing bond issue; the Governor created the Urban Development Corpora-tion. By the time Rockefeller resigned from office in 1973, 14 months before the state faced possible default and bankruptcy, New York's off-budget debt stood at $13.3 billion, approximately four times the amount of on-budget, voter-approved debt outstanding.[13]

The poor performance of off-budget governmental enterprises in New York eventually drove the state to the brink of bankruptcy. For example, the state's Urban Development Corporation (UDC) was formed in April 1968 to carry out Rockefeller's plans for housing construction. Within a year, 50 projects were underway in 23 cities with estimated construction costs of about $2 billion (total *on-budget* state government expenditures for all programs in 1968 were $5.5 billion). Emphasis was placed on speed—an extraordinarily careless policy. The UDC's first director, Edward J. Logue, stated that his agency had "a directive to go out and build, build, build," and the agency's construction methods soon became known as "fast track-ing."[14] This approach required simultaneous work on several aspects of a project; commencement of construction before final project drawings and specifications were completed; negotiated rather than competitive bidding with contractors, which raised contract prices; proceeding with projects without signing final construction contracts or agreements to deliver performance bonds; and commencement of construction before UDC was given title to the land upon which construction was taking place.

This kind of carelessness is not characteristic of private contractors who must invest their own money in a project or even of on-budget governmental agencies that are under more public scrutiny. Predict-ably, the UDC was soon so grossly inefficient that by February 25, 1975—with over $1 billion in partially completed construction, over $1 billion in outstanding debt, and operating costs of about $1 million per day—the financial markets closed to the UDC and it went into default. The UDC could not pay its outstanding obligations, and banks were unwilling to give it new financing. The UDC was eventu-ally bailed out by the taxpayers of New York and it still operates. Because there have been few fundamental changes in its operations, however, it remains a financially precarious institution.

Although the UDC, like all other OBEs, is ostensibly a nonprofit organization, many have found its activities to be quite profitable. The New York State Comptroller conducted an audit of the UDC in 1983 and concluded that "the outside legal fees, consultant contracts, bond underwriting selections, public relations retainers, and other discretionary expenditure items . . . show a clear pattern of imprudent spending, waste, favoritism, politics, duplication, high living, and poor public policy."[15] Moreover, "there seems to have been a general attitude that the [UDC] should be run for the convenience and benefit of the technocrats and political insiders with disregard for the taxpayers or the urgency of austerity elsewhere in government."[16] The Comptroller cited many examples: One attorney with "good contacts in the Carey administration" was paid $5 million in legal fees over a three-year period, although 94 percent of all the legal work was done by secretaries or paralegals; two vice presidents billed a four-day, $6,300 trip to Las Vegas to the agency; other outside legal counsel billed the agency at a rate of $190 per hour, despite a state law that limited such compensation to $125 per hour; approximately half of the UDC's outside legal fees went to one attorney because there was no competitive bidding; and law firms simply submitted bills to the UDC listing the amount charged without identifying the work performed, the number of hours billed, or the hourly rate. Others also profited, including investment bankers who sold the organization's bonds; construction firms and labor unions that benefited from building construction; and architects, engineers, accountants, bureaucrats, and others involved in the projects.

The Washington Public Power Supply System

The Washington Public Power Supply System (WPPSS), known as "Whoops," became notorious in the early 1980s because of what *Fortune* magazine labeled "squalor and fantastic waste."[17] This OBE is an organization of 23 governmentally owned utilities that in 1957 joined together to form an off-budget "municipal corporation" of the state of Washington. Its broad purpose was to construct, finance, operate, and sell electric power from nuclear generating plants.

The "squalor and waste" was a reference to the scrapping of all but one of the five partially completed power plants WPPSS had set out to build. This action left Washington state utility customers with $2.25 billion in debt outstanding as of 1983, a debt that is estimated to increase to $7.2 billion by the year 2018 when all outstanding bonds for those plants are retired. The initial cost estimates for all five WPPSS plants was $4.2 billion; because of mismanagement, the figure was revised to over $24 billion by 1984. All five plants were scheduled to be completed by 1977, but as of 1987 only one was operating; the others had been cancelled or their operation postponed indefinitely. Several of them were being torn down and scrapped. Rapidly escalating construction costs on the WPPSS plants are expected to at least quadruple electric bills in the Northwest within ten years and to push the outstanding debt of some member utilities to 70 or 80 percent of the value of all property in their jurisdictions.

One explanation for the WPPSS fiasco is that WPPSS, like other OBEs, was almost completely unaccountable to the taxpayers. WPPSS management had virtually no regard for cost effectiveness; as one of its directors explained, whenever there were cost overruns and cash was low, "we would just toddle down to Wall Street."[18] As long as WPPSS directors could borrow to finance construction and the financial markets were willing to buy their bonds, there was little incentive for cost consciousness. In a study of the causes of WPPSS's financial failures, the state's Senate Energy and Utilities Committee concluded that the major problem was "mismanagement." For example, WPPSS board members, mostly local politicians, made the political decision to give work to as many contractors as possible, hiring from 45 to 65 general contractors per job site. In contrast, Commonwealth Edison, a lower-cost private producer of power plants, generally uses only three general contractors.[19] The confusion over who should do what on various job sites led to long delays and inflated construction costs. Adding to the mayhem was a featherbedding requirement that each contractor have his own support staff and equipment, so each construction site was littered with from 50 to 60 cranes. At other nuclear plant construction sites, nine or ten cranes are usually sufficient.

The Committee's report also noted the use of "fast track" construction methods, similar to those used by New York's UDC. The Committee concluded that the practice of commencing construction before architectural and engineering design work was completed made it necessary to renegotiate many contracts. The Committee found that contract renegotiation delayed construction by as much as five years and increased costs by approximately 1,200 percent.[20]

In sum, the effects of WPPSS on ratepayers in the Northwest have been disastrous. In less than a decade they have gone from having the most abundant and least costly power in the nation to defaulting on nearly $8 billion in outstanding debt. The 1983 WPPSS default was the largest in the history of municipal finance up to that time.

We do not mean to imply here that all nonprofit organizations are likely to be managed in as haphazard a manner as the UDC and WPPSS. These examples do illustrate, however, the importance of incentives to economic performance. The UDC and WPPSS managements were permitted to use their organizations to pursue their own personal interests at the expense of the public interest. They enriched themselves without benefiting even those segments of the public they were mandated to serve—housing consumers and electric ratepayers. There are literally thousands of OBEs like the UDC and WPPSS in the U.S., many of which are experiencing similar financial problems.[21]

In summary, both OBEs and CNEs have greater latitude in their decision making than either private enterprises or on-budget governmental enterprises. Consequently, CNEs are prone to experience many of the same performance problems that OBEs do.

The "Problem" of Commercialism

Because they are "nonprofit" organizations, the motives of CNEs are less suspect than private businesses that operate "only for profit." Some scholars have even advanced the theory that people who are more selfless and altruistic by nature will tend to seek employment in nonprofit organizations, whereas those who are more selfish and materialistic will gravitate toward the private sector.[22] Thus, despite the well-known incentive problems of nonprofit organizations, the absence of a capitalistic mentality is said to be an advantage that CNEs have over private enterprises. Good performance allegedly stems from good intentions and vice versa. According to this theory, good intentions may be sufficient to overcome the incentive problems in nonprofit organizations. This type of thinking gives CNEs another type of competitive edge over for-profit firms.

Bennett Schultz, a private producer of educational materials, testified about this particular CNE advantage at hearings held by the federal government's Small Business Administration:

> Tax-supported institutions are provided with federal funds to create curriculum materials. Because of the university imprimatur, the material is automatically assumed to be valid. . . . A goodly portion of this material could not survive the rigors of a

free market. Commercial producers would be afraid to put their names on much of what is offered by the universities.[23]

While Mr. Schultz's views may be suspect on the grounds that his business competes with CNEs, it is reasonable to believe that a university connection is likely to invoke a feeling of trust among consumers, even if that feeling may not be warranted.

The image of nonprofit organizations as comprised of selfless, beneficent public servants has helped them to maintain or extend their involvement in a number of fields, such as the provision of health care. Nonprofit institutions themselves have advanced the notion that certain services, such as hospital care, should not be left to the for-profit sector, because it is immoral for someone to profit from the misery of others. Something as critical to life as hospital care, we are told, should not be provided by profiteers.

This line of reasoning may initially seem attractive and intuitively appealing, but on closer inspection it is not convincing. If hospital care is best provided by nonprofit organizations, for example, it is not clear why other equally important goods and services are not provided by the nonprofit sector as well. Why do we have private grocery stores and farms when food is crucial to survival? Clothing and housing are also considered necessities of life, but their provision is dominated by private, profit-seeking businesses. The list of such crucial goods and services is long. Moreover, CNEs coexist in industries with many private businesses, providing evidence that the profit motive creates no inherent problem in those industries. In fact, it is *because of the profit motive* that there are markets for such products. As Adam Smith pointed out more than 200 years ago, it is not because of altruism that the butcher and baker provide us with meat and bread but because of their regard for their own self interest. This insight is as relevant today as it was then. The absence of a profit motive is not an argument *for* nonprofit organizations providing services but an argument *against* it.

The profit motive involves both the carrot of reward and the stick of punishment. Those businesses that satisfy consumers with high quality products at competitive prices will be rewarded with profits; failure to do so results in losses or bankruptcy. The absence of these incentives is a major *disadvantage* for nonprofit organizations. Furthermore, the more "important" a service is, the stronger is the case for private sector provision.

In the important area of hospital care, for example, one can clearly see the problems related to the elimination of the profit motive by observing the failures of socialized health care in Great Britain. Eliminating the profit motive through nationalization has led to the reduced quality and quantity of health care, higher costs, and the flight of many medical professionals to the United States and Canada where rewards are more closely linked to performance.[24]

Undoubtedly, many nonprofit organizations are managed by compassionate, altruistic individuals who undertake those charitable activities that they believe neither government nor the private sector does enough of. Personal profit seeking does not appear to play a dominant role in such organizations (e.g., churches and charities), but *commercial* nonprofit organizations are another matter. Because they are legally "nonprofit" organizations, they enjoy the same charitable image as churches, the United Way, and the March of Dimes. However, not all of them deserve that reputation.

There are many examples of how "nonprofit" status is used by profit-seeking individuals to gain an unfair competitive edge and to make profits. For instance, the American Association of Retired Persons (AARP) and the National Retired Teachers Association (NRTA) have been sued for serving as a front for a large commercial insurance company. A former executive director of AARP has testified in court that the two associations have been used to direct business to the Colonial Penn Group of Philadelphia, which sells insurance, travel packages, and other services. The director and principal stockholder of Colonial Penn was also one of the founders of AARP and NRTA. According to the suit, Colonial Penn's director "has become a millionaire from the sale of insurance and other services to elderly people who are systematically misled into believing that the primary purpose of the associations is the best interest of the elderly. The fact is that AARP was designed and created to be, and NRTA was turned into, a group for insurance purposes."[25]

AARP and NRTA efforts have apparently been quite profitable: "Colonial Penn is one of the nation's most profitable insurance firms. . . . The company's after-tax return on capital [in recent years] averaged 30.5 percent, placing it in the top three companies with sales of 250 million dollars or more."[26] Other profit-making "nonprofit" organizations in the insurance industry are the Knights of Columbus life insurance program, which has about $4 billion annually in nontaxed business, and the Lutheran Brotherhood, which sells about $8 billion worth of (untaxed) insurance annually.[27]

Because there is profit seeking in the commercial "nonprofit" sector, the alleged beneficence of CNEs should be met with the same skepticism given to any businessman who claimed to be an altruistic, socially responsible philanthropist. In short, there are good reasons to heed the advice of Adam Smith, who claimed to have "never known much good done by those who affected to trade for the public good."

The Problem of Consumer Ignorance

One justification for governmental support of commercial nonprofit enterprises is a specific type of "market failure." It is alleged that because consumers may be incapable of accurately evaluating the quality of goods or services, private-sector producers can charge excessive prices for inferior goods. Professor Henry Hansmann of the University of Pennsylvania has described how the market "fails" in this regard:

> In situations of this type, consumers might be considerably better off if they deal with nonprofit producers rather than with for-profit producers. The nonprofit producer, like its for-profit counterpart, has the capacity to raise prices and cut quality in such cases without much fear of customer reprisal; however, it lacks the incentive to do so because those in charge are barred from taking home any resulting profits. In other words, the advantage of a nonprofit producer is that the discipline of the market is supplemented by the additional protection given the consumer by another, broader "contract," the organization's . . . commitment to devote its entire earnings to the production of services. As a result of this institutional constraint, it is less imperative for the consumer either to shop around first or to enforce rigorously the contract he makes.[28]

This theory appeals to many economists and legal scholars and has generated further research on the problem of "contract failure" by private producers. One research project, for instance, recently concluded that "nonprofit firms may be superior to for-profit firms if the output cannot be costlessly observed."[29] One problem with a conclusion like this, however, is that it seems trivial because *nothing* can be "costlessly" observed. Elementary economic theory teaches that *every* activity has an opportunity cost—that is, the value an individual places on the most highly valued alternative use of his time.

Aside from this point, however, there is a more fundamental problem with the "contract failure" rationale for commercial non-profit enterprise. There are two different ways for consumers to gain knowledge about the quality of a product or service. First, they can rely on a business's reputation, past performance, and contractual obligations, for example, 30–day warranties and service contracts. In short, consumers can rely on the marketplace to discipline businesses that provide inferior products at inflated prices.

Second, consumers can rely on the edicts of governmental authorities. For instance, governmental regulation of product standards is one way in which bureaucracy, rather than markets, generates information about product quality. Government now regulates nearly every consumer product imaginable and attempts to provide consumers with safety and product quality information by informing them when products have passed certain government tests or by mandating product standards. Once a product has been granted governmental approval, however, producers have weaker incentives to assure that the product is of a high quality because many consumers are likely to believe the government's evaluation. This is especially true of goods or services whose quality is difficult to judge until after the purchase has been made. In other words, a government stamp of approval can easily give consumers a false assurance of a product's safety or quality.

Governmental regulation of product quality can also be counterproductive by increasing the product's cost, by limiting consumer choice, by slowing the rate of innovation, and even by making products more dangerous. The regulation of drugs is a case in point. New drugs cannot be sold unless they are approved by the Food and Drug Administration, and there is growing evidence that this regulation has done more harm by retarding progress in the production and distribution of valuable drugs—sometimes life-saving drugs—than it has done good by preventing harmful drugs from entering the market.

As a result of FDA regulation, the number of new drugs introduced each year in the U.S. has fallen by more than 50 percent since 1962. In addition, it now takes much longer for a new drug to be approved, which has substantially increased the cost of drugs. According to one estimate, between 1962 and 1978 regulation caused a hundred-fold increase in the cost of developing new drugs and a quadrupling of the time needed to bring a new drug to market.[30] This so-called drug lag has caused many drugs to be unavailable in the U.S. that are routinely used elsewhere, all to the detriment of American consumers. In the late 1970s, for example, new drugs called "beta blockers," which apparently can sharply reduce the probability of death after a heart attack, were introduced in Europe but were not available in the U.S. until years later. If these drugs had been available at an earlier date in the U.S. they could have saved thousands of lives.[31] Another "cost" of substituting governmental edicts for market discipline to judge product quality is that such edicts are sometimes wrong, and the results can be quite harmful. For example, in 1973 the Consumer Product Safety Commission banned certain types of aerosol spray adhesives as potential health hazards. The ban was based on the preliminary findings of an academic researcher who claimed they could cause birth defects. Further research failed to corroborate the initial study, so the ban was lifted. Despite the government's commendable correction of the mistake, "it seems that at least nine pregnant women who had used the spray adhesives reacted to the news of the commission's initial decision by undergoing abortions. They decided not to carry through their pregnancies for fear of producing babies with birth defects."[32] Relying on governmental edicts or standards rather than on the marketplace can be very costly and even harmful.

Finally, government-imposed product standards make the introduction of new products more costly. This creates a barrier to entry, which protects the profits of incumbent business firms. In other words, governmentally mandated product standards can lead to monopoly. Monopolists have weaker incentives to be concerned with product quality than do more competitive businesses. Ironically, governmentally mandated product quality standards may result in reduced product quality.

In light of this discussion the claim that commercial nonprofit enterprises can be trusted to provide better quality services than competitive, profit-seeking firms should be greeted with skepticism. Those who *assert* that CNEs are more likely to be concerned with product quality than private enterprises advocate replacing the discipline of the marketplace with governmental edicts—that is, the edict that the products of "nonprofit" organizations are necessarily of high quality. Like product quality regulation, however, this can give consumers a false sense of product safety or quality. Moreover, there is little convincing evidence to support the notion that CNEs provide higher-quality goods and services than private businesses because of "contract failure." If anything, the evidence points in the opposite direction, especially if one compares the products of governmental enterprises to those of private enterprises. There is strong evidence that quality is superior in the latter (see chapters 4 and 6).

Finally, a fatal flaw in the "contract failure" rationale for unfair competition is its assumption that CNE managers cannot benefit from the organization's profits and so will devote all of the organization's resources to improvements in service quality. As mentioned above, managers, board members, and others involved with CNE operations can and do personally benefit from the profits. In fact, since competitive pressures are weaker in the nonprofit sector, a strong case can be made that CNE managers are even more prone than private sector managers to use their organization's resources for personal benefit rather than for improving service quality. The WPPSS and UDC examples illustrate how the managers of "non-profit" organizations can personally benefit at the expense of their customers, and additional examples will be given in later chapters.

Why CNEs?

Contract failure—the difficulty in judging product quality—is not an adequate explanation of why governmental policy allows CNEs to unfairly compete with private enterprises in so many industries. There are likely to be many reasons, but one in particular stands out in the recent literature on nonprofit enterprises. Consider some statements made by Lester Salamon, the director of a long-term research project on the nonprofit sector at The Urban Institute, a nonprofit research organization in Washington, D.C. After five years of research and the publication of several dozen books and monographs by the Urban Institute staff, Salamon observed that "the nonprofit sector experienced its greatest growth during the period of most dramatic government expansion."[33] In addition,

in the domestic sphere . . . government— particularly the federal government—does very little itself. What it does it does through other entities: states, cities, counties, banks, hospitals, private social service agencies, and so forth. The United States has created an elaborate system of "third-party government" in which the government raises resources and sets objectives for their expenditure through a democratic political process but leaves the actual provision of services to a host of . . . nongovernmental third parties. Nonprofit organizations have been major beneficiaries of this pattern of third-party government. . . . [34]

The result is

> an intricate pattern of government financing of nonprofit activity through grants, purchase of service contracts, and third-party payments. In fact, nonprofit organizations now receive a larger share of their income from government than from all private charitable giving combined. . . . As of 1980, for example, the federal government alone provided approximately $40 billion in support to . . . nonprofit . . . agencies. Private charity, by contrast, provided only $26 billion. [35]

This means that federal direct subsidies to nonprofit organizations amount to approximately $400 per year for each American taxpayer.

In *The Endangered Sector*, Waldemar Nielson echoes Salamon's view: "Government has been an active partner and financier of the [nonprofit] sector to a much greater extent than is commonly recognized."[36] The result, according to Nielsen, is that "the interdependence of the two sectors is now more extensive than ever before. . . ."[37]

Salamon also found that the federal government has *created* numerous nonprofit organizations specifically to help carry out governmental policies. "Under the social programs of the Great Society era of the 1960s, the federal government has taken on . . . a . . . role [of] stimulating the birth of new nonprofit institutions to help carry out Great Society goals."[38] For example, the Secondary Education Act of 1965 provided for federal funding of at least twenty regional "educational laboratories." President Lyndon Johnson indicated that the role of such laboratories was

> to build links with other Federal programs. . . . The laboratories should be related to the supplementary centers provided for in the Elementary and Secondary Act of 1965, to the teacher training programs of the Office of Education and the National Science Foundation, to appropriate activities of the Office of Economic Opportunity and the National Institutes of Health.[39]

Typical of the twenty regional laboratories is the Central Midwestern Regional Educational Laboratory, incorporated as a private nonprofit organization in 1965. The extent to which it acts as an agent of the federal government can be seen in its bylaws, which state:

The purposes of the organization are . . . to implement all aspects of Public Law 89–10, Title IV, and such other titles, as are appropriate for the planning and operation of an educational laboratory operating as part of the National Program of Educational Laboratories authorized by Public Law 89–10, Title IV. . . . To implement any and all appropriate aspects of any subsequent legislation related to, complementing, extending, or in any way modifying the National Program of Educational Laboratories authorized by Public Law 89–10, Title IV.[40]

Such laboratories compete with many private, for-profit educational laboratories throughout the country (see chapter 6).

The federal government has also created nonprofit "communnity action" organizations to perform functions ranging from family planning to voter education to consumer assistance. The government established hundreds of such organizations during the 1960s and, even though they are ostensibly private, they are strongly controlled by the federal government. For example, the federal government established controls over the organizations' personnel practices, mandating that it is to approve any starting salary over $5,000 or any promotion involving a salary increase of over 20 percent.[41] An average of 80 percent of the funding of such agencies came from the federal government during the 1960s and 1970s. To receive government funds, the agencies have to submit to the government's specifications regarding functions to be performed, methods of operation, personnel practices, methods of contracting for goods and services, and many other items.[42]

There are many research and development centers located at universities that generally operate under a long-term, continuing relationship with the federal government. The National Science Foundation reported that such centers "in most instances were established to meet a particular R&D need of a federal agency. . . . The supporting federal agency determines the objectives of these organizations."[43] Examples of these research centers include the Applied Physics Laboratory at Johns Hopkins University, the Lincoln Laboratory at MIT, and the Lawrence Radiation Laboratory at the University of California, Berkeley.[44] Research centers like these are all closely controlled by the federal government, which gives them funds on a continuing basis. The centers are all closely identified with a single government agency and have contractual responsibilities for furthering the interests of that agency. Accordingly, federal agencies impose constraints on the centers' personnel policies.[45] Because of federal support, these centers also unfairly compete with private research labs.

Finally, the military has also used nonprofit enterprises, such as the Rand Corporation, the Institute for Defense Analysis, and Research Analysis Corporation, to provide it with systems analysis. Similar analyses are also carried out by private, profit-making research organizations.

These observations reveal a possible answer to the question of why governmental policy gives such preferential treatment to commercial nonprofit enterprises: The federal government apparently views many CNEs as "third-party governments." When the federal government grants CNEs tax exemptions, provides them with direct grants, and gives them special privileges, there are inevitably strings attached: CNEs' activities must meet the approval of federal government authorites and comply with their regulations and directives. Because of this arrangement the distinction between the public and commercial nonprofit sectors of the economy becomes blurred. Referring to CNEs as part of the "third sector"[46] is inaccurate. It is not clear that there is a significant, fundamental difference between the public sector and the "voluntary" nonprofit sector. The latter is not as voluntary as is commonly believed, given that over 60 percent of all nonprofit income was derived from compulsory federal taxes in 1980, not including state and local governmental subsidies. And it certainly isn't "nonprofit."

In short, a strong case can be made that governmental policies that favor CNEs are a means of expanding the government's powers over resource allocation. This is one more dimension of the government crowding out the private sector. Direct subsidies, selective tax exemptions, and selective regulatory relief for CNEs are ways in which government reallocates resources. This ultimately means that more resources are allocated according to the wishes of political decision makers rather than the preferences of consumers. To our knowledge, previous studies of the "crowding out" issue have not recognized the symbiotic relationship between the governmental and commercial nonprofit sectors, a relationship that has been described as a "partnership with government that makes it possible [for CNEs] to tap public revenues."[47]

The Politics of Unfair Competition

A 1969 law provided that revenues from radio and television stations operated by Loyola University in New Orleans would not be taxable. Instrumental in securing the provision were two powerful Louisiana politicians, Senator Russell Long and the late Representative Hale Boggs. One of Loyola's television stations ranked number one in the New Orleans market at the time, and its competitors were indignant over what they perceived as an unfair advantage. According to one competing station executive: "It's a difficult, competitive situation. They [Loyola's station] have more readily available money to invest in their product—programming—and in equipment. They're well managed, but they play by different rules."[48]

To understand why such unfair public policies exist it is essential to realize how important constituent services are to legislators. Each legislator has strong incentives to use government's taxing, spending, and regulatory powers to bestow benefits on his or her constituents to ensure reelection. CNEs are among the instruments used to dispense these benefits. Perhaps this is one reason why CNEs are created, nurtured, and expanded by governmental policies, even when they impose costs on private competitors. It is simply good politics for a member of Congress to do favors for "nonprofit" organizations, even if the organization is essentially a commercial enterprise. In the Loyola University example, it is relevant that the university's employees, alumni, and supporters are well-organized and politically active. In sheer numbers and political influence, their interests become more important than the interests of those harmed by the policy. In terms of a legislator's political calculus, therefore, it pays to advance such policies, even if they are inherently unfair. This is not to say that politicians are necessarily unfair people but that the political process creates incentives to enact such policies for political survival. Politicians pursue their own self interests just as managers do in both for-profit and nonprofit enterprises.

When those who are harmed by such policies complain—especially small businesses—government's response has not been to eliminate the cause of the damage, but instead to attempt to "buy off" the small business sector with taxpayer subsidies through, say, the Small Business Administration. These policies create even further economic distortions, because not all businesses receive the subsidies (less than 1 percent of all small businesses benefit from the Small Business Administration). Consequently, those businesses receiving no subsidies find it even harder to compete with those that do. Moreover, small businesses that accept such subsidies can no longer credibly criticize CNEs for accepting theirs.

The Hidden Costs of the Commercial Nonprofit Sector

Governmental policies that favor CNEs over private commercial enterprises may be good politics, but they are very costly to society and are inherently unjust. The costs of such policies are well hidden. For instance, CNEs often charge prices that are lower than those charged by their private-sector competitors. This is misleading, however, for consumers ultimately pay more than just the explicit money price because of the economic side effects of governmental subsidies to the commercial nonprofit sector.

Consider the CNE exemption from corporate income taxation. Corporate income taxes are always partly passed on to consumers in the form of higher prices and to workers in the form of lower wages. Thus, eliminating the corporate income tax liability to CNEs would appear to be a break for both consumers and workers. But these benefits are not likely to be realized; the corporate tax burden is not eliminated but only shifted. To the extent that CNEs are exempt from corporate income taxes, those taxes are likely to be paid by private, profit-making businesses and, ultimately, by consumers and individual taxpayers. One of the biggest complaints about the U.S. tax system has been that loopholes allow many individuals and businesses to escape taxation while others must make up for the revenue loss by paying higher taxes. The tax exemption of CNEs is clearly one example of these loopholes.

The burden of additional taxes on private businesses is widely dispersed and well hidden but is very real. Specifically, higher taxes will make investment in those industries less profitable; the return on investment will fall and impose costs on investors, primarily pension funds, banks, insurance companies, and colleges and universities. As investment becomes less profitable because of taxation, there will naturally be less of it. Since businesses are less able to invest in new plants, equipment, and machinery, their future productive capacity is reduced. With a smaller productive capacity, fewer goods and services will be produced. This reduction in the future supply of goods and services will cause prices to be higher than they otherwise would be. In terms of labor market effects, a reduced productive capacity will also lead to fewer employment opportunities and lower wages, reducing living standards. Thus, consumers and workers both share in the indirect costs of exempting CNEs from taxation.

The essence of governmental policies that favor CNEs is that they contribute to the crowding out of the private sector. The so-called crowding-out controversy has gained the attention of economists, policy makers, and others for decades, for it is well known that governmental spending and borrowing policies that crowd out private-sector business activity is costly to workers, consumers, investors, and many others. The same concern over government policy toward the commercial nonprofit sector is warranted because of the costs—both direct and indirect—imposed on the private sector.

Smaller businesses are especially harmed by CNEs since they have fewer assets than larger corporations to fall back on when they incur losses from competing on such a skewed basis. The crowding out of small businesses means the loss of a major source of employment, technological development, and competition in the economy. Moreover, as CNEs replace private businesses consumers are forced to pay at least three times for it. First, they pay through taxpayer subsidies to CNEs. Second, because CNEs are inherently less efficient than private, competitive businesses, the loss of private enterprises will eventually cause prices to rise. Third, crowding out will deprive federal, state, and local governments of business, employment, property, and sales tax revenues as tax-exempt enterprises are substituted for taxpaying businesses; governments are likely to make up for this loss by raising individual taxes.

Conclusions

Governmental policies of unfair competition that cause tax-exempt CNEs to crowd private, taxpaying businesses out of the market are likely to reduce the quality and raise the price of goods and services provided by these organizations. Because of the absence of property rights and the profit motive, nonprofit organizations are inherently less efficient than private, competitive businesses with which they compete. Commercialism is a virtue, not a vice, as far as the quality of serice provision is concerned.

Various assertions of the superior efficiency and accountability of nonprofit organizations to profitseeking firms—usually made by CNE management—were examined and all were found wanting. Nor is there reason to believe that CNEs will necessarily provide a more equitable distribution of services. Several examples were given of how some CNEs use their special legislative privileges to serve a relatively affluent clientele, sometimes at the expense of the less well off. Other

examples will be given throughout the book. The "consumer ignorance" rationale for unfair competition was also found to be weak.
Economic reasoning suggests that competitive pressures are the most
reliable means of assuring product quality, and those pressures are
weaker in the commercial nonprofit sector than in the private sector.
The "consumer ignorance" rationale predicts that the quality of
goods and services provided by CNEs will be superior to those
provided by private firms, but the evidence does not support this
theory, as shown in chapters 4 through 7.

A likely reason for the special legislative treatment of CNEs is that
many of them are creatures of the federal government. They were
created by the federal government as extensions of "Great Society"
spending programs and, consequently, governmental authorities
have granted them special legislative privileges that enable them to
compete on an unfair basis with private businesses. This explanation
does not necessarily apply to all CNEs, but it clearly applies to
hundreds of nonprofit organizations in many different industries.
Thus, CNEs may be viewed as an extension of government. Accordingly, it should not be surprising that CNEs are granted legislative
privileges almost identical to the privileges enjoyed by governmental
enterprises.

The economic consequences of unfair competition are that governmental policy is crowding out the private sector to a greater extent
than is realized. This imposes many indirect costs on businesses,
workers, consumers, and taxpayers. The next four chapters provide
case studies that illustrate the political economy of unfair competition.

Notes to Chapter III

1. Henry Hansmann, "The Role of Nonprofit Enterprise," *Yale Law Journal*
(April 1980), p. 880.
2. Gordon Tullock, *The Politics of Bureaucracy* (Washington, D.C.: Public
Affairs Press, 1965).
3. Thomas J. DiLorenzo, "Corporate Management, Property Rights and
the X-Istence of X-Inefficiency," *Southern Economic Journal* (July 1981), pp.
116–24.
4. Sheila Pires, *Competition Between the Nonprofit and For-Profit Sectors* (Washington, D.C.: National Assembly of National Voluntary and Social Welfare
Organizations, Inc., January 1985).

5. Ibid.

6. Ibid.

7. "Putting on the Ritz at the Y," *Time*, July 21, 1986.

8. Ibid.

9. Ibid.

10. James T. Bennett and Manuel Johnson, *Better Government at Half the Price* (Ottawa, IL: Caroline House Publishers, 1981); Robert Poole, *Cutting Back City Hall* (New York: Universe Books, 1979); and E.S. Savas, *Privatizing the Public Sector* (Chatham, NJ: Chatham House Publishers, 1982).

11. Thomas J. DiLorenzo and Ralph Robinson, "Managerial Objectives Subject to Political Market Constraints: Electric Utilities in the U.S.," *Quarterly Review of Economics and Business* (Summer 1982), p. 236.

12. James T. Bennett and Thomas J. DiLorenzo, *Underground Government: The Off-Budget Public Sector* (Washington, D.C.: Cato Institute, 1983).

13. New York State, *Annual Report of the Comptroller*, various volumes.

14. New York State Mooreland Act Commission, *Restoring Credit and Confidence: A Program for New York State and Its Public Authorities* (Albany, NY: State Printing Office, 1976).

15. New York State Comptroller, *Audit of the Use of Legal Consultants by UDC and MLC*, cited in Jack Newfield, "Abuse of Authority: Private Empires in the Public Sector," *Village Voice*, March 29, 1983.

16. Ibid.

17. Peter Bernstein, "A Nuclear Fiasco Shakes the Bond Market," *Fortune*, February 22, 1982.

18. Ibid.

19. Washington State Energy and Utilities Committee, *WPPSS Inquiry* (Seattle: Senate Energy and Utilities Committee, January 12, 1981).

20. Ibid.

21. Bennett and DiLorenzo, *Underground Government: The Off-Budget Public Sector*.

22. Henry Hansmann, "The Role of Nonprofit Enterprise," p. 882.

23. Statement before the U.S. Small Business Administration hearings on "Government Competition With Small Business," Des Moines, Iowa, August 28, 1979.

24. John Goodman, *The Regulation of Medical Care* (Washington, D.C.: Cato Institute, 1980).

25. "For Many, There Are Big Profits in Nonprofits," *U.S. News and World Report*, November 6, 1978.

26. Ibid.

27. Ibid.

28. Henry Hansmann, "The Role of Nonprofit Enterprise."

29. David Easly and Maureen O'Hara, "The Economic Role of the Nonprofit Firm," *Bell Journal of Economics* (Autumn 1983), p. 220.

30. William Wardell and Louis Lasagna, *Regulation and Drug Development* (Washington, D.C.: American Enterprise Institute, 1975).

31. Ibid.

32. Murray Weidenbaum, *The Costs of Government Regulation*, Formal Publication no. 12 (St. Louis: Center for the Study of American Business, Washington University, 1977).

33. Lester Salamon, "The Invisible Partnership: Government and the Nonprofit Sector," *Bell Atlantic Quarterly* (Autumn 1984), p. 1.

34. Ibid.

35. Ibid.

36. Waldemar Nielson, *The Endangered Sector* (New York: Columbia University Press, 1979).

37. Ibid.

38. Ibid.

39. Central Midwestern Regional Educational Laboratory, *Central Midwestern Regional Educational Laboratory, Inc. for Educational Research, Innovation, Diffusion, Implementation* (St. Ann, MO: CMREL, 1966), p. 4, cited in Murray Weidenbaum, *The Modern Public Sector* (New York: Basic Books, 1969), p. 97.

40. Central Midwestern Regional Educational Laboratory, Inc., *Progress Report to the U.S. Commissioner of Education on Contract O.E.C.–6–000535* (St.Louis, MO, April 1, 1966), cited in Weidenbaum, *The Modern Public Sector*.

41. U.S. Office of Equal Opportunity, *Designation and Recognition of Community Action Agencies Under the 1967 Amendments to the Economic Opportunity Act*, Feb. 15, 1968, cited in Weidenbaum, *The Modern Public Sector*, p. 100.

42. See Clarence H. Danhoff, *Government Contracting and Technological Change* (Washington, D.C.: Brookings Institution, 1968), p. 375.

43. U.S. National Science Foundation, *Scientific Activities at Universities and Colleges* (Washington, D.C.: U.S. Government Printing Office, 1964), p. 32.

44. Ibid., Appendix B.

45. Danhoff, *Government Contracting*, p. 314.

46. Diane Disney et al., *Partners in Public Service* (Washington, D.C.: Urban Institute, 1984).

47. Ibid.

48. "For Many, There Are Big Profits . . . ," *U.S. News and World Report*.

IV.

Unfair Competition in the Hospital and Medical Care Industries

Although nonprofit hospitals comprise less than three percent of all nonprofit organizations, they dominate the sector's expenditures: In 1982, nonprofit hospitals accounted for more than half of all non-profit-sector expenditures—53.7 percent, or $70.3 billion.[1] In addition, the health care sector itself is dominated by nonprofits, for all but a small fraction of all hospital beds in the U.S. are in nonprofit hospitals. The hospital and medical care industries, then, are a natural starting point for analyzing unfair competition. Nonprofit health care organizations not only enjoy the privileges accorded to all charitable entities (see chapter 2), but they also receive other forms of governmental assistance that further enhance their competitive position relative to their for-profit counterparts. Unfair competition has become so intense in this sector of the economy that the for-profit hospital has almost become a curiosity. Research on the economics of medical care, particularly on the operation of nonprofit hospitals, has provided interesting insights into the question: "Who profits from nonprofits?" The justification for nonprofit status for medical care organizations is based on the concept of "contract failure"; that is, health care consumers cannot adequately assess the quality of services being provided. When consumers lack the expertise required to make informed decisions before purchasing a service, many believe that for-profit providers have a strong incentive to reduce the quality of care and to charge excessive prices; supposedly, nonprofits do not have this incentive. Thus, the nonprofit hospital and medical care

73

industries offer an opportunity to explore some of the major issues surrounding unfair competition.

Nonprofit vs. For-Profit Hospitals

It has been estimated that in 1910 56 percent of the 4,359 hospitals in the U.S. were for-profit entities. Since that time, the number has declined dramatically. By 1928, only 36 percent of the 6,852 hospitals in the country were proprietary; the remainder were private nonprofit and governmental facilities.[2] The American Hospital Association reported that of the 6,782 hospitals that existed in 1984 (including long and short term, general purpose, psychiatric, TB and respiratory, and "other"), 51.5 percent (or 3,534) were private nonprofit facilities; 33.9 percent were operated by local, state, or federal governments; and fewer than 15 percent (1,002) were proprietary.[3]

The decline in the number and importance of proprietary hospitals has not been accidental. Public policy has consistently favored nonprofits and permitted them to compete unfairly with for-profits, and the special privileges have been especially beneficial for hospitals. Contributions to nonprofit hospitals are tax-deductible and charitable giving has been generous. Between 1960 and 1966, philanthropic giving provided between 26 and 34 percent of all funds for capital expansion of nonprofit hospitals. To an extent, charitable contributions support the current operating expenses of nonprofits.[4]

Government has also subsidized nonprofit hospitals through the Hospital Survey and Construction Act of 1946 (P.L. 79–725), better known as the Hill-Burton Act. During the Great Depression, privately-financed hospital construction virtually ceased, and nearly 800 hospitals closed between 1928 and 1938.[5] New construction was also limited during World War II because of wartime exigencies. One of the major objectives of the Hill-Burton Act was to remedy the situation by funding the construction of "public and nonprofit hospitals." Under the act, for-profit hospitals were not eligible to receive support for either new facilities or the expansion of existing facilities. From July 1, 1947 through June 30, 1971, $3.7 billion in federal funds supported a total of 10,748 projects, creating 470,329 in-patient care beds and assisting more than 3,000 out-patient and other health-care facilities.[6] The Hill-Burton program provided a massive stimulus to the expansion of nonprofit hospitals.

The Hill-Burton Act also required that states license hospitals as a condition of federal support, and there is evidence that state agencies have used these regulatory powers to impede the development of proprietary hospitals and nursing homes and to reduce their ability to compete with nonprofits.[7] Economist John C. Goodman has found

two examples of how regulatory authority can be used to discriminate against proprietary hospitals . . . [in] New York City. In 1964 the city's hospital code was revised to limit the practice of surgery in proprietary hospitals to board-certified surgeons. In a test case in which the law was upheld, a court ruled that a general practitioner could not continue practicing surgery in proprietary hospitals despite the fact that he had done so for many years and that there was no apparent indication that he was unqualified to continue doing so. In a more dramatic case in 1976, the mayor of New York City attempted to exercise his authority by forcing the outright closure of nine proprietary hospitals operating in the city.[8]

The judiciary has favored nonprofit over proprietary hospitals through the interpretation of a traditional rule which forbids the "corporate" practice of medicine. The chain of logic proscribing corporations from practicing medicine is somewhat tortured. Although a corporation is a "person" in the legal sense, it cannot be licensed to practice the learned professions because these professions require licensing after a test of knowledge. Because a corporate entity is not capable of taking the test, it cannot be licensed.[9] In some courts, this rule has been applied to for-profit hospitals but not to nonprofits.[10] State legislatures have also used this rule to hamper proprietary hospitals. In New York, for example, where corporations can operate nonprofit hospitals, proprietary hospitals can be operated by individuals or by partnerships but not by corporations.[11] This distinction severely hampers the development of proprietary hospitals. Without the corporate form of ownership, it is much more difficult for proprietaries to obtain funds for construction or renovation and to finance costly, high technology equipment that is increasingly used in providing quality medical care.

During the 1960s, all hospitals prospered with the rapid increase in Great Society social spending. "Third parties," such as insurance companies and government agencies, typically reimbursed health service providers on the basis of costs incurred or the amount charged for service. Between 1960 and 1970, the proportion of hospital costs paid by government more than doubled, from 18.8 percent to 37.8 percent. During the same period, the proportion of hospital costs paid by individuals continued to decline markedly, from 49.6 percent in 1950 to 11.9 percent in 1975. Private insurers paid for the remainder.[12] There were few effective restraints on consumer demand for hospital care and on the procedures practiced by physicians. Consequently, expenditures by government and private insurers on hospital care skyrocketed. Medical expenditures were rising faster than national income, and government's share of these expenditures was increasing faster than medical expenditures because of Medicare and Medicaid. During the early 1980s, the federal government and private insurers initiated significant changes to restrain soaring medical costs, especially hospital costs. In 1983, major changes were made in the provision of health services in an effort to lower both public and private expenditures on hospital care:[13]

> The [federal] government introduced diagnostic-related groupings, which generally defined how long patients should be hospitalized for their illness and what physicians and hospitals should be paid for their treatment. Private insurers also changed coverage, and then health-maintenance organizations and their emphasis on short hospital stays became popular.[14]

Alternative forms of service delivery, such as out-patient surgery facilities and neighborhood emergency clinics, are being offered in an attempt to reduce hospital costs. These initiatives reduced the income of hospitals—occupancy rates dropped as fewer patients entered hospitals and, on average, stayed fewer days. As a result, hospitals have been actively seeking alternative sources of revenues.

When nonprofit hospitals compete with for-profit entities, unfair competition is unavoidable, because nonprofits enjoy special privileges. Unfair competition by nonprofit hospitals, however, differs from the pattern of unfair competition found in other industries: Nonprofit hospitals not only compete with proprietary hospitals but they also compete outside the traditional health care sector. Because of unfair competition between nonprofits and for-profits, nonprofit hospitals have all but forced proprietaries out of the market. As a result, there are now few opportunities for nonprofits to increase their revenues by taking patients from proprietaries. Instead, nonprofit hospitals have diversified:

> Faced with shrinking patient rolls and reduced federal support, hospitals across the country are offering a wide variety of new

and—for them—unconventional services to bolster their finances. Although the services themselves aren't always profitable, hospital administrators hope the programs will give their facilities a positive image and persuade customers to return when they need medical care.[15]

In 1987, with patient censuses down by as much as 20 percentage points over levels three years earlier (to an average of 60 to 65 percent of capacity), the food and laundry operations of many hospitals were operating far below their capacity.[16] To make use of these facilities, hospitals are operating commercial laundries, catering services, and restaurants; some are even entering the hotel business. For example, Day Kimball Hospital in Putnam, Connecticut, established Special Occasions, a subsidiary that offers prepared foods "for such things as a World Series party for 10 people, a wedding reception for 50 and a birthday party for 15."[17] Christian Hospital Northeast in St. Louis caters wedding receptions ("down to the ice sculpture and champagne fountain") and sells frozen meals to institutions and people who cannot cook for themselves.[18] The entry of hospitals into catering has become a nationwide phenomenon:

> St. Rose Hospital in Hayward, Calif., for example, has started a catering service. The under-used hospital kitchen provides the food for weddings and champagne receptions, and has an annual contract to cater the Shriners' Christmas dinner. Donald Stafford, vice president of general services at St. Rose, says such services—if performed in a professional manner—can benefit the hospital. "If people see something at a wedding or reception and like the food presentation," he says, "they feel they'll get something of comparable value at the hospital."[19]

Women's Hospital of Texas in Houston "provides food service to a nearby hospice, and has catered private parties."[20] Pikes Peak Mental Health Center in Colorado Springs leased part of its property to a Wendy's restaurant,[21] and a Chicago hospital leases space in its lobby for a McDonald's franchise.[22]

In search of revenues, hospitals have gone far beyond cooking, cleaning, and doing laundry. The North Florida Regional Hospital in Gainesville operates the Excess Express, a taxi service for those who have been drinking. Florence General Hospital in Florence, South Carolina, operates a day care facility for the elderly.[23] The Roanoke Hospital Association, a nonprofit organization that runs several hospitals in Virginia, "purchased an advertising agency to go along with its other for-profit ventures, including two health clubs, an interior decorating firm, a pharmacy and a helicopter ambulance service."[24] The entrepreneurial spirit among hospitals and health care managers is especially apparent in the Washington, D.C. area. For example,

• The Fairfax Hospital Association, a group of four Northern Virginia hospitals, has invested nearly $3 million in venture capital during the past five years in commercial projects. They include walk-in clinics, an in-vitro fertilization center, a weight-loss program, a home health equipment company and a bill collection agency. These businesses produced $1.9 million in profits last year on $22 million of revenue. . . .
• The Arlington Hospital Foundation established STAT Tele-communications, an answering and paging service for physicians.
• A foundation linked to the Greater Southeast Community Hospital bought a company that sells wheelchairs and other durable medical equipment. This organization has a real estate firm that operates two physician office buildings.
• An affiliate of Providence Hospital, DePaul Corp., set up a subsidiary that offers billing and consulting services for physicians.[25]

Nonprofit hospitals have established health clubs and fitness programs; hotels; restaurants; child care and senior citizen centers; dry-cleaning, janitorial, laundry, and printing services; class instruction in everything from bicycle repair to clowning; and a wide range of commercial services, some of which stray far afield from health and medical care.[26] Nonprofit hospitals have gone to great lengths to restore their sagging financial fortunes by starting commercial enterprises. The *Wall Street Journal* reported: "A 1985 survey of 700 nonprofit hospitals by the accounting firm Ernst & Whinney found that one in three were involved in for-profit joint ventures and most others were considering them."[27] For-profit hospitals have experienced the same problems as nonprofits and have also responded by trying commercial ventures. But there is a difference. Unfair competition does not occur when a for-profit hospital competes with existing businesses, because the for-profit hospital has no special privileges that provide a competitive advantage. The issue here is not competition *per se*, but whether or not one group of competitors operates under a different set of rules than another. The special privileges enjoyed by nonprofits can have unintended consequences that cause or at least intensify serious social problems.

The Less Savory Side of Nonprofits

Prescription drugs are a critical part of the nation's health care system, and the pharmaceuticals purchased by consumers must be safe and effective. But, special privileges granted by Congress to nonprofit hospitals and health care organizations have inadvertently contributed to the degradation of prescription drugs by encouraging their "diversion" and counterfeiting:

In 1936, Congress determined that large sellers and buyers in the drug and grocery marketplace were exercising substantial buying power in a way that discriminated against small buyers. Congress enacted the Robinson-Patman Act to make it unlawful for a seller to sell to a customer who would, in turn, resell in competition with another customer at a discriminatory price.

In 1938, Congress passed an exemption to the Robinson-Patman Act [the Nonprofit Institutions Act] to address a concern that charitable institutions—who had previously obtained goods from sellers at lower prices because they were used for . . . charitable purposes—would not be able to do so as a result of the Act. These institutions, typified by almshouses or pauper hospitals, were supported by subscription and were making their services available to people who could not pay for the services. Today, nonprofits that are engaging in commercial activities with for-profit firms that pay Federal, state, and local taxes for the privilege of doing business, claim the protection of that exemption. . . . Few, if any patients, receive free care from such organizations. In order to obtain care from them, you must be a paying member, or be covered by Medicare or Medicaid.[28]

The Nonprofit Institutions Act permitted manufacturers to sell drugs to nonprofit hospitals and charitable organizations at substantially lower prices than they charged the wholesale and retail drug trade as long as the drugs were for "their own use." The price differential between profit and nonprofit purchasers averages

40% to 50% across the board, and in the case of some items is much more. For instance, a month's supply of one brand of birth control pills is sold to nonprofit pharmacies for between 65 and 95 cents. It costs [a retail pharmacy] $10.81. . . . The cost to a private doctor for one brand of DPT (diptheria, tetanus and whooping cough) vaccine is $171 for a 15–dose vial. The cost to the state is $45.15.[29]

Such large price differences encourage unfair competition. Stephen Sims and David Nelson, staff members of the House Subcommittee on Oversight and Investigations, have reported that "an entire industry has sprung up whose sole purpose appears to be to solicit nonprofit hospitals to purchase excess pharmaceuticals using their special discount. . . ."[30] The excess is sold at a higher price to a broker or wholesaler and eventually finds its way to the retail market. Companies in California, Texas, New Jersey, and Florida have been identified as existing primarily to induce pharmacists at nonprofit hospitals to divert their drugs:

> One of the more active companies is Healthcare Marketing Services, Inc., a broker located in Encino, California. According to its literature, HMSI represents "a licensed wholesale pharmaceutical distributor in the State of California," but the name of the company is not listed. The company is apparently Marchar Laboratories of Walnut, California. . . . The literature offers the hospital "the ability to share in tremendous profits" by purchasing pharmaceuticals at the hospital discount price and immediately reselling them to HMSI. The hospital can receive an immediate payment of cost plus eighteen percent for handling and profit, or half the profit after resale by HMSI less twenty percent handling cost. The solicitation promises a profit for a one-hundred bed hospital of between $2,700 and $8,000 per month.[31]

Nonprofit institutions feed the market by purchasing pharmaceuticals at very attractive prices in quantities that far exceed their internal needs. Stanley Kowitt, an active participant in the diversion market for 12 years, testified before a congressional subcommittee that in 1974 one small hospital in Florida purchased "12 units of eyedrops for a total worth of $59.00. In 1975 when they started diverting, the figures shot up to 45,457 units with a total value of $41,011." This hospital also bought "96,000 tablets of . . . tranquilizer Miltown in 2 months or 5 times as much as every patient taking the manufacturer's recommended dosage could consume in that time period; and . . . 539,200 tablets of muscle relaxant Soma/Soma Compound in 8 months, or 7 times what every patient taking the suggested dosage every day could consume."[32] Drug diversion can be profitable for hospitals of even modest size.

In July 1985, congressional testimony indicated that "the volume of merchandise and the number of diversions from nonprofit institutions appear to have increased dramatically."[33] As nonprofits search for additional revenues, the large-scale diversion of drugs appears to be an attractive way to increase income with little risk or effort. This diversion of pharmaceuticals by nonprofits is illegal under the Robinson-Patman Act, because the drugs were never intended for internal use by the nonprofit institution. The Federal Trade Commission is responsible for enforcing the act, but it is unlikely that the FTC will do anything about the diversions. The offending nonprofits are off-limits for the FTC, whose enabling legislation prevents it from taking action against entities that do not conduct business for profit.

Concern about the diversion of drugs by nonprofits goes far beyond the issue of unfair competition. The diversion market is supplied from many questionable sources, including stolen or expired drugs and counterfeits. When nonprofit institutions supply drugs for diversion, they lend credibility and legitimacy to an enterprise that operates to the detriment of consumers:

> the existence and method of operation of a wholesale submarket . . . the "diversion market" . . . prevents effective control over, or even routine knowledge of, the true source of merchandise in a significant number of cases. As a result, pharmaceuticals which have been mislabeled, improperly stored, have exceeded their expiration dates, or are bald counterfeits, are injected into the national distribution system for ultimate sale to consumers.[34]

As an example of the risks the drug diversion market presents, consider the counterfeit birth control pills sold in the U.S. In the fall of 1984, G.D. Searle and Company discovered that nearly two million Panamanian counterfeits of its Ovulen 21 pills had been introduced and distributed throughout the U.S. via the diversion market. "The primary reason that counterfeits like Ovulen 21 could easily be introduced into the distribution system is the existence of the . . . diversion market."[35] Marchar Laboratories of Walnut, California, was found to have purchased and resold 3,551 units of counterfeit Ovulen 21 in June 1984.[36] Without supplies from nonprofits, the diversion market would be limited to drugs obtained under false or fraudulent pretenses, samples, foreign goods that are relabeled or repackaged prior to U.S. sale, domestic pharmaceuticals sold to foreign buyers and then re-exported to the U.S., stolen merchandise, counterfeits, and expired drugs. The diversion market would be much smaller in size and the merchandise would come from less desirable sources if nonprofits did not participate. In this way, the special privileges given to nonprofit hospitals have produced unintended and undesirable consequences that literally threaten the nation's health care system. In testimony before the House Committee on Energy and Commerce, U.S. Attorney Larry D. Thompson reported:

> The FDA [Food and Drug Administration] has rigid safeguards for the handling and packaging of drugs, including among other requirements, sterile hand, head, beard, body, and feet coverings in rooms with no windows having special air-filtering systems. Those who deal in adulterated and misbranded drugs disregard all safeguards consisted [sic] essential by Congress and by health experts in this country.
>
> Drugs [in the diversion market] were shucked or removed from their original packaging and labeling for a number of reasons. . . . [and] were stored and resold in open boxes, used paper grocery sacks, cellophane bread wrappers, old soft drink bottles, plastic baggies, and other unauthorized containers. Many of these pills had been expired for over 5 years.
>
> The presence of diverted, adulterated, and misbranded drugs in the prescription drug system is a national problem. At least one drugstore in every city, town, and village involved in the FBI investigation, was found to be dispensing such medications.[37]

Because of misbranding, repackaging, and removal of identifying numbers on drugs peddled in the diversion market, it is impossible to remove dangerous or ineffective drugs from the marketplace.

It is no exaggeration to assert that the diversion market represents a significant threat to the nation's health, and the root of this problem can be found in the special privilege granted to nonprofits by the Nonprofit Institutions Act, because

- without the benefit of price discrimination, a nonprofit institution would not buy in excess of its needs and illegally resell the surplus.
- without the benefit of price discrimination, companies or individuals would have little or no incentive to obtain pharmaceuticals from manufacturers through false or fraudulent pretenses.

- without the benefit of price discrimination, what incentive would there be to re-export back to the United States pharmaceuticals produced in the U.S. and sold to foreign buyers?
- without the benefit of price discrimination, no diversion black market would exist to facilitate the introduction into the drug distribution system of adulterated, counterfeit, and stolen prescription drugs.[38]

The special privileges enjoyed by nonprofits have consequences that go far beyond the issue of unfair competition.

Who Profits from Nonprofit Health Care?

Conventional wisdom has long held that nonprofit hospitals are charitable institutions that provide medical care to poor people who would be turned away from for-profit, proprietary hospitals. This suggests that the poor and indigent are major beneficiaries of nonprofit hospitals. But, there is little evidence that nonprofits benefit the poor more than for-profits, even though nonprofit hospitals would like the public to think that this is the case. P.D. Fliessner, president of the Oregon Association of Hospitals, has predicted that "if the legislature takes away tax exemptions, then some hospitals may have to deny access to people who cannot pay for the cost of their care."[39] Jeffrey Selberg, executive vice-president and chief of operations for the Good Samaritan Hospital in Portland, Oregon, has charged that "for-profit hospitals are not leading the fight over the tax status of nonprofit hospitals because they want to keep a low profile on the issue of charity care."[40] But nonprofits can rarely be considered charitable institutions. In a Utah court case, *Intermountain Health Care* v. *Utah County*, evidence showed that the nonprofit Intermountain Hospital chain, the largest non-utility employer in the state, had a profit margin of 10.9 percent in 1985. Yet, "Intermountain was losing an amount equivalent to only 3.3 percent of revenues on patients who couldn't pay, while for-profit hospitals in the state were losing 4 percent to 5 percent."[41] The Utah Supreme Court "found a nonprofit hospital system to be no different than profit-making systems, and refused to give it state property tax exemption."[42]

Understandably concerned about the precedent established in the *Intermountain* case, the American Hospital Association (which represents nonprofits) has begun a public relations campaign to protect the tax-exempt status of their members. The editorial pages of the April 19, 1987, *Washington Post* carried an advertisement under the headline "Not-For-Profit Hospitals' Tax Exemption: A Bargain for the American Public" in which association president Carol M. McCarthy argued for retaining the tax-exempt status of nonprofit hospitals. After noting that "eighty-five percent of our community hospitals are not-for-profit and tax-exempt," McCarthy described how nonprofits benefit their communities and listed the economic pressures they face:

> During the past five years alone, these hospitals provided more than $22 billion in charity care. Add paid but unprofitable services: burn and trauma units, pediatric and cardiac intensive care, research and education, emergency care, and a range of social services such as care for the homebound.
>
> How do hospitals finance these services while coping with intense competition and demands for lower prices? Some hospitals generate income from taxable business activities to help subsidize care. But other sources such as philanthropy are on the wane (philanthropy would virtually dry up were tax-exempt status revoked), making tax exemption even more important.
>
> Tax exemption can make a crucial difference. It often means that working capital is available so a hospital has dollars needed to support ongoing programs of care. It means access to less-expensive investment capital so changing community needs can be met.[43]

Despite McCarthy's argument, the *Intermountain* case raises serious doubts about the degree to which nonprofits are willing to serve the poor relative to proprietaries. Evidence from cases brought under the terms of the Hill-Burton Act also raises questions about nonprofits' charitable intentions. In order to receive funds under the Hill-Burton Act, hospitals must agree to be available to "all persons residing in the territorial area" of the facility and to make available "a reasonable volume of hospital services to persons unable to pay therefor."[44] But the act never seems to have achieved its intended effect:

> Despite its good intentions . . . the Hill-Burton program has been a giant giveaway to private [nonprofit] hospitals, which have received 60 percent of the grants. For the first twenty-five years after the act's passage, the government did nothing to insure that recipient hospitals were meeting their obligations to provide

community service and free health care. Most Hill-Burton recipient hospitals turned away patients who could not pay, who did not have a private physician, or who were on Medicaid. Critically ill patients were even refused admission to emergency rooms.[45]

In 1970, the first of numerous suits were filed claiming that indigents had been denied services at nonprofit hospitals which had received Hill-Burton funds.[46] This litigation has been summarized in the following way:

> When, in the early 1970s, health rights activists filed lawsuits against recalcitrant hospitals, U.S. attorneys sided with the health industry, arguing that the courts had no jurisdiction to enforce the community service provisions. The courts rejected that position, however, and after a series of adverse decisions, the government was forced to issue a new set of regulations spelling out the hospitals' obligations in detail. Those rules were adopted in 1979, and last summer [1984] they survived a challenge by the American Hospital Association when the Supreme Court declined to review lower court rulings upholding them.
>
> Nevertheless, the government is dragging its feet on enforcement. An April 1982 Government Accounting Office investigation disclosed that among hundreds of other deficiencies, over the preceding two years only 17 of 690 complaints pending against hospitals had been resolved by the Department of Health and Human Services, the agency responsible for insuring compliance.[47]

Nonprofit hospitals appear to be getting a bargain at the expense of the taxpayers.

There is mounting evidence that tax-exemption and other special privileges granted to nonprofits do little to ensure that the poor receive medical services. In a study conducted by Harvard University professors Regina E. Herzlinger and William S. Krasker, Herzlinger reported they:

> could find no difference between for-profit and nonprofit hospital chains in the amount of care given to patients who are uninsured or have low-paying Medicaid insurance.
>
> But as things now stand, it is not up to the for-profit hospital to provide care for the uninsured, any more than it is a supermarket's responsibility to feed the poor. The nonprofit hospital, on the other hand, has received a tax exemption primarily in

exchange for treating those who cannot afford to pay for their health care. Dumping by nonprofits is a grave violation of this social contract.[48]

Despite the claims of nonprofit hospitals, for-profits appear to do as much, if not more, to serve the needy. There is little evidence that the poor and indigent are the major beneficiaries of nonprofit hospitals and would not receive medical care if nonprofits did not exist.

In their study, Herzlinger and Krasker analyzed the performance of 14 major hospital chains—6 for-profit and 8 nonprofit—in 1977 and 1981. Their sample consisted of 725 hospitals representing 90 percent of the hospital beds in the for-profit sector and 68 percent of the beds in the nonprofit sector in the U.S. The researchers made adjustments so that accounting data for both types of hospital were comparable and corrected for factors that could influence financial performance, including location, scope of services, the presence of teaching and research activities, care to indigent patients, quality of care, size, and prices charged for services. Based on this comprehensive analysis, Herzlinger and Krasker reported four major findings:

1. While nonprofit hospitals receive more social subsidies than for-profits, they do not achieve better social results. They are not more accessible to the uninsured and medically indigent, nor do they price less aggressively. They are also more oriented toward short-term results, replacing plant and equipment much more slowly than for-profits.

2. Nonprofits, however, do more to maximize the welfare of the physicians who are their main consumers. These hospitals make large numbers of staff and beds available to the physicians, and they finance these benefits through social subsidies, tax exemptions, and delays in replacing plant and equipment. Today's physicians are subsidized by current taxpayers and future patients.

3. For-profit hospitals, in contrast, produce better results for society and require virtually no societal investment to keep them afloat. They are more efficient than nonprofits, reinvest their earnings in newer plant and equipment, and offer just as broad a range of services to a large number of patients, including the medically indigent.

4. Our data suggest that, at the very least, nonprofit hospitals do not inevitably improve social welfare in their communities. Indeed, the hospital's professional staff—and not the patients or

society—may be capturing many of the benefits inherent in the nonprofit form. This imbalance is unlikely to happen in a for-profit organization subject to stock market discipline.[49]

According to Herzlinger and Krasker, nonprofits have not "fulfilled their social promise."[50] In fact, the quality of services may be higher at for-profits than at nonprofits and at comparable prices. The "contract failure" rationale that has been used to justify tax-exempt status for nonprofit hospitals, cannot withstand close examination.

Nonprofits are subject to weaker controls than for-profits are. Managers of for-profits are disciplined by the ever-present threat of a takeover if management becomes inefficient. Because of the weaker controls on nonprofits, Herzlinger and Krasker "found that nonprofit hospital chains acted for the self-interest of the professionals within them, not just for the welfare of society. They increased professional staffs' comfort level through tax exemptions and the deferral of capital replacement without providing better, cheaper, or more accessible health care in return."[51] The special privileges given nonprofits have lowered their operating costs, but the savings have been used to create a comfortable working environment for staff physicians by making an excessive number of beds available, by offering a wide range of services, and by acquiring a large support staff. In this way, nonprofits have become much less efficient than their for-profit counterparts.

The trustees and staff of nonprofits have also personally benefitted from the lack of controls and market discipline. Amitai Etzioni and Pamela Doty have charged that

> omissions, ambiguities, and loopholes in the laws and regulations governing not-for-profit corporations make it possible for the trustees and staff of not-for-profit corporations to engage in a variety of financial practices which bring them personal profits over and above the fees, salaries, and fringe benefits due them for work performed. The practices in question are not those generally termed "fraud," i.e., kickbacks, double billing, charging for services never performed, etc., which are clearly illegal whether they are practiced in for-profit or not-for-profit corporations. Rather we refer to forms of profit making which are at odds with the underlying rationale of not-for-profit corporations, not as currently written in existing laws and regulations but as widely held and understood as legitimate expectations by members of society.[52]

Etzioni and Doty identified four "avenues" through which individuals at nonprofit hospitals could personally profit: (1) income tied to entrepreneurial activity rather than work; (2) self-dealing; (3) real estate transactions; and (4) unreasonable and uncustomary fees, salaries, and fringe benefits.

It is common practice for certain medical specialists, including pathologists, radiologists, and anesthesiologists, to receive all or part of their remuneration based on a percentage of their department's gross or net income. Pathologists, for example, have a rule stating that "I shall not accept a position with a fixed stipend in any hospital. . . ."[53] Because the rule could violate civil service regulations, an exception was made for governmental and university hospitals. In 1972, pathologists at hospitals in the Washington, D.C., area earned as much as $500,000 a year; their salaried counterparts were paid about $26,600.[54] In 1969, the U.S. Department of Justice brought suit against the College of Pathologists because the practice was monopolistic; to settle the suit, the College dropped the anti-salary rule. The practice has persisted, however, because of informal pressures by pathologists and because the Joint Commission on Hospital Accreditation requires that hospital laboratories be run by pathologists. The situation endures even though many independent commercial laboratories charge far less for the same tests than their in-hospital counterparts that use the "percentage of profit" rule.[55] For-profit hospitals have the incentive and market discipline to obtain services at the lowest cost; nonprofit hospitals do not. Furthermore, when salaries are determined by the level of services, there is a strong motivation to over-utilize the service, regardless of the patients' needs. As a result, patients incur unnecessary financial burdens and health risks.

Etzioni and Doty refer to the second avenue through which individuals at nonprofits can personally benefit as "self-dealing." This occurs when the two parties to a trade or transaction appear on both sides, that is, as both buyer and seller. A 1975 General Accounting Office study found cases of "overlapping interests," or self-dealing, among trustees or key employees at 17 of the 19 hospitals investigated.[56] In 6 of the 19 hospitals, 25 percent or more of the board members had overlapping interests. For example, a Washington, D.C. hospital

was governed by a 42–member board of trustees (including emeritus members). The hospital also had three honorary trustees with no voting authority. Twelve board members and all honorary trustees, or 33 percent, had overlapping interests. The primary overlapping interest involved banks servicing the hospital, although board members were also identified with legal, investment, and three other types of firms.

Seven board members were associated with a bank which maintained a hospital savings account; checking account; and custody of hospital property, such as stocks and bonds. . . .

Two members were associated with two other banks where the hospital maintained various checking and savings accounts. . . .

Three board members were associated with two firms providing legal services to the hospital. . . .

One member was associated with a group of eight radiologists providing radiology services to the hospital. . . .

In addition to the 15 board of trustees members [GAO] identified 2 nontrustee officers of the hospital, 3 action committee members [who make investment decisions and revise by-laws], and 3 administrative employees with overlapping business interests. One officer owned stock in a bank that serviced the hospital; an employee owned stock in two firms doing business with the hospital; and another employee received half of his salary from the company which provided food service to the hospital.

Overlapping interests of the other nontrustee hospital personnel involved stock ownership in, or association with, the firm which had provided the hospital with computer service. The firm's services were based on a May 1970 agreement between hospital officials and the computer services firm president, who was also the hospital's assistant administrator-controller from 1967 to 1972. No record of competitive bidding was available at the hospital to indicate that other firms had been considered. The computer services cost the hospital about $680,000 in 1972.[57]

In 1970, Jose A. Blanco was controller and assistant administrator of Washington Hospital Center, the largest private, nonprofit hospital in the District of Columbia. Blanco, who managed the hospital's data-processing operations at an annual salary of $39,000, decided that the existing system needed improvement, so he formed a private company—Space Age Computer Systems, Inc. He was certain of one customer, Washington Hospital Center. As the October 13, 1972 *Washington Post* reported:

Blanco's boss, Richard M. Loughery, administrator of the hospital, accepted stock free of charge in the new company, and became one of its directors. Blanco concedes that five other administrative officials of the hospital, including the assistant controller and the internal auditor, bought stock in Space Age at $1 a share.

To further help the new company along, it was given $50,000 by the hospital. The payment was described as a "deposit."[58]

Examples such as this are typical. Instances of self-dealing have become so common that Herbert S. Denenbery, a Pennsylvania insurance commissioner who has investigated hospital finances, has observed that nonprofit hospitals are "public institutions and they ought to be above suspicion, but you'd never know it from the way they operate." Concurring, Marilyn G. Rose, head of the Washington office of National Health and Environmental Law Program, complained that "There's no such thing as a nonprofit hospital. The money goes to the staff, trustees, and administrators through high salaries and various arrangements."[59]

One of those arrangements involves the sale or lease of land or facilities. Mary A. Mendelson in *Tender Loving Greed*, her book on nursing homes, reported that it is standard for a proprietary nursing home to be sold or leased to a nonprofit corporation at a highly inflated price. The artificially exaggerated value of the property may then be used to increase the reimbursement for rent under Medicaid.

In her investigation of the Acacia Care Center in Cleveland, Ohio, Mendelson described owner Sanford Novak as "typical of many operators" of nursing homes who were interested in making profits from nonprofit status.[60] Under his ownership, the Acacia Care Center was heavily mortgaged; the Cleveland Trust Company held a first mortgage for $1.1 million and a second mortgage for $195,000. Nevertheless, Novak managed to sell the nursing home to the Emmanuel Baptist Church, a nonprofit organization, at a highly inflated price. As a result,

> the nursing home, which had been built with little or no down payment, and was purchased with no down payment at all, now served as collateral for debts totaling $2,695,000. The mortgage obligations had doubled, and the home now enjoyed the advantages of nonprofit status. As for Novak, he had turned a debt of $1.1 million owed *by* him into a debt of $1 million owed *to* him.[61]

Mendelson also traced a complicated lease transaction in which a doctor and his wife built a nursing home in New York City with an

FHA-insured mortgage for more than $4 million. They leased the facility to themselves to operate it as a proprietary organization and then sold the lease to a newly created nonprofit corporation. The couple administered the home, owned the home through their proprietary corporation, and was on the board of directors of the nonprofit organization. According to Mendelson, for their $80,000 investment, the doctor and his wife received a profit in excess of $1 million. She concluded: "The term 'nonprofit' clearly does not include the [owners'] share of the deal."[62]

Mendelson determined that nonprofits are susceptible to such transactions because "the image of nonprofit carries with it a halo of probity in a capitalist society: one imagines the gentle administrator of a church-owned nursing home who spends his time in good works for the benefit of his patients, rather than in calculating new ways to beat the government."[63] But, reality is very different:

The term "nonprofit" does not mean what it would seem to mean: there are plenty of opportunities for profit in a nonprofit operation. All it means is that the home by law does not produce profits for tax purposes: it does not return cash dividends to its owners. A church or a fraternal order or a union or a group of individuals can set up a nonprofit entity to run a nursing home. Once having achieved nonprofit status, the home enjoys some important advantages. It does not pay income taxes, in some states it does not pay the local property tax, and in various places it is exempt from water taxes. It also enjoys official favor. The federal government and foundations prefer nonprofit operations in giving grants for special projects. In some states, health insurers like Blue Cross will only pay for care in nonprofit institutions.[64]

The last type of self-dealing identified by Etzioni and Doty is the most obvious: the payment of excessive fees, salaries, and fringe benefits to executives and employees of nonprofits. Income does not violate the nonprofit concept *per se*, and it is difficult to establish in each instance what is reasonable compensation for work performed. It is sufficient to note here, however, that there is ample opportunity for abuse, as shown in the case of the hospital pathologist whose income far exceeded the income of pathologists employed on a salaried basis.[65]

More and more, the primary beneficiaries of nonprofit hospitals are not patients or the poor but administrators and professional staff members. Through various devices, these self-interested parties have been able to use the subsidies given to nonprofits to make their work environment more pleasant and to increase their personal incomes. There is no convincing evidence that nonprofit hospitals act altruistically or that they provide better or less expensive care to patients than their for-profit counterparts.

Other Examples of Unfair Competition in Health Care

Unfair competition extends far beyond the nation's hospitals and nursing homes. In some states, "sheltered workshops," which receive preferential treatment from public agencies, produce eyeglasses. For example, Disc Village, a drug and alcohol rehabilitation center in Woodville, Florida, established

> an optical laboratory . . . which has begun turning out prescription eyeglasses and safety goggles for industry. Supervised by a licensed optician who draws a salary, the lab work is done by anywhere from four to eight residents. Olk [the director of the facility] received a $10,000 grant from the state of Florida to purchase equipment, and then looked for customers. He approached state officials first, and got a contract to supply glasses for a community-run children's clinic. "As a sheltered workshop, we can sell to the state. They save money this way because we can produce at a competitive price," Olk says. "It's a matter of utilizing the state's 'use laws.' "
>
> The state of Florida runs six large hospitals, and virtually every community has a children's medical service, so Olk sees his market for lenses expanding rapidly. "You do some politicking, persuading, explaining, and that gives us the opportunity to grow," he says. "I want to see us at the point where we're supplying most of the state's demand for eyeglasses. We've also been talking to the military and local Lion's Clubs about doing work for them. The market is unlimited. You just have to go out and talk and sell."[66]

When asked about Disc Village being in competition with the private sector, Olk responded: "There's no fear of competition here."[67] Given its special status, the sheltered workshop had little to fear from for-profit competitors; the private firms that pay taxes to subsidize such operations likely view the situation quite differently.

Disc Village has even taken the process a step further. Olk reported that the profits from making eyeglasses would "get rolled back into buying more equipment and funding other entrepreneurial ventures," including a printing operation.[68] In this way, unfair competition with private sector producers of eyeglasses generated revenues for a foray into unfair competition in the printing business.

Unfair competition also occurs in laboratory testing for medical and other purposes. Nonprofit hospitals commonly charge higher fees to in-patients in order to subsidize the fees charged to out-patients. For example, in Portland, Oregon, "the in-patient fee for one lab test at Good Samaritan Hospital is $74.25; the same test for an out-patient is $15. At Providence Hospital, one test for in-patients costs $35; the same tests for out-patients is $10."[69] The University of North Carolina obtained a $700,000 federal grant from the National Science Foundation to purchase a secondary ion mass spectrometer for research and teaching, but "5% of its time is used to do work for clients such as General Electric Co., International Business Machines Corp., and Union Carbide Corp." The University charges fees to these customers that are lower than those of its for-profit competitors.[70] Similarly, the Department of Physics at the State University of New York at Albany regularly performs tests for corporate clients at rates that undercut profit-seeking labs. Michigan Technological University offers an array of low-priced laboratory services to corporate clients.[71] Many colleges and universities throughout the nation are using equipment purchased with government grants to compete unfairly with for-profit laboratories.

Until a decade or so ago, the market for hearing aids was served almost exclusively by private firms. Since 1980, sales of hearing aids have almost doubled, but the sales volume of most private firms has not markedly increased. Private firms have not received the expected benefit of increased demand because of the entry of nonprofit competitors into the market. In St. Louis alone, 13 nonprofit hospitals have entered the hearing aid market since 1980, and other parts of the country have experienced a similar trend.[72] These nonprofits have not hesitated to use their special status to acquire customers. In Seattle, for example, Northwest Hospital's Speech and Hearing Center persuaded several radio and television stations to run ads promoting free hearing tests for the public. Because the hospital is nonprofit, its ads were aired at no charge as a "public service." When a for-profit company asked for advertising at no cost to promote its own free hearing tests, all of the stations refused.[73] Unfair competition can take many subtle forms.

As a final instance of unfair competition in the health care sector, consider pharmacies that are operated by nonprofit hospitals or by tax-exempt membership groups, such as the American Association of Retired Persons. Because of special treatment by law, nonprofits can purchase drugs at a fraction of the costs that for-profits must pay. This special privilege has taken its toll on retail druggists, as reported by *Oregon Business*:

> There used to be 300 independent pharmacies in the Portland [Oregon] area; now there are about 70. People think it would create a "social disaster" if a not-for-profit hospital had to close . . . but an average of 2.5 independent pharmacies go out of business every day in the United States "and nobody seems to think about those jobs."[74]

In sum, the primary beneficiaries are those who oversee, manage, and work in nonprofit organizations, rather than their customers or society as a whole. Nonprofits can be extremely profitable for those who are associated with them.

Summary and Conclusions

Unfair competition has become prevalent in the nation's hospital and medical care industries. The special privileges that government has given nonprofit hospitals have generated serious, unanticipated social problems, such as the dangerous growth in the diversion market for pharmaceuticals. Nonprofits have attempted to justify their special status by claiming to care for the poor and indigent, but there is no convincing evidence that nonprofits aid the poor more than for-profits do. Rather, the principal beneficiaries of nonprofit hospitals seem to be their trustees, administrators, and professional staffs.

The "contract failure" rationale for the existence of nonprofit health care facilities has little validity. Consumers are by no means ignorant and "given a choice between two organizations that offer the same service, the American consumer is more likely than ever to pick the one with better performance, no matter what its form."[75]

Given that for-profits are more efficient producers of hospital care than nonprofits and that there is no strong justification for the special privileges accorded to nonprofit health providers, it is difficult to disagree with the conclusion drawn by Herzlinger and Krasker: "we believe nonprofit managers could perform even better if they were freed of the limitations imposed by the nonprofit setting and could operate in a for-profit environment with its clearer incentives and measures of performance."[76] If nonprofits operated in a for-profit environment, unfair competition, which has become so prevalent in this sector of the economy, would no longer exist.

Notes to Chapter 4

1. Lester M. Salamon, "Nonprofits: The Results Are Coming In," *Foundation News* (July/August 1984), p. 17.

2. Bruce Steinwald and Duncan Neuhauser, "The Role of the Proprietary Hospital," *Law and Contemporary Problems* (Autumn 1970), p. 819; see Table 1.

3. American Hospital Association, *Hospital Statistics, 1985 Edition* (Chicago, IL: AHA, 1985), pp. 8–11, Tables 2A, 2B.

4. Dorothy Rice and Barbara Cooper, "National Health Expenditures, 1950–66," *Social Security Bulletin* (April 1968): 3–22. See also Cotton M. Lindsay and James Buchanan, "The Organization and Financing of Medical Care in the United States," in *Health Services Financing* (London: British Medical Association, 1970), p. 548.

5. "The Hill-Burton Act, 1946–1980: Asynchrony in the Delivery of Health Care to the Poor," *Maryland Law Review* (1979), p. 318.

6. Judith R. Lave and Lester B. Lave, *The Hospital Construction Act: An Evaluation of the Hill-Burton Program, 1948–1973* (Washington, D.C.: American Enterprise Institute for Public Policy Research, 1974), p. 14, Table 3. No appropriations have been made under the Hill-Burton program since 1974; see 43 Fed. Reg. 49,954.

7. See Philip Kissam, "Physicians Assistant and Nurse Practitioner Laws: A Study of Health Law Reform," *Kansas Law Review* (1975), p. 53.; David Kalkever, "Competition Among Hospitals," in *Competition in the Health Care Sector: Past, Present and Future*, ed. Warren Greenberg (Germantown, Md.: Aspen Systems Corporation, 1978), pp. 150–51.

8. John C. Goodman, *The Regulation of Medical Care: Is the Price Too High?* (Washington, D.C.: Cato Institute, 1980), p. 61.

9. See Alanson W. Wilcox, "Hospitals and the Corporate Practice of Medicine," *Cornell Law Quarterly* (1960), p. 438.

10. Edward Forgotson, Ruth Roemer, and Roger Newman, "Innovations in the Organization of Health Services: Inhibiting vs. Permissive Regulation," *Washington University Law Quarterly* (1967), p. 403.

11. Steinwald and Neuhauser, "Role of the Proprietary Hospital," p. 835.

12. See Martin Feldstein and Amy Taylor, *The Rapid Rise of Hospital Costs* (Cambridge, MA: Harvard Institute of Economic Research, Harvard University, 1977).

13. See "The Big Business of Medicine," *Newsweek*, October 31, 1983.

14. D.J. Wilson, "Hospitals Diversify to Boost Business," *Houston Post*, February 22, 1987.

15. Laralyn Sasaki, "Hospitals Offer Unconventional Services in Hopes of Attracting Future Patients," *Wall Street Journal*, August 1, 1985.

16. Wilson, "Hospitals Diversify."

17. Richard L. Madden, "For Hospitals, New Ventures and New Profits," *New York Times*, January 25, 1987.

18. Judith Vandewater, "Hospital Services Changing," *St. Louis Post Dispatch*, February 16, 1987.

19. Sasaki, "Hospitals Offer Unconventional Services."

20. Wilson, "Hospitals Diversify."

21. "Why Nonprofit Businesses Are Booming," *U.S. News and World Report*, January 16, 1984.

22. Wendy Swallow, "Nonprofit Hospitals and Their Profits on the Side," *Washington Post* (Health Supplement), April 3, 1985.

23. Saski, "Hospitals Offer Unconventional Services."

24. Michael Abramowitz, "Nonprofit Hospitals Venture into New Lines of Business," *Washington Post*, February 15, 1987.

25. Ibid.

26. Sasaki, "Hospitals Offer Unconventional Services."

27. Udayan Gupta, "Hospitals Enlist Profit-Minded Partners for Ventures to Generate New Business," *Wall Street Journal*, January 23, 1987.

28. Charles M. West, Executive Vice-President of the National Association of Retail Druggists, statement for the House Committee on Energy and Commerce, *Prescription Drug Diversion and Counterfeiting—Part I, Hearings Before a Subcommittee on Oversight and Investigations*, 99th Cong., 1st sess., 1985, p. 455.

29. "A Headache for Druggists," *Oregon Business* (August 1986), p. 21.

30. Stephen F. Sims and David W. Nelson, "Statement Before the Subcommittee on Oversight and Investigations of the Committee on Energy and Commerce, July 10, 1985," mimeograph, p. 2.

31. Ibid.

32. Stanley Kowitt, testimony before the House Committee on Energy and Commerce, *Prescription Drug Diversion and Counterfeiting—Part I, Hearings Before a Subcommittee on Oversight and Investigations*, 99th Cong., 1st sess., 1985, pp. 116–17.

33. Stephen F. Sims and David W. Nelson, testimony before the House Committee on Energy and Commerce, *Prescription Drug Diversion and Counterfeiting—Part I, Hearings Before a Subcommittee on Oversight and Investigations*, 99th Cong., 1st sess., 1985, p. 6.

34. Ibid., p. 5

35. Ibid.

36. Ibid.

37. Larry D. Thompson, U.S. Attorney, Northern District of Georgia, testimony before the House Committee on Energy and Commerce, *Prescription Drug Diversion and Counterfeiting—Part I, Hearings Before a Subcommittee on Oversight and Investigations*, 99th Cong., 1st sess., 1985, pp. 300–1.

38. West, Statement for the House Committee on Energy and Commerce, pp. 454–55.

39. "Healthy Competition," *Oregon Business* (August 1986), p. 20.

40. Ibid.

41. Laura Sanders, "Profits? Who, Me?" *Forbes*, March 23, 1987.

42. Nancy M. Davis, "The Competition Complex," *Association Management*, August 1986, p. 26.

43. Carol M. McCarthy, "Not-For-Profit Hospitals' Tax Exemption: A Bargain for the American Public," *Washington Post*, April 19, 1987.

44. Title VI, P.L. 79–725, Section 622(f), 60 Stat. 1042–43.

45. Michael S.Balter, "Broken Promises," *The Nation*, June 12, 1985.

46. For a summary of this litigation, see "The Hill-Burton Act, 1946–1980."

47. Balter, "Broken Promises."

48. Regina E. Herzlinger, "Nonprofit Hospitals Seldom Profit the Needy," *Wall Street Journal*, March 23, 1987.

49. Regina E. Herzlinger and William S. Krasker, "Who Profits from Nonprofits?" *Harvard Business Review* (January/February 1987): 93–106.

50. Ibid., p. 93.

51. Ibid., p. 104.

52. Amitai Etzioni and Pamela Doty, "Profit in Not-For-Profit Corporations: The Example of Health Care," *Political Science Quarterly* (Fall 1976), p. 434.

53. See Ronald Kessler, "Pathologists: More Profits, More Pay," *Washington Post*, November 1, 1972.

54. Ibid.; U.S. General Accounting Office, *A Proposal for Disclosure of Contractual Arrangements Between Hospitals and Members of Their Governing Boards and Hospitals and Their Medical Specialists (MWD-75-73)* (Washington, D.C.: GAO, 1975), p. 23.

55. Kessler, "Pathologists."

56. U.S. General Accounting Office, *A Proposal for Disclosure of Contractual Arrangements*, p. 2.

57. Ibid., pp. 7–8.

58. Ronald Kessler, "Hospital Center Officials Used Connection to Reap Profits," *Washington Post*, October 31, 1972. For additional insight into self-dealing at the Washington Hospital Center, see Ronald Kessler, "Conflict of Interest Marks Hospital Center Management," *Washington Post*, October 30, 1972. See also William Stockton, "Bank with Officers on Blue Cross and Blue Shield Boards Use Their Funds," *New York Times*, August 5, 1987.

59. Kessler, "Hospital Center Officials."

60. Mary A. Mendelson, *Tender Loving Greed* (New York: Alfred A. Knopf, 1974), p. 5.

61. Ibid., p. 200.

62. Ibid., p. 205.

63. Ibid., p. 195.

64. Ibid., pp. 196–7.

65. For more examples, see Etizoni and Doty, "Profit in Not-for-Profit Corporations," pp. 450–3.

66. James C. Crimmins and Mary Keil, *Enterprise in the Nonprofit Sector* (Washington, D.C.: Partners for Livable Places, 1983), pp. 62–3.

67. Ibid., p. 63.

68. Ibid.

69. "Healthy Competition," p. 20.

70. Michael W. Miller, "Colleges Bids for Work Rile Private Labs," *Wall Street Journal*, August 12, 1983.

71. Ibid.

72. Sanders, "Profits? Who, Me?"

73. Kendall J. Wills, "The Battle for Hearing Aid Sales," *New York Times*, May 5, 1985. See also Erik Calonius, "There's Big Money in the 'Nonprofits,'" *Newsweek*, January 5, 1987.

74. "A Headache for Druggists."

75. Herzlinger and Krasker, op. cit., p. 94.

76. Ibid., p. 104.

V.

Unfair Competition in the Physical Fitness Industry

Americans spend billions of dollars annually on recreation and physical fitness activities, and their concern about health and fitness is an important one. Studies have shown that how one *maintains* one's health is the most important determinant of overall physical well being. In a study of health care in the U.S., Professor Victor Fuchs of the Stanford University Medical School concluded: "In the United States, our health has less to do with what we spend on medical care than with our heredity, environment, and personal lifestyles."[1]

This point is illustrated by the link between physical fitness and cardiovascular diseases, which annually claim more American lives than all other natural causes of death combined. Medical professionals have long been concerned with how sedentary lifestyles may lead to heart disease and have encouraged the population to become more active. For example, an international symposium on physical fitness and coronary heart disease addressed the question: Should the medical profession encourage the public . . . to exercise more than they do? The participants in the symposium were fifty heart specialists from around the world who concluded that "the answer [to this question] should be yes."[2] In other words, the old adage that an ounce of prevention is worth a pound of cure is as trite as it is true.

Heart disease is not the only health problem that has been linked to sedentary lifestyles. Other problems that have been diagnosed include insomnia, iron deficiency, osteoporosis, obesity, back pain, and bursitis. The health and fitness industry, therefore, is an important ingredient in health maintenance and, consequently, in holding down health care costs. The international symposium on physical fitness and coronary heart disease recognized this by further stating that "the only way to improve the physical condition of the population seems to be by making the training procedure a pleasure, readily accessible and socially attractive."[3]

This chapter discusses the impact of unfair competition by CNEs, primarily YMCAs, and governmental enterprises on the physical fitness industry. To the extent that unfair competition reduces the economic vitality of the private physical fitness industry, the industry's potential to contribute toward a healthier population—and to help hold down health care costs—will be impaired.

Regulated Competition in the Physical Fitness Industry

There are thousands of private sector recreational facilities in the U.S., including health spas, racquetball courts, swimming pools, skating rinks, bowling alleys, tennis courts, vacation resorts, and golf courses. The marketplace has responded to the public's diverse preferences by providing facilities for every type of physical activity imaginable, from aerobics to yoga.

A major competitor of private firms in the recreation business is the YMCA, a tax-exempt organization whose ostensible purpose is to improve "the spiritual, mental and physical health of the young," especially the less privileged.[4] In providing recreational services to the poor and underprivileged, the YMCA supposedly "provides a service to the portion of the population it is not profitable to serve."[5] In theory, the YMCA helps fill a gap in the marketplace that is purportedly left by the unwillingness or inability of private enterprises to serve the poor and underprivileged.

As a charity the YMCA has long held nonprofit status and has enjoyed all the advantages of CNEs. It is exempt from state and federal income taxes; it can raise capital through tax-deductible, charitable donations; it is exempt from sales, property, and corporate income taxes; it pays lower postal rates; it uses volunteer labor; it receives direct governmental subsidies; and it is excluded from costly and time-consuming regulations imposed by the U.S. Federal Trade Commission and state "consumer protection" regulations.

The YMCA (like other CNEs) especially benefits from regulations that impose heavy costs on their profitseeking competitors, but from which YMCAs are exempt. Consider the Maryland law concerning the regulation of private health clubs. The law was enacted

> for the purpose of imposing certain registration and renewal fees on each person who sells health club services in this state; requiring a person who sells health club services to purchase a certain surety bond; requiring a person who sells health club services at a facility under construction to maintain a certain surety bond; creating a health club administration fund for certain purposes; altering the manner in which a buyer of health club services may cancel an agreement for health club services; requiring a seller of health club services to disclose certain information to the buyer regarding the buyer's right to cancel the agreement; requiring a seller to disclose certain information to the Consumer Protection Division of the Office of the Attorney General at a certain time; making each sale of health club services that violates this act an unfair or deceptive trade practice . . . ; and generally relating to the regulation of health club services.[6]

The Maryland law creates an obvious competitive imbalance by further stating that these regulations do not apply to "any nonprofit public or private school, college, or university; the state, or any of its political subdivisions; or any nonprofit, religious, ethnic, community, or service organization."[7] Thus, in the name of deterring "unfair trade practices" the law mandates unfair trade practices.

The Maryland law also imposes extensive record-keeping requirements on private health clubs but not on CNEs by stipulating that "any person who sells health club services shall maintain accurate records, updated as necessary, of the name, address, contract terms, and payments of each buyer of health club services."[8] The law denies private health club owners and managers individual rights to privacy by further insisting that "these records shall be open to inspection by the Division at any time. . . . The Division may revoke the registration of any person who fails to maintain or produce the records described." The due process clause of the U.S. Constitution is also trampled upon: "If this Division determines that a person is selling health club services in violation of this [law], the Division may issue a cease and desist order *without conducting a hearing*" (emphasis added).[9]

The Maryland law effectively establishes a partial governmental takeover of the private health club industry in that state by giving state regulators the ability to influence or direct management decisions regarding the purchase of surety bonds, contract terms offered to customers, and other business matters. Private health club owners are treated as though they do not have the same constitutional rights as other citizens. In the name of enhancing the financial security of the private health club industry these regulations will do the opposite by imposing costs on them that their "nonprofit" competitors need not bear. And, ironically, the private health clubs are forced to pay for this system, a system which undermines their livelihood, by making payments to a "health club administration fund."

Maryland's neighboring state of Virginia has a similar law, as do at least twenty-seven other states. The Virginia law claims that its purpose is "to safeguard the public interest against fraud, deceit, and financial hardship, and to foster and encourage competition, fair dealing and prosperity in the field of health spa services."[10] But fostering competition and "fair dealing" appear inconsistent with another part of the law that states:

> The term 'health spa' shall not include nonprofit organizations, including, but not limited to, the Young Men's Christian Association, Young Women's Christian Association, . . . any facility owned or operated by the United States, any facility owned or operated by the Commonwealth of Virginia or any of its subdivisions, and any nonprofit public or private school, college or university."[11]

One example of how the Virginia law fosters unfair competition is that it requires *private* health clubs to grant full refunds to customers who either do not use the club's facilities for a period of time or who become physically disabled, but specifically exempts nonprofits from this requirement. As discussed below, most private health clubs have long granted refunds for legitimate purposes such as job transfers or physical injuries. Many YMCAs, however, do not grant refunds under any circumstances.

The Business of the YMCA

As one of the nation's most popular charitable institutions, the YMCA's well-deserved reputation has been earned through more than 100 years of charitable acts benefitting the underprivileged, the young, and many others. The modern-day YMCA, however, is very different. Many, though not all, YMCA branches no longer direct their activities primarily at the young or the underprivileged. Rather, their customers are among the most affluent consumers in America. Many YMCA chapters have abandoned their original purpose of working with the poor and have become "essentially health clubs for yuppies, with very expensive fees. . . . in direct competition with . . . private clubs."[12] The *Wall Street Journal* has documented this national phenomenon:

> State-of-the-art Ys are cropping up all over the country, serving downtown business clients and upscale suburbanites. Forty-four new YMCA fitness centers opened last year; a YMCA brochure boasts that a major YMCA project is begun or completed in a U.S. community almost every day. "Ys are moving into office complexes, shopping malls, condominiums and even the New Orleans Superdome," crowed the YMCA's 1984 annual report.[13]

Time also reported that "in cities and suburbs across the country, the Y is shedding its image of serviceable shabbiness and putting up gleaming facilities that rival the ritziest of private clubs."[14] As one example: "This fall [1986] a 110,000 square foot Y will open in the most prestigious area of downtown Los Angeles. Among its attractions: a large pool, indoor running track and six racquetball and handball courts. It's the poshest athletic club ever built in Southern California."[15] Another example is the YMCA of Metropolitan Washington, D.C., described by its executive director as "the prototype of the Y of the future. In Nashville, Portland, and Hartford, YMCAs are taking routes similar to that of the Washington Y."[16]

Journalist Arthur Levine reported on the nature of the route taken by the Washington Y after a tour of its facilities:

> What I saw was a long way from the traditional Y. The new, red brick building cost $6.5 million, and it looks it. In the lobby there are paintings and plush carpeting—and an eerie quiet. There were no shouts, no echoing of balls against wood; it didn't sound like a gym. Some of the locker rooms I saw had orange carpeting and tan lockers, and there were uniformed black attendants to pick up your dirty towels after you got out of the shower. . . . Upstairs, there was an open area full of athletic luxuries: massage tables, sauna, sun-room, and other YMCA equipment. To the right of the massage tables was the lounge, complete with Sony color TV. . . . On the fourth floor, I had a look at the Y's cardiovascular fitness testing center. It had an EKG machine and treadmills and resembled . . . a hospital lab.[17]

Mr. Levine was obviously impressed with the facilities and "was ready to join the Y" until he discovered that an "athletic center membership" would cost him $745 per year. "In contrast, the chic Watergate Hotel Health Club looked positively cheap with its $495 annual fee."[18] Despite its facade as a charitable institution, the Washington Y is essentially a private health club for affluent Washingtonians. Eighty percent of its members are in the highest income brackets,[19] and about one third of them are lawyers.[20]

Moreover, there is no membership arrangement at the Washington YMCA for those whom the Y is ostensibly in business to serve: the young and the poor. Children of adult members can only use the facilities when accompanied by their parents and only during certain weekend hours. The reason for the "no-kids" policy, according to one YMCA employee, is that the Y is "trying to sell [itself] as a country club. . . . As long as we keep kids out of the . . . businessmen's faces, everyone will be happy."[21] A YMCA member voiced disappointment over the Y's no-kids policy: "I've been very appalled at the lack of response to young people. . . . [The Y] has such an exclusive air, like it's geared only to male heart attack prevention. . . . When I brought my son there, all these older men with paunches were grumbling about little kids getting in their way."[22] The Washington Y's management has explained its no-kids policy: "This is a specialized facility, . . . not a children's Y. Within a six-block radius, there are less than 2,000 children."[23] According to the Y's management, then, there are not enough children in downtown Washington, D.C. to justify offering youth memberships. This argument could not hold water with anyone who has ever walked through the DuPont Circle area where the new Y is located, which is one of the most densely-populated neighborhoods in the city.

Although the Washington YMCA claims that it is "not a children's Y" and all but totally excludes children, it still has youth-oriented advertising. In a promotional slide show for potential members the Y claims:

> The YMCA of Metropolitan Washington . . . strengthens family structures . . . helps change the conditions that foster alienation, delinquency, and crime. And it strengthens physical and mental health, and develops in youth values for living—a faith to live by.[24]

The programs sponsored by the Washington Y, however, do not seem to fit this stated purpose. In addition to all its cardiovascular equipment, for example, it holds financial planning classes with such topics as "Our Changing Tax Laws," "Building Your Estate," and "Preserving Assets."

Who Benefits?

The Washington YMCA has become a vehicle through which a small group of relatively affluent individuals can organize its own private health spa and reap the advantages of a tax-exempt institution by merely promising to promote "youth values." The YMCA boards of directors are elected at annual meetings attended by the most active local volunteers. In Washington, D.C., and in many other cities, this includes businessmen, politicians, and other professionals. It is not surprising that these boards establish essentially commercial enterprises that appeal to their own preferences and that they price "undesirables," that is, young people and the underprivileged, out of the market. As one board member candidly admitted, "This facility reflects what the leadership . . . wished it to be."[25]

The managers and employees benefit from the Y's transformation because of a more pleasant (and financially rewarding) work environment.

> After all, [the Washington Y's director] didn't become the leader of "the prototype Y of the future" or get access to the "top echelon of people" by refurbishing some drafty old gym. And the well-to-do, it often turns out, are so much more pleasant to deal with. They pay their bills, their problems can be solved, they make good lunch companions.[26]

The membership of a commercial nonprofit enterprise such as the Washington YMCA also benefits indirectly from the Y's profits. While the Washington Y's membership fees are high, it is apparently still a bargain considering all of the amenities. Because it does not have to pay taxes on income earned through membership fees or on the sale of property, the Washington Y can make capital improvements and purchases that private health clubs cannot afford. For instance, when their old YMCA building was sold, the Washington Y was able to keep the full $5 million selling price. In addition, it held a fund-raising drive and raised another $700,000 in tax-deductible contributions.

It is not surprising, then, that members rebelled when the Y's management announced a plan to attract more female members. Several hundred members formed the "Members' Association for a Safe YMCA" to discuss ways of blocking the proposed admission of 1,500 women to the 5,000–member club.[27] At a YMCA where one third of the members are lawyers, there was also, naturally, much talk of litigation. The Members' Association claimed that the Y was unsafe because of overcrowding so that the women should not be admitted. One spokesman for the group explained:

> It's . . . the premier health facility of the city . . . I want to come out of the pool feeling unfettered with the world's cares. I really believe after this expansion [of membership], I'm going to come out of the pool feeling more frustrated than when I dove into it. I'm not there to wring my hands, gird my loins and battle other swimmers, thank you very much.[28]

With the prospect of an expanded membership, the subsequent crowding means that the net benefits to members would decline. This would eventually render the YMCA no more attractive to members than some of the local private health clubs, which are not nearly as prestigious as "the premier health facility of the city."

Not only does the Washington YMCA not serve its supposed constituents—the young and underprivileged—but its affluent members have even sought to block membership by other well-off members of the community on the basis of sex. The Washington Y has strayed far from its original ideal of fostering "the spiritual and mental conditions of young men" and has become, effectively, an exclusive, private health club.

Other Examples

Another "prototype of the new Y" is the Los Angeles YMCA, which openly admits that "it is not and never was our intention to work only with the poor. . . . We service the mainstream and always have."[29] In short, the Los Angeles Y does not deny that in practice it is the equivalent of a private health club. For tax purposes, however, it still claims to be a "charity" and still enjoys the benefits of its nonprofit status.

Because of its superior facilities the fees charged by the Los Angeles YMCA are slightly higher than those charged by nearby private health clubs. According to one of its recruiters, its members are mostly "executive types, from nearby Security Pacific Bank and the World Trade Center." Moreover, said the recruiter, "Our target is clerical workers and governmental employees. That's who we built our facility for."[30] This may explain why the Los Angeles Y received a $1.5 million federal grant and a $3 million federally guaranteed low-interest loan for its investments in new facilities in 1985.[31]

In order to preserve the organization's tax-exempt status the president of the YMCA of Metropolitan Los Angeles claims that it is a "charitable" institution. But about 30 percent of the membership is described as "middle class"; the remainder is even more affluent. This purportedly creates a charitable setting, according to the Y's president: "Giving somebody upscale a locker right next to someone starting out in life, I think that's charity."[32] Furthermore, he stated, "In my opinion, 100 percent of what we do is charitable. The definition of charity under which we operate is improving the wellness of the community."[33] This definition, of course, can apply to any private sector health club. If what the Los Angeles YMCA is doing is charitable and worthy of tax exemption, so must be the activities of every private health club.

The Glendale, California, YMCA has a similarly strained definition of charity. It is lobbying for legislation that would broaden the state's definition of charitable organizations and has hired one of the nation's largest publicity firms to assist it.[34] The Glendale Y openly admits that it provides services identical to a private commercial health club. But it apparently does not wish to compete on an equal basis with the private clubs. It seeks to ensure its nonprofit status and its unfair competitive edge through the legislative process. When asked about the prospects of losing its tax-exempt status, the Glendale Y's general manager stated that he was not worried about the consequences: "We haven't even tried to compete [with the private clubs]—if they want competition they'll see competition they'd never believe."[35] If the general manager of the Glendale Y is genuinely confident in its ability to compete with private health clubs, however, he would not be lobbying for laws that would spare him from having to compete.

Direct Subsidies

Even if it was recognized that the YMCA is not primarily a charitable organization and its tax exemption was removed, it would still enjoy special advantages because of other types of subsidies.

For instance, the new YMCA being built in Roswell, Georgia, an Atlanta suburb, is estimated to cost about $900,000, with $400,000 being contributed by the Roswell city government. It does not appear, however, that this governmentally funded facility is charitable. A city councilman stated that, with this project, "We feel like we are tops in recreation in Atlanta."[36] Special rooms are being built for slimnastics, aerobics, karate, and classes in ceramics, pottery making, and yoga—not exactly the activities that are of special interest to the underprivileged and to young people.

The special competitive advantage given to the Roswell Y by direct governmental subsidies was clearly stated by the Roswell Y's director: "The [new] center has been a dream for five years, but we couldn't see a way to finance it . . . without the [government] grant."[37] In the words of a local politician, "Roads are not the only public works that need to keep pace with the expanding population of Roswell—ample recreation facilities are important too."[38] How slimnastics, yoga, and pottery classes can be considered "public works" is unclear. Such recreational activities are purely private services that are also provided by unsubsidized private enterprises. Local government officials who provide such subsidies are praised for their generosity (with taxpayers' money) and public spiritedness, but they are rarely criticized for contributing to the elimination of small, private health clubs and the accompanying loss of jobs and tax revenues.

Local governments are not the only entities that grant subsidies to local YMCAs. Nonprofit organizations received more than $40 billion in federal subsidies in 1980 (see chapter 3). One example of this kind of largesse is a $480,000 grant to Baltimore's YMCA from the Department of Housing and Urban Development.[39] The Baltimore Y also expected to finance its renovation projects with an additional $1 million from the federal government and $500,000 in revenue bonds from the city of Baltimore. The Baltimore Y, and many others, also qualifies for United Way contributions.

Finally, it is important to note that governmental subsidies to some of the most exclusive YMCAs in the country constitute a regressive redistribution of income. The janitor who cleans a corporate executive's offices each evening, for example, is paying taxes to subsidize the executive's membership fees at an expensive health spa. Moreover, the health spa may be financially off limits to the janitor's family, even though they are precisely the ones the YMCA is supposed to be serving.

Abandoning the Poor

One particularly clear example of how the "new Y" has abandoned its traditional, charitable function is found at the Philadelphia YMCA. Until 1985, the Philadelphia Y operated a residence hall. In that year, however, the residence hall was sold for $13 million to Evans-Pitcairn, a large commercial developer, and the hall's 300 residents were evicted. According to the president of the Philadelphia Y: "The sale will allow the . . . YMCA to get out of the shelter business and to pour millions of dollars into renovation of the Central Branch's athletic and office space. . . . Renting rooms is no longer part of the Y mission. Our emphasis today is on health enhancement."[40] Even though the Philadelphia Y has abandoned one of its charitable functions in favor of a commercial one, the tax-exempt $13 million can still be applied to new investment projects. "We're going to put in a new indoor track, increase our locker facilities, enlarge our exercise facilities, and expand our women's health-fitness center."[41]

The Y's Center City branch in Philadelphia includes staff offices and new office space, which is rented by the commercial developer who purchased the building. The developer anticipates that "because we're only a block from City Hall, we expect to attract the interest of legal firms. . . . Also, two of our floors will have very high ceilings, which will appeal to architectural firms."[42] This is a good indication of the type of clients that will be frequenting the renovated Y, which is located in the same building. The Y's lower-income tenants have been replaced by lawyers and architects, and the organization expects to earn a handsome profit from the change by more than doubling its membership from 2,200 to 5,000. Many of the new clients will probably leave the membership rolls of the city's private, taxpaying health clubs that do not have 13 million tax-free dollars available.

The Dallas, Texas, YMCA has been accused of abandoning its traditional role of serving the poor, the disadvantaged, and average residents by withdrawing resources from an older facility "which offers the simplest enjoyments: a Universal weightroom, an outdoor pool, two aging tennis courts and an expanse of weedy soccer and baseball fields."[43] The organization's resources have been redirected toward higher-income neighborhoods as the Y has sought to attract "a predominantly white, middle- and upper-class clientele."[44]

In downtown Dallas, the Y does it up with flourish: five, going on six, levels of gleaming fitness amenities; three gymnasiums,

19 handball/racquetball courts, forests of Universal, Nautilus and Cam II weightlifting machines. Rubberized running tracks, motorized treadmills with cardiac monitors, spacious locker rooms graced with sauna, whirlpool, color TV, masseuse and masseur.[45]

The new facilities are a stark contrast to YMCAs in Dallas's poorer neighborhoods.

The Oak Cliff Y hasn't received a major improvement in several years. The East Dallas Y has a single, cramped men's shower. The Lewisville branch uses private backyard pools to give swimming lessons. There is no YMCA in West Dallas.[46]

As in the other cities surveyed thus far, the Dallas YMCA has become a specially-privileged, tax-exempt, commercial enterprise that has largely abandoned its charitable role. Furthermore, it has competed unfairly with unsubsidized private health clubs, sometimes even bankrupting them. As one private club owner said: "At the time [the new Y] opened, we just got wiped out."[47]

Similarities Between Nonprofit and For-Profit Health Clubs

A survey of YMCAs in eighteen metropolitan areas across the United States, which compared the policies and practices of modern YMCAs with a sample of private health clubs, concluded that the "YMCAs and health spas provide essentially the same services, at approximately the same costs, through similar promotional vehicles." The survey continued: "The facilities and services offered by YMCAs for full-service memberships and the facilities and programs of standard full-service health spa memberships appear to be similar."[48]

The YMCAs included in the survey did charge slightly higher prices, on average, than the private health clubs in the sample. "The average price for two years full-service membership among the 18 YMCAs surveyed is $560. The average two year membership price in the three health spa companies surveyed is $469." These comparisons may not be entirely accurate, however. Although membership dues to the YMCA are not tax deductible because they are fees for services, it is likely that many individuals deduct them just as they would, say, union dues. Many YMCA members may not understand the distinction between a contribution to the YMCA and dues, and even if they do they may deduct it anyway, given the small probability of an IRS audit. The IRS audits only about 2 percent of all tax returns, and even a taxpayer caught fudging pays only the small amount of tax owed and a small fine. In short, given the likelihood that many YMCA members deduct their dues from their taxes, the *after-tax* price may be lower than prices charged by private recreational facilities.

Both YMCAs and private health clubs surveyed offered credit options such as Master Card, Bank Americard, bank loans, extended payments and preauthorized bank drafts. These kinds of arrangements are expected at expensive, private clubs, but not at facilities that supposedly serve underprivileged youth. The acceptance of major credit cards as a way to pay for YMCA memberships is a good indication of how affluent new YMCA members are.

The survey also found evidence of monopoly power among some YMCAs, which are able to ward off competition from private health clubs because of their legislative privileges. For instance, fifteen of the eighteen YMCAs surveyed refused to grant refunds under any circumstances. By contrast, private health clubs generally grant refunds for medical or relocation reasons. Private health clubs also typically offer consumers a three- to seven-day "cooling off period" immediately after a membership contract has been signed during which customers can withdraw from the club. The YMCAs surveyed offered no such terms. Many of the YMCAs did not permit patrons to transfer their memberships to other Y branches. Private health clubs, by comparison, have formed the International Physical Fitness Association as a vehicle for facilitating reciprocity arrangements among member companies. Private clubs are probably compelled to offer the superior terms because of competitive pressures—pressures that YMCAs often don't experience due to their legislative privileges. The survey concluded: "the only difference between the full service memberships sold by YMCAs and [private] health spas, then, is that YMCAs would not be subjected to . . . regulations governing health spas and would thus have a substantial competitive, financial and economic advantage."[49]

In light of this evidence, there is no doubt that many YMCAs are commercial, not charitable enterprises. This becomes especially apparent in the new YMCAs' advertising and promotional activities. Charitable institutions have legitimate reasons to advertise their activities to raise funds and to inform the public. It is both a way for potential beneficiaries to learn of services available to them and a way to attract and court potential donors. But much of the YMCAs' advertising falls into neither of these categories. The advertising is identical to that done by commercial firms and is directed at the customers of private health clubs which the YMCA hopes to lure away.

For example, New York City's West Side YMCA advertises by comparing its prices and services to six private health clubs (see Appendix Table A5.1). The advertisement makes it clear that the West Side YMCA considers itself to be a competitor of some of the ritziest health clubs in New York City, including the Vertical Club, which costs $1,150 per year to join. Claiming to be *superior* to the private clubs, the advertisement's theme is "Don't settle for less." This is typical of the advertisements used by YMCAs throughout the U.S. As the YMCA/health club survey revealed, a comparison of the advertising and promotional activities of YMCAs and private health clubs reveals little discernible difference.

Examples from Abroad

The transformation of YMCAs from charitable organizations to commercial, but untaxed, health spas has also occurred outside the U.S. The first YMCA was founded in London in 1844 "to improve the spiritual condition of young men in the drapery business."[50] Today the London YMCA is similar to many of the American Ys in that it serves a relatively affluent clientele rather than the young and under-privileged. A promotional brochure for the London Y announces:

> There has never been anything like it. . . . A modern hotel—built by the London Central YMCA . . . in the very heart of London that includes squash courts, a gymnasium, a 25–meter swimming pool, shops and underground parking. Come to the Y Hotel and relax in comfort. The lounges, with color television, bar, two types of restaurant services and all the facilities await you.[51]

A similar facility exists in Toronto, Canada. As reported in the *Toronto Star*:

> The Y has obviously abandoned its historic roots of non-exclusivity—a conscious move best symbolized by its decision not to provide cheap accommodation in the new building. Today, it seems to be trying to imitate a private club. While this may suit

the downtown singles crowd, it represents the loss of an important community resource to many people.[52]

Like many American Ys, the Toronto Y is large and bureaucratic. "The sales staff is large enough to form an army platoon. . . . If you encounter a problem . . . be prepared to devote a lot of time to solving it. You'll be sent from one bureaucrat to another, none of whom knows what the others are doing."[53]

The Toronto Y also has a "no-kids" policy. Children under twelve years old are not permitted in the pool area unless accompanied by a parent, because "not all children are strong enough to swim by themselves." Some parents have suggested that the Y apply its well-developed testing levels to determine a child's ability, but the suggestions have been rejected. One Y employee said "We're thinking about that, but the building is still new."[54] Another similarity between the affluent American Ys and the Toronto Y is its no-refund policy. One of its employees explained why:

It isn't affordable for us to give refunds. If we gave back money, we'd lose money, and we have to be careful not to lose money. After all, we get about 10 requests for refunds each day.[55]

Rarely does a private businessman, let alone an employee of a supposedly charitable institution, admit such an overriding concern for profit. And the Toronto Y, like its American counterparts, still insists that it is a nonprofit and charitable institution.

These brief examples only suggest the nature of nonprofit physical fitness activities abroad. They support the notion that the new Y, in the U.S. and abroad, has become a commercial enterprise. Thus, the commercialization of the YMCA appears to be a general phenomenon. The "new Y" is, in most instances, a commercial enterprise, but the laws still treat it as though it were a charity.

Tax Exemption Challenged

The shift in many YMCAs' purpose and membership has not gone unnoticed by the courts. In May 1985, the the Columbia-Willamette YMCA in Oregon was placed on the Multnomah County tax roles. The county tax court ruled that even though property used for charitable purposes is exempt from taxes, the YMCA did not qualify because it was spending too little of its resources—only 11 percent—

on charity. According to the county tax assessor: "Based on those figures, my determination was that the YMCA was not primarily a charitable institution." The Y appealed that ruling to the Oregon Department of Revenue. In November, 1987 the Department ruled that several of the Y's fitness clubs are in fact not charities and don't qualify for tax exemption. According to Oregon tax laws, an organization that is labeled a "charity" does not necessarily qualify for a property tax exemption. In order to qualify an organization must 1) "in some way lessen the normal burdens of government," and 2) "A degree of gift giving must be present. . . . If no gift is involved, there is no charity." The Oregon Department of Revenue ruled that several branches of the Columbia-Willamette Y met neither of these criteria and, on that basis, withdrew their tax exemption. The Revenue Department concluded that the Y was primarily restricted to adults, which "forecloses assistance to needy children."[56] This judgement is consistent with current federal tax laws, which stipulate that for an operation to be tax exempt its *primary activity* must be charitable. However, even the 11 percent of its budget spent on charitable activities probably overstates the Columbia-Willamette Y's charitable function. This is because YMCAs receive United Way contributions which are used to finance their charitable activities, freeing up the profits from membership sales to finance commercial activities.

The Metro Center Y in Portland, Oregon has also been placed on the tax roles because its primary purpose was judged to be commercial, not charitable, as was the Rock Island, Illinois YMCA in 1984. The YMCA has appealed all three of these decisions. The president of the Columbia-Willamette YMCA has warned that if his appeal is unsuccessful, "taxing charitable organizations would result in their decline."[57] This statement confounds the issue, however, for his organization is clearly not charitable.

The best way to preserve the tax-exempt status of charitable institutions is to ensure that they continue to engage in charitable activities. If they choose to enter commercial businesses, they should do so through a for-profit subsidiary that is subject to all the rules and regulations that affect private businesses (see chapter 8). The Columbia-Willamette YMCA's decline in charitable activities is a cause, not a result of its withdrawn tax exemption. The loss of tax-exempt status can be traced directly to the Y's managers and directors, not to the county tax court or the private health clubs which brought the suit. The most expeditious route to regaining its tax exemption would be to resume its charitable functions, but the Columbia-Willamette Y has decided instead to lobby for an expanded definition of "charitable activities" in the state's tax code. Their new definition would include slimnastics, aerobics classes, and even financial planning seminars. How such activities could be called "charitable" stretches the wildest of imaginations.

Governmental Competition in the Physical Fitness Industry

Crowding out small businesses in the physical fitness industry does not occur solely at the hands of commercial nonprofit enterprises such as the YMCA. Federal, state, and local governments also provide physical fitness and recreational services using the taxpayers' money.

In the area of health and fitness, local governments are probably the most active competitors. In 1982—the latest year for which complete census data are available—local governments spent $6.2 billion on "parks and recreation."[58] This constitutes a compulsory "membership fee" in local government recreational facilities of approximately $60 per year for each taxpayer. State governments spent an additional $1.3 billion in 1982; during the same year the federal government spent approximately $1 billion on the national park system. The average state spent $124 million on parks and recreation in 1981–82, ranging from the $4.1 million spent in Vermont to California's $1.1 billion (see Appendix Table A5.2).

Why Government?

Local governments operate such recreational facilities as swimming pools, water slides, racquetball courts, Nautilus machines, jogging tracks, tennis courts, golf courses, ice skating rinks, bowling alleys, "fitness centers," squash courts, "adult education" classes, dance, art classes, music and theater productions, saunas, jacuzzis, vacation resort hotels, and much more. Virtually all the recreational activities provided by local governments are also provided by the private sector. Thus, there is no "market failure" problem in the recreation industry, for private markets supply similar services and facilities in great abundance. Nor can a case be made that local government expenditures on parks and recreation rectify any inequitable distribution of income, because so many of the beneficiaries are relatively affluent.

All taxpayers in a metropolitan area must pay taxes to support the local park authority, but the facilities are often disproportionately located in more affluent areas. In these instances, lower-income taxpayers provide benefits for higher-income individuals. In fact, this may be a dominant reason for governmental involvement in the recreation industry, because the affluent are more politically active than are the less affluent. It should come as no surprise that the former group uses the political process to get others to pay for some of its *private* goods.

Thus, a more plausible reason for local governments' involvement in the physical fitness and recreation industries is politics. Governmental provision of recreational services is a way for politicians to win votes and dispense patronage jobs. They also win votes by providing benefits to politically active voters while dispersing the costs across the entire taxpaying population.

Local governments provide recreational services through a variety of institutional arrangements. There are literally thousands of local government recreational districts and "authorities," city or county recreation departments, public school systems, and governmentally funded "community centers" (See Appendix Table A5.3). But governmental enterprises compete with private suppliers in these industries on an unfair basis. They pay no taxes; they are financed by compulsory taxes; they can borrow money at preferred interest rates by issuing either general obligation or revenue bonds; they pay no rent; they need not comply with many regulations; they pay lower utility rates than private firms do; sometimes they use the government's power of eminent domain; they can obtain special zoning variances; they do not post performance bonds; and they receive state and federal government subsidies (of the $6.2 billion spent by local governments on parks and recreation in 1982, $5 billion came from state and federal sources).[59]

Governmentally Owned Recreational Facilities in Fairfax, Virginia

In Fairfax County, Virginia, a wealthy suburb of Washington, D.C., there are dozens of private recreational facilities that offer many types · of activities. Governmental agencies are also quite prevalent, with the activities of the Fairfax County Park Authority, the Fairfax County Department of Recreation and Community Services, the public schools, and the recreation departments of various municipal governments. The Department of Recreation and Community Services provides such services as "social, recreational, and other leisure activities" for senior citizens; gymnasiums; dance, art, music, and theater productions; and classes in fitness, scuba diving, and "popular interest" subjects.[60]

Municipal governments offer similar services. In their pursuit of profit they often concentrate on activities for which fees are charged, as does the Fairfax County Park Authority and various governmentally funded community centers. As a study of the government operated recreational facilities done for the Fairfax County government stated: "The Fairfax County Park Authority is heavily oriented toward fee class programming. In . . . 1983, some 2,000 . . . classes attracted over 20,000 participants and fee class revenue is a major source of financial support."[61]

Governmental authorities in Fairfax County seem to be more concerned about interagency rivalry than about competition from the private sector. The study prepared for the Fairfax County government warned: "There is a substantial overlap of . . . effort between the Fairfax County Department of Recreation and Community Services, municipal recreation departments, and community groups."[62] Because of this overlap, the study cautioned, "in the future . . . as Park Authority recreation centers are constructed throughout the county, the impact of the overlap [on revenues] will become more apparent."[63]

The study did not even mention the numerous private recreational facilities in the county as a competitive threat. Because of the legislated advantages that governments have over private enterprises in the industry, 64 percent of the participants in indoor recreational activities in Fairfax County use government-owned facilities. This compares to a 25 percent market share for private health clubs or fitness centers.[64]

Like the YMCA, many of Fairfax County's recreational facilities are aimed at an affluent clientele. For instance, one of the objectives of the Fairfax County Park Authority is "maximization of revenue potential through provision of specialized facilities and programs."[65] To accomplish this requires new facilities "which can attract new users" by offering "unique recreational and leisure time experience." One such experience is provided by the county government's "wave pool" in which

> wave action can be created by means of compressed air. The pool is capable of operating in both non-wave and wave modes. In the non-wave mode the pool can be used in much the same manner as a standard pool, for recreational and competitive swimming. . . . During programmed periods of wave action, the . . . pool will have an especially strong appeal to teenagers and young adults. . . . The popularity of the . . . pool has been well documented. . . . Numerous pools have been developed by the public sector based on revenue potential, and the pool has been the focal point of an increasing number of commercial aquatic parks.[66]

The Park Authority recognizes that wave pools have been profitable in the private sector and wants in on the profits. Private enterprise would operate the facility more efficiently, but it can hardly compete with taxpayer-subsidized facilities.

Another example of the Park Authority's pursuit of profit is its construction of new fitness centers in high income neighborhoods. In 1986 the county began building a new $7.6 million fitness center in the Spring Hill area of McLean, Virginia, one of the wealthiest suburbs in the entire country. The new center is being designed "to attract a more sophisticated, fitness conscious individual," and will provide an experience "that is somewhat more socially oriented than the traditional recreation center."[67] The new facility will include a 25 yard by 25 meter indoor pool (glass-enclosed on two sides), offices and staff rooms, two racquetball courts, weight rooms, a spa, whirlpool, locker rooms with sauna, large multipurpose rooms for dance and exercise classes, a lounge and snack bar with an outdoor eating area, a nursery, and baseball and soccer fields.[68] A second phase of the project is planned, so that the services provided by the McLean facility will eventually "match those at similar county facilities."[69]

The county government clearly expects to take business away from commercial health clubs and fitness centers in the area. The study recommending that the county build the new facility pointed out that the area "already has a well-developed array of [private] health and fitness centers," but that "providing a unique and . . . upgraded facility" the revenue potential "should be maximized" despite the "competitive environment." Being able to spend $7.6 million in taxpayers' funds, the Fairfax County government is not too concerned about competition from private enterprises. Private enterprises will lose money, lay off employees, and possibly go out of business (thereby reducing county tax revenues); the beneficiaries will be the affluent residents of McLean, the managers and employees of the new facility, and the county political authorities, who will take credit for the benefits provided by the facilities, but deny blame for the costs imposed.

The Northern Virginia Regional Park Authority also operates as a cooperative (some might say collusive) arrangement between six local government jurisdictions. Like the Fairfax County Park Authority and other local governments in the area, the park authority operates many commercial enterprises, including five regional swimming pools, twelve vacation cottages, two 18-hole golf courses, five mini-golf courses, two frisbee golf courses, a skeet and trap range, an indoor archery shooting center, and five hundred camp sites. Even though it is ostensibly a "nonprofit" organization, the Park Authority describes itself as "a business conglomerate which generates $3 million annually. . . . This is almost two-thirds of the total operating budget of the authority."[70] The remainder of the budget comes from tax revenues from the six member jurisdictions and from state and federal grants.

The Northern Virginia Regional Park Authority also describes itself as "a large, complex organization operating dozens of facilities and programs, including a country music jamboree and a "nationally significant dog show."[71] Some of the facilities run by the Park Authority sound like exclusive (and expensive) private vacation hideaways. For instance, one promotional brochure recommends that people "ask about the VIP cottage, complete with spa tub" at one of the twelve new riverfront rental cottages that are "completely equipped, with designer decor."[72] Patrons can also "reserve riverfront cottages for reunions, guests, conferences, and hold . . . business meetings at the new conference center/club house."[73]

The "nonprofit" Regional Park Authority is in the business of offering vacation packages. It does so at a considerable advantage over private resorts, however, having spent approximately $28 million in taxpayers' money to acquire nearly 9,000 acres of land.[74] As a nonprofit organization, it has also attracted millions of dollars worth of tax-deductible donations in cash and in land.

Educational institutions, especially universities, constitute another type of CNE competition with private health and recreational facilities. For example, George Mason University in Fairfax, Virginia, invites members of the community to use its "recreation and sports complex," with 64,000 square feet of indoor space, a 400–meter track, six basketball courts, seven tennis courts, seven volleyball courts, golf and archery nets, racquetball courts, fencing lanes, saunas, sports medicine area, and so forth by making a *tax-deductible* contribution to the university's athletic booster club. Stressing the tax deductibility of the contribution, the university's advertising materials also offer season tickets to sporting events, priority parking privileges, a sweater, a key chain, a coffee mug, and invitations to "social events." Private recreational facilities find it almost impossible to compete with such taxpayer-supported facilities. This type of unfair competition occurs throughout the U.S., as nearly every university offers the use of its facilities in return for tax-deductible "contributions."

Economic Implications

Although local governments may appear to offer low prices for their recreational facilities and are often praised for keeping prices so affordable, the announced price for such facilities is not the full price. With millions of dollars of taxpayer subsidies, taxpayers also pay a hidden price. By contrast, private enterprises cannot hide the costs of their services. With private enterprises, what you see is what you get, which makes it easier for consumers to make more accurate decisions regarding personal expenditures on services. Because part of the costs of governmentally provided services are hidden but the benefits are well advertised and promoted, consumers are led to spend more of their income on these services than they would if they had more accurate information. It is unlikely, for example, that the average taxpayer knows precisely how much of his local taxes are used for parks and recreation, how much for police protection, for public schools, and so on. Taxpayers are compelled to financially support activities they might not want if they were better informed. With government-financed recreational facilities, consumers' choices are often restricted—especially if private suppliers have been driven out of the market. Moreover, if costs rise because of bureaucratic inertia in a government bureaucracy, they may not be reflected in higher *explicit* prices but in increased general taxation. Consumers may end up subsidizing a large local governmental bureaucracy without really being aware of it.

Once government bureaucracies replace private enterprises in the recreation industry they can be expected to continue to offer benefits to small groups of politically active voters at the expense of the less active taxpaying public. In other words, they can be expected to continue to invest in more land and more facilities, which will ultimately increase the tax burden to local taxpayers. Bureaucratic empire building is as natural as it is inevitable. And as more governmentally owned facilities drive private enterprises out of the market, tax burdens will increase even further because of pressures to raise taxes to compensate for the loss in business tax revenue. This is an additional hidden, long-run cost of the governmental provision of recreational and physical fitness services.

Bureaucracy and the Environment

The proclivity of government bureaucracies to be costly, inefficient, and unresponsive to taxpayers is well known. These outcomes are the result of the types of incentives that bureaucrats face, not their ill intentions, laziness, or lack of knowledge. In the context of the recreation industry, an understanding of bureaucratic incentives can also help explain some of the land-use decisions made by governmental authorities.

Local governments are involved not only in providing services that are similar to those provided by private health clubs—swimming, racquetball, dance classes, and so forth—but they also own and operate thousands of parks. There are over 1,000 local government special park districts in the U.S., in addition to numerous park "authorities" operated by municipal, county, and township governments.

Governmentally owned parks, however, are likely to be run very differently from privately owned parks. The two property rights systems—government ownership and private property—produce strikingly different sets of incentives and different methods of resource management and use. As biologist and environmentalist Garrett Hardin has written, government ownership can have tragic effects on the environment because of what he called "the tragedy of the commons."

> Picture a pasture open to all. It is to be expected that each herdsman will try to keep as many cattle as possible on the commons. . . . As a rational being, each herdsman seeks to

maximize his gain. Explicitly or implicitly, more or less consciously, he asks, "What is the utility *to me* of adding one more animal to my herd?" The utility has one negative and one positive component. . . . The positive component is a function of the increment of one animal. Since the herdsman receives all the proceeds from the sale of the additional animal, the positive utility is nearly 1. . . . The negative component is a function of the additional overgrazing created by one more animal. Since, however, the effects of overgrazing are shared by all the herdsmen, the negative utility for any particular decision-making herdsman is only a fraction of –1. Adding together the component partial utilities, the rational herdsman concludes that the only sensible course for him to pursue is to add another animal to his herd. And another. . . . But this is the conclusion reached by each and every rational herdsman sharing a commons. Therein is the tragedy. Each man is locked into a system that compels him to increase his herd without limit—in a world that is limited. Ruin is the destination toward which all men rush, each pursuing his own best interest in a society that believes in the freedom of the commons. Freedom in a commons [i.e., government ownership of land] brings ruin to all.[75]

By contrast, private ownership provides incentives for the care and preservation of natural resources and allows owners to capture the full capital value of their resources. The owner of a particular resource will want to benefit from it now, tomorrow, and in the indefinite future. Thus, according to Robert J. Smith, "We can see why the buffalo nearly vanished, but not the Hereford; why the greater prairie chicken is endangered, but not the red grouse of Great Britain; why the common salmon fisheries of the United States are overfished, but not the private salmon streams of Europe or the private trout farms in many American states."[76] Smith makes his point even more forcefully in the following series of questions:

Why do people litter public parks and streets, but not their own yards? Why do people dump old refrigerators and rubber tires in the public or common streams, rivers, and swamps, but not in their farm ponds or their swimming pools? Who is most likely to carefully clean the leaves out of a gutter, a homeowner or someone who is renting the house? Is private housing or public housing better maintained? Why do cattle and sheep ranchers overgraze the public lands, but maintain lush pastures on their own property? Why are the national forests so carelessly logged and overharvested, while private forests are carefully managed, cut on a sustained-yield basis, and reforested with "super trees" grown on costly nursery tree farms? Why are many of the most beautiful national parks suffering severe overuse to the point of the near destruction of their recreational values, but many private parks are maintained in far better condition?[77]

The answer to these questions is that government ownership inevitably leads to the tragedy of the commons, whereas private ownership induces conservation. Hardin has described a problem that has plagued the national parks and is likely to affect local government parks as well:

> The National Parks present another instance of the . . . tragedy of the commons. At present, they are open to all, without limit. The parks themselves are limited in extent—there is only one Yosemite Valley—whereas population seems to grow without limit. The values that visitors seek in the parks are steadily eroded. Plainly, we must soon cease to treat the parks as a commons or they will be of no value to anyone.[78]

In summary, by purchasing land for parks, local governments are not only driving competitors and potential competitors out of the market, they are also causing environmental damage. The problems are caused by the political urge to provide park services for "free" or at a low *explicit* cost. When resources are free, they tend to be overused. Thus, some of the taxes paid to local governments are used to subsidize environmental degradation. Local government officials surely do not intentionally degrade the environment; such outcomes are just the natural consequence of the tragedy of the commons.

Local government involvement in parks and recreation also crowds private individuals and businesses out of the market because of unfair competition. The private sector has long been a source of campgrounds, shooting preserves, fee fishing areas, swimming sites, marinas, rifle ranges, campsites, vacation farms, skiing resorts, vacation cottage sites, winter sports areas, and other activities. Since they are privately owned, these lands have provided many opportunities for outdoor recreation as well as the preservation of their natural beauty. The U.S. Department of Agriculture once recognized that such activities could be an important source of additional income for the nation's farmers, whose earnings are sometimes disastrously volatile.

Individual initiative and private enterprise should continue to be the most important force in outdoor recreation, providing many and varied opportunities for a vast number of people, as well as goods and services used by people in their recreation activities. It should stimulate desirable commercial development, which can be particularly effective in providing facilities and services where demand is sufficient to return a profit. . . . Our national policy should encourage private enterprise to provide outdoor recreation opportunities and services wherever feasible.[79]

In recent years, however, national policies of unfair competition have encouraged the governmental takeover of more and more privately-held land and has thereby precluded the opportunities available to private landowners such as the nation's farmers.

Conclusions

The physical fitness and recreation industries are clear examples of grossly unfair competition. The courts have begun to recognize that some YMCAs are not distinguishable from private health clubs and have withdrawn their tax exemptions. However, this has occurred in only a few instances; many other CNEs in the physical fitness industry continue to benefit from tax exemptions, subsidies, and exemption from regulations that their private-sector competitors must comply with. In the name of charity YMCAs continue to build lavish health spas for the affluent with their tax-exempt profits while private health clubs suffer the consequences of unfair competition.

Government involvement in the physical fitness and recreational industries is also a big business. There are no sound economic reasons for governmental involvement in these industries, for they have long been the domain of the private sector. With their special legislative privileges, however, governmental enterprises in these industries have sometimes become "giant conglomerates," as the Northern Virginia Regional Park Authority was described by one of its managers. They have taken advantage of their governmental powers to crowd private businesses out of a lucrative market. Unless fair competition is restored, the future of private enterprise in the physical fitness industry appears bleak. Governmental enterprises are naturally inclined to grow rapidly and expand their domain, and CNEs, such as the YMCA, also have very significant advantages over their private-sector competitors because of their special legislative privileges.

Notes to Chapter V

1. Victor Fuchs, *Who Shall Live?* (New York: Basic Books, 1974), inside front cover.

2. R.O. Malmborg, ed. *Coronary Heart Disease and Physical Fitness* (Baltimore: University Park Press, 1971), p. i.

3. Ibid.

4. "Putting on the Ritz at the Y," *Time*, July 21, 1986.

5. Robert L. Hill, "What's Fair is Fair," *Oregon Business* (August 1986).

6. Senate of Maryland, Bill no. 966, Consumer Protection/Health Club Services Act, July 1986.

7. Ibid.

8. Ibid.

9. Ibid.

10. Virginia Health Spa Act, 59.1–295, 1986.

11. Ibid.

12. Ellen Hume, "YMCA's New Elite Clubs Prompt Charge That It Abuses Its Tax-Exempt Status," *Wall Street Journal*, March 31, 1986.

13. Ibid.

14. "Putting on the Ritz."

15. Ibid.

16. Arthur Levine, "Serving the Rich: The Washington Y," *The Washington Monthly* (December 1978), p. 14.

17. Ibid.

18. Ibid, p. 12.

19. "At the YMCA," *Insight*, April 28, 1986, p. 32.

20. Elizabeth Kastor, "No Room at the Pool," *Washington Post*, January 28, 1986.

21. As quoted in Levine, "Serving the Rich."

22. Ibid.

23. Ibid.

24. Ibid.

25. Ibid.

26. Ibid.

27. Kastor, "No Room at the Pool."

28. Ibid.

29. Deborah Anderluh, "YMCA Gives Health Spas Run for the Money," *Los Angeles Herald Examiner*, May 23, 1986.

30. Gary Libman, "Health Clubs, Downtown YMCA Go to the Mat," *Los Angeles Times*, June 29, 1986.

31. Ibid.
32. Ibid.
33. Ibid.
34. Richard Swearinger, "Health Clubs Square Off Against YMCAs," *Glendale* (CA) News-Press, July 7, 1986.
35. Ibid.
36. Ibid.
37. Ibid.
38. Ibid.
39. As described in a June 13, 1985 newsletter from the YWCA of Greater Baltimore.
40. Gregory Byrnes, "The Y Goes Off in a New Direction," *Philadelphia Inquirer*, July 2, 1985.
41. Ibid.
42. Ibid.
43. Ibid.
44. David Fritze, "Swank YMCAs Accused of Failing the Poor," *Dallas Times Herald*," May 13, 1986.
45. Ibid.
46. Ibid.
47. Ibid.
48. *YMCA Survey*, Association of Physical Fitness Centers, 5272 River Road, Suite 500, Washington, D.C.
49. Ibid.
50. As cited in Levine, "Serving the Rich."
51. Ibid.
52. Louis Sweet, "The Y Is No Longer My Friend," *Toronto Star*, April 4, 1986.
53. Ibid.
54. Ibid.
55. Ibid.
56. Michael Rollins, "YMCA Loses Charitable Status," *The Oregonian* (December 10, 1985), p. 1; and Paul Koberstein, "YMCA Fitness Facilities Lose Tax Exemption," *The Oregonian* (November 17, 1987), p. A–1. Also see the preliminary ruling issued by the Oregon Department of Revenue on Nov. 16, 1987.
57. Ibid.
58. U.S. Department of Commerce, Bureau of the Census, *Census of Governments* (Washington, D.C.: U.S. Government Printing Office, 1983).
59. Ibid.
60. Economic Research Associates, *Fairfax County Park Authority Recreation Center Feasibility Study*, Washington, D.C., March 1984.
61. Ibid.
62. Ibid.

63. Ibid.
64. Ibid.
65. Ibid.
66. Ibid.
67. "Work Begins on $7.6 Million Spring Hill Recreation Facility," *Fairfax Journal*, Oct. 13, 1986.
68. Ibid.
69. Ibid.
70. "Regional Communications and Cooperation," Northern Virginia Regional Park Authority, 11001 Popes Head Road, Fairfax, Virginia 22030.
71. Ibid.
72. Ibid.
73. Ibid.
74. Ibid.
75. Garrett Hardin, "The Tragedy of the Commons," *Science*, December 13, 1968, p. 1244.
76. Robert J. Smith, "Privatizing the Environment," *Policy Review* (Spring 1982), p. 11.
77. Ibid.
78. Hardin, "The Tragedy of the Commons."
79. U.S. Department of Agriculture, "Report by the Outdoor Recreation Resources Review Commission," Spring 1962, as cited in Clodus Smith, Lloyd Partain, and James Champlin, *Rural Recreation for Profit* (Danville, IL: Interstate Publishers, 1966), p. 9.

TABLE A5.1
Health Club Comparison Chart

As of 3/1/85	Swimming Pools	Court Time	Exercise Areas	Permanent Storage	Running Track	Cost to Join
West Side YMCA (212) 787-4400 5 West 63rd Street New York, NY 10023	2 pools small-60' × 20' large-75' × 25'	No charge	Nautilus & Universal	$25/yr.– $75/yr.	1/23 of a mile Tartan	$330– $420/yr.
New York Health & Racquet Club 110 West 56th Street New York, NY (212) 541-7200	1 small pool 50 feet	$8/45 min.	Nautilus Machines	$46–$96/yr.	1/30th of a mile Concrete	$895
Club LaRacquette 119 West 56th Street New York, NY (212) 245-1144	1 small pool 20' × 40'	$8.50–$18/hr.	Nautilus Machines	$50–$100/yr.	1/30th of a mile	$575/yr. for courts $850/yr. for courts pool
Vertical Club 330 East 61st Street New York, NY (212) 355-5100	1 small pool 20' × 40'	$8–$20/hr.	Nautilus & Universal	None Available	1/10th of a mile	$1,150/yr.

Jack LaLanne B'way at 75th Street New York, NY (212) 877-1111	None	No courts	Nautilus Machines	None Available	None	$960/yr.
Aerobics West Fitness 131 West 86th Street New York, NY (212) 787-3356	20' × 40'	No courts	Nautilus Machines	Limited Availability $5/mo.	None	$494/yr.
Paris Health Club 131 West 86th Street New York, NY (212) 749-3500	50' pool	No courts	Nautilus Machines	$60/yr. $5/mo.	None	$743.60/yr.
Lincoln Squash Club 1 Harkness Plaza New York, NY (212) 265-0995	None	$8/45 min.	Nautilus Machines	$100–$120	None	$250/yr. $295/yr. with Nautilus
205 Third Ave. #17G New York, NY 10003						

Source: West Side YMCA, New York, NY.

TABLE A5.2
Local Government Expenditures on Parks and Recreation, 1981–82
(millions of dollars)

State	Expenditure	State	Expenditure
Alabama	$ 70.2	Montana	$ 13.6
Alaska	44.5	Nebraska	32.3
Arizona	92.6	Nevada	50.1
Arkansas	14.9	New Hampshire	9.0
California	1,068.2	New Jersey	158.5
Colorado	131.2	New Mexico	33.2
Connecticut	66.1	New York	516.4
Delaware	3.4	North Carolina	100.6
Florida	437.8	North Dakota	14.6
Georgia	87.7	Ohio	217.6
Hawaii	44.2	Oklahoma	82.1
Idaho	12.0	Oregon	81.9
Illinois	447.6	Pennsylvania	159.3
Indiana	68.8	Rhode Island	12.3
Iowa	69.2	South Carolina	32.4
Kansas	49.3	South Dakota	14.7
Kentucky	33.1	Tennessee	100.1
Louisiana	95.9	Texas	350.5
Maine	10.3	Utah	44.9
Maryland	161.3	Vermont	4.1
Massachusetts	75.5	Virginia	122.2
Michigan	215.9	Washington	151.9
Minnesota	189.1	West Virginia	19.5
Mississippi	20.5	Wisconsin	152.6
Missouri	86.4	Wyoming	34.1

Source: U.S. Department of Commerce, Bureau of the Census, *Census of Governments* (Washington, D.C.: U.S. Government Printing Office, 1983).

TABLE A5.3
Examples of Government Recreational Facilities
That Compete Directly with Private Enterprises

Chicago, Illinois. 540 park districts, including 4 major districts. Each district contains recreational centers, including racquetball, handball, aerobic dance, weight lifting, swimming pools, etc. Most of these activities are offered at below-market rates. The Chicago park district shows nontaxed revenue for 1984 at $21,426,000.

Hartford, Connecticut. 21 governmentally owned gymnasiums that include weight lifting, aerobics, tennis courts, swimming pools, exercise classes.

Knoxville, Tennessee. 37 governmentally owned recreational centers that offer aerobic dance, weight lifting, swimming, tennis, and so forth.

Detroit, Michigan. 35 governmentally owned recreational centers, including outdoor and indoor swimming pools, weight lifting, universal gyms, aerobic dance, racquetball courts, body-building facilities, jazzercize classes, physical fitness areas.

Cleveland, Ohio. 17 governmentally owned recreational centers, all of which have indoor pools and some outdoor pools. Most include saunas, steam rooms, racquetball courts, weight lifting, and aerobic dance.

Los Angeles, California. 150 governmentally owned recreational centers that include weight lifting, aerobic dance, and indoor and outdoor pools.

Pontiac, Michigan. 4 governmentally owned recreational centers offering swimming, aerobic dancing, physical exercise programs, and other activities.

St. Louis, Missouri. 3 governmentally owned recreational facilities including calisthenics, swimming, tennis, and aerobics.

Atlanta, Georgia. 39 governmentally owned recreational facilities, all of which have outdoor pools, aerobic dancing, exercise classes, etc. Many have weight lifting, indoor pools, and indoor track.

Miami, Florida. 29 governmentally owned facilities offering outdoor swimming, indoor swimming, racquetball courts, weight lifting, jazzercise, and other activities.

Orlando, Florida. Multiple recreational facilities, including racquetball courts, gymnasiums, tennis courts, free weights, universal equipment, aerobic dancing, etc.

Dallas/Fort Worth, Texas. 38 governmentally owned recreational facilities including gym activities, body building, swimming, gymnastics, jazzercise, coed exercise, aerobic dancing, weight lifting, Nautilus equipment, jogging, and stretching classes.

Denver, Colorado. 29 governmentally owned recreational centers, including 14 indoor and 22 outdoor swimming pools. Most centers offer body building, aerobics, weight lifting, swimming, and other activities.

Houston, Texas. 54 governmentally owned recreational centers.

Source: Survey taken by the Business Coalition for Fair Competition.

VI.

Unfair Competition in the Audiovisual and Computer Software Industries

For at least half a century, a U.S. industry has produced, promoted, and distributed audiovisual materials for schools, libraries, colleges and universities, businesses, and government agencies that use the products to educate, communicate, and train. Despite its long participation in the marketplace, however, little is known about the structure and composition of this industry, beyond the fact that it is made up of a large number of geographically dispersed small companies. It has been estimated that in 1981 95 percent of audiovisual firms had annual revenues under $5 million, with total sales for the entire industry falling between $300 and $400 million.[1] The typical firm, then, is essentially a "mom and pop" operation.

The audiovisual industry is highly fragmented and widely dispersed:

> Of more than a million persons who earn their living using AV media or supplying the products or services, a fifth (some 210,000 people) are suppliers manufacturing, producing, or selling products and services. In the AV industry there are more than 15,000 companies and institutions—the great majority private businesses. Nearly 1,000 are institutions, such as public libraries and university film libraries, serving education and the public. Another 2,000 sources of educational materials are not in the AV business per se.

Some 4,000 producers and services that make media software comprise the largest category in the AV industry. Many of these companies are very small, even one-person operations. Probably half produce educational media that are sold either through education distributors direct to schools or through AV dealers.[2]

The development of microcomputers over the past decade has had a major impact on instructional techniques, and for our purposes, the educational software industry may be regarded as part of the audiovisual industry. The development, promotion, distribution, and sale of instructional software is a rapidly growing field that serves the same clientele as the audiovisual industry. Many of these software firms are small operations that often specialize in programs for specific applications, such as class scheduling or accounting systems for schools. Both the audiovisual and microcomputer industries are experiencing intense competition from the commercial nonprofit sector, particularly from tax-exempt educational institutions and government agencies.

It is no surprise that colleges and universities have moved into the audiovisual market. These institutions not only use audiovisual materials, but many also offer both undergraduate and graduate degrees in "communications" with a specialty in developing instructional materials. Members of the faculty are available to provide production expertise as well as to develop programs. In fact, a case can be made that the initial entry of educational institutions into the media market was purely a matter of chance. Consider, for example, the Instructional Media Center (IMC) at Michigan State University:

> The marketing division at Michigan State University grew from expressed needs within the university. During the late 1960s and early 1970s, extensive slide/tape and video programs were developed by faculty for use within their classes. As often happens, requests for copies of these programs were soon coming in from other institutions. The lack of a centralized system of quality control, reproduction, packaging, shipping, invoicing, collection, and distribution of income made it difficult to fill the requests. At this early stage, the business office and consulting staff of the instructional media center (IMC) produced all media formats except video and maintained a business office so this seemed to be a reasonable arrangement.[3]

From these modest beginnings, IMC quickly expanded into a commercial operation. A statement of policy was developed and approved by the university's board of trustees, which also approved the allocation of royalties: 50 percent to the authors, 20 percent to the academic department, and 30 percent to the university. With these arrangements in place, Michigan State University, a nonprofit, tax-payer-supported organization, entered the market as a competitor: "The IMC agreed to fund two full-time positions until general support from the university became available. Our objective was to make the marketing division into a self-supporting operation while filling a growing service need within the university."[4]

Higher education was not facing budget exigencies during the late 1960s and early 1970s, so IMC's marketing activities at the time might be interpreted as an effort to provide a service to the academic community on a self-supporting basis. In addition, the extent of IMC's involvement in the marketplace was limited by an explicit restriction that IMC could promote only those educational materials developed by MSU faculty. From IMC's perspective, the operation has been a major success:

> Since its beginnings, the marketing division's sales have shown a steady increase. Continued growth will depend to a large extent on additions to the nearly 400 program titles currently offered. Our instructional materials have been purchased nation-ally and internationally. . . . The emphasis on innovative, effective instructional techniques and consistently superior production/reproduction quality has resulted in a growing list of clients.[5]

When the economic climate for education dramatically changed in the early 1980s during the most severe recession since the Great Depression, educational administrators sought alternative sources of revenue. The successful commercial ventures that had been established earlier by educational institutions, such as IMC, provided an excellent prototype. Educational institutions and school districts pursued entrepreneurial activity with a vengeance. For example, when the Montclair, New Jersey, school district was faced with a $600,000 reduction in federal funds for the 1981–1982 school year, the school board approved several commercial activities:

> Expanding the school district's data-processing center and paying someone to sell data services to 31 surrounding school districts.
>
> Publishing books and pamphlets on education topics written by the district's administrators and teachers, printed in its shop and promoted by three of its public-relations people.

Bidding on Federal Government contracts for such things as military-educational materials, sex-education pamphlets for parents and running desegregation workshops nationwide.

Establishing an education center for the district's emotionally disturbed students and taking in tuition-paying students from adjacent districts.

Operating a public restaurant as a vocational training program at a planetarium built with a foundation grant.[6]

The New Jersey State Commissioner of Education endorsed these plans and described the Montclair school district as a "lighthouse in education."[7]

Whether nonprofit competition with private firms in the audiovisual industry began by serendipity or by design, the result is the same: Both private firms and the economy suffer as nonprofit organizations use their tax-exempt status and other special privileges to engage in unfair competition. This chapter explores the nature of this unfair competition in the audiovisual and computer software industries and provides examples that illustrate the extent to which it exists.

Unfair Pricing in the Audiovisual and Computer Industries

Commercial nonprofit enterprises enjoy special privileges granted by government, giving them a substantial cost advantage relative to their competitors in private industry (see chapter 2). When government grants and contracts finance research and development and equipment purchases or provide personnel and facilities, a CNE enjoys substantial cost advantages relative to competing firms that have not received taxpayers' money. It does not necessarily follow, however, that lower costs will cause CNEs to set prices to undercut those in the private sector. Economic theory indicates that if CNEs maximize profits, they will price their goods and services competitively, even though they have a cost advantage. There is ample evidence that CNEs engage in predatory pricing, that is, they charge lower prices than their private counterparts do. Promotional materials developed by CNEs often stress that their prices are "at cost" or "breakeven"; in some cases, customers receive goods and services at a purely nominal or even zero price. There are a number of reasons why predatory pricing behavior occurs among CNEs.

In Fairfax County, Virginia, for example, the county library system offers patrons videotapes at no charge. Private companies that rent the same tapes to customers require payment of membership fees and daily rental charges. The library, supported entirely by tax revenues, competes directly with private firms and actively pursues a predatory pricing policy—no commercial entity can routinely provide services at zero price. This practice is widespread: "many public libraries loan films at little or no charge. College and university film rental libraries rent 16mm film (and occasionally video tapes) at costs lower than commercial distributors."[8]

Another example of predatory pricing can be found in WGVC-TV, a public television station licensed to Michigan's Grand Valley State Colleges. In anticipation of reductions in taxpayer funding, WGVC began soliciting video production business by direct mail. All of the equipment owned by WGVC offered for commercial use in its rate card, including a mobile unit, minicams, and studio facilities, was either obtained wholly or partially with state or federal funds, originally for student training and the production of local programs.[9] In 1981, the station manager announced that WGVC had one of the best-equipped studios in the region for television and field production.[10] With 36 percent of WGVC's annual operating budget coming from state and federal taxes, private, taxpaying firms in western Michigan are, in effect, subsidizing a competitor that charges only one-third to one-half the rates that commercial companies must charge.[11]

There are many other examples of CNEs that price their services only to recover all or part of their costs.[12] The Occupational Curriculum Laboratory at East Texas State University in Commerce, for example, is one of "four centers within the Texas Curriculum Network funded by the Texas Education Agency. . . . [which] is currently developing and disseminating competency-based materials for both secondary and postsecondary programs."[13] The OCL's product catalog notes that "complimentary copies are not available because the OCL operates on a cost recovery basis."[14] Similarly, the National Dissemination and Assessment Center, Los Angeles (NDAC-LA), located at California State University is "funded by the Office of Bilingual Education to provide support services to all other bilingual programs at State, Post-Secondary and School District Levels." An NDAC-LA promotional brochure indicating "a growing inventory of texts, booklets, visuals [sic]," is accompanied by a cover letter announcing that all the materials are "available at cost plus mail charges." The brochure reports that "the NDAC-LA's central function is to receive, find, edit, and print materials judged to fill the needs of bilingual programs. The printing and reproduction capabilities of the Center cover all possibilities, the only limitation being cost."[15]

The Oklahoma State Department of Vocational and Technical Education established a "productivity division that links vocational education with a pressing need of American business and industry— developing a work force that understands its role in productivity." Two state employees:

> travel throughout the state to provide orientation, training, and other services in a variety of settings. They have at their fingertips an array of materials and approaches to meet the individual training needs of employers—seminars, workshops, quality circles, case studies, analytical problem solving, lectures, films, videotapes and slide-tape programs. . . . The only cost to companies using this program through the productivity division is for the materials used."[16]

IMC at Michigan State University also uses "cost-recovery" pricing:

> We have tried to set prices so that at least 25 percent of the sale price goes to the authors as royalties. This helps compensate for the fact that authors are not prepaid for developmental costs. Before we calculate royalties, our other expenses must be recovered. If a particular program requires the duplication of print materials, special packaging preview stock, advertising, or other types of promotion, the marketing division advances these monies with the expectation of recovering the advances from future sales. If the initial risk investment is too large, then some alternatives must be sought. On occasion, MSU Press has published student texts while the marketing division distributed the audiovisual components and the instructor's manuals. A second alternative is the Educational Development Fund, which is the recipient of the university's share of royalties. Without these alternative sources, worthwhile and innovative programs could not be distributed because of high initial capital requirements.[17]

In 1980, Apple SWAP (an acronym for Software with a Purpose) was established as an independent, nonprofit national clearinghouse for educational programs written for Apple microcomputers. "To access the library of Apple programs, participants must initially provide the library with a blank Apple disk, a disk of programs, and one dollar in return for another disk of programs. After that, participants need only provide a disk of their programs and one dollar for each disk of programs they wish to receive."[18] No private firm could possibly compete with this arrangement.

CNEs that base their prices on production costs have a significant advantage over their for-profit competitors. In addition to being exempt from taxes and standard postal charges, the production costs of many CNEs are also heavily subsidized. CNEs obtain equipment through government grants and contracts or from tax revenues; and those that are agencies of state or local governments, such as colleges or schools, have much of their "overhead" paid by taxpayers. Audiovisual centers at colleges and universities may pay little for offices and production space, telephone service, heat and utilities, and other services. When this is the case, even cost-recovery prices do not have to reflect these expenses. In other words, any CNE can set prices at a level that private competitors would consider predatory and still be able to cover costs simply because its costs are so heavily subsidized.

Several reasons may be offered to explain why CNEs practice predatory pricing in the market for audiovisual instructional materials and microcomputer software programs. First, political considerations can induce CNEs to offer goods and services at either below market or at zero prices to consumers. Gordon Tullock has observed that "the overwhelming majority of government activities are . . . the provision of private goods, which could be better provided by the private market. . . ."[19] Tullock argues that government produces private goods and services because it benefits the politically powerful—that is, the middle and upper classes. Government is a vast apparatus for transferring income from one group to another, but the transfers are rarely made in cash. Instead, tax revenues are used to subsidize the provision of private goods and services to politically active groups: "People have made use of the government to transfer funds to themselves. This should surprise no one. The average profit-seeking individual will seek his profits where he can find them, and there is no reason why he should be more reluctant to use the government for profit seeking than the market."[20] Thus, libraries may offer videotapes and films at nominal or no charge as a way of transferring income to constituents who are likely to provide active political support for such programs.

A second reason why CNEs may practice predatory pricing has to do with the quality of goods and services offered. In many cases, a CNE's product is of lower quality than that provided by the private sector. At educational institutions, for example, teachers may donate text- or script-writing time even though they are not professionals in the field; an administrator with no credentials in broadcasting may be selected to record or narrate the material; and students with no previous experience may be recruited for acting, artwork, filming, and other production services. For example, Apple SWAP has reported that of the more than 8,000 programs submitted in 1980–1981 by educators from half the states and seven foreign countries, only 15 percent were useful enough to accept into its library for public access.[21] Gerald Gleason, professor of educational psychology at the University of Wisconsin, Milwaukee (which produces and distributes vocational education materials), has written that

> a major source of programs [is] educators. The teachers probably have not had any formal training or experience in programming techniques, and this is likely to be reflected in their products. Again, some of these programs may be useful and effective, but most will not meet the quality standards we should expect. . . . One only has to examine some of the programs offered for sale to realize that there is far more to CAI [Computer-Assisted Instruction] programming than learning to operate a microcomputer.[22]

Educational experience alone is not sufficient to ensure quality, nor is experience in nonprofit publishing. For example, in a review of "Our Political System," a National Geographic filmstrip/cassette package for grades 5–12, Dwain Thomas, supervisor of the Instructional Services Department at Lake Park High School in Roselle, Illinois, writes that "the National Geographic Society typically is synonymous with quality photography. This new kit on our political system does contain striking visuals, but it lacks much in terms of instructional objectives and content substance. . . . Not recommended for purchase."[23] In contrast, the commercial marketplace has little tolerance for shoddy merchandise and private, profit-seeking firms have a strong incentive to provide high quality materials. Gleason asserts that

> major publishers of educational instructional materials are beginning to invest substantial effort in the development of CAI programs for microcomputers. . . . While some may reject this marketplace mentality, I believe that major publishers do have resources, organization, and experience which should result in high quality programs.[24]

If competition operates in the marketplace to drive firms that produce poor quality products out of business, why do the same forces not operate in the same way with regard to CNEs? In part, this question may be answered by noting that while private firms usually allow purchasers to preview audiovisual materials before they are purchased or rented, CNEs typically give users only two options: rental or purchase. Consider the policy stated in Cornell University's *Audio-Visual Resource Catalog*:

> *Preview for Purchase.* Preview prints are available on the same basis as rental films listed in this catalog. If the previewed film is purchased within sixty (60) days of the preview date, any paid rental fee will be deducted from the film purchase price. Return of films is the user's responsibility.[25]

The restrictions are even more stringent for slide sets: "Requests for *previewing purchase slide sets* cannot be honored. . . ." Rental is not even an option with Cornell's audio tapes, "because of the high costs of handling orders relative to the purchase price."[26] By imposing costs on customers who want to screen materials in advance, CNEs often limit the opportunities for prospective customers to evaluate the quality of the materials to be rented or purchased. Even if consumers recognize the inferior quality of a CNE's product, they may still purchase it because the price difference is disproportionately larger than the difference in quality. There are also customers who are educators themselves who have a natural bias toward the products of a particular educational institution.

There is a bias toward nonprofit organizations in general, which have acquired a *pro bono publico* (for the good of the public) image. Marc Lane, author of the *Legal Handbook for Nonprofit Organizations*, has charged that that "even if we put aside possible tax advantages, the nonprofit entity has an unfair advantage [relative to private firms] owing to the public image of nonprofit status."[27] Thus, a third reason that CNEs charge lower prices than private-sector competitors is because of this image they enjoy. By definition, nonprofits do not operate to earn a profit, and any CNE that charged the same prices as a private firm for similar goods and services would appear to be operating to make a profit. One means of affirming to the public that CNEs are nonprofit organizations is that they charge lower prices than those charged by private firms. But this does not necessarily mean that a CNE makes no profit, only that its profits are less than would be earned if, other things equal, prices were closer to those charged by private firms.

Finally, a CNE manager's income is not directly related to the organization's level of profits. In educational institutions, especially state schools, salaries are set by administrators or by civil service regulations. Even if CNEs could earn a greater profit by raising prices to competitive levels, managers cannot benefit personally, unless those profits were used to obtain more perquisites. Moreover, if CNEs were to charge the same prices as private firms, CNE employees would have to be much more aggressive in marketing their products and services; they would no longer have the advantage of below-market prices to induce customers to patronize their organization. A relaxed pace of work is an important perquisite enjoyed by employees in the public sector and in other nonprofit organizations. Predatory pricing may be regarded as a means of obtaining this benefit.

The Rationale for Nonprofit Competition

Applying the criteria developed in chapter 2 for public goods to the audiovisual and to the instructional software industries, it is clear that these goods and services cannot reasonably be regarded as public goods. Films, slide sets, videotapes, and computer programs have the characteristics of private goods and are being produced, promoted, and distributed by private firms.

The basic rationale for nonprofit organizations to become involved in these industries is the "thin market" argument, which states: "There are too few customers for this product to entice a for-profit company to provide it." This argument might well be applicable in a few cases where audiovisuals deal with highly technical materials which tend to reflect the specialized research equipment and professional staff that are available at educational institutions. For example, Massachusetts Institute of Technology's Center for Advanced Engineering Study provides videotape materials for engineers involved in continuing education. The Center's catalog contains many films that are obviously intended for a specialized audience, such as "Interaction Between Spherical Double Layers—Schiller Layers and Other Experiments on Double Layer Interaction," and "Colloid Stability—Lyotropic Effects—Repeptization."[28] Not all of the MIT films, however, are aimed at a limited audience; there are also films on basic calculus, basic probability theory, principles of economics, and energy conservation. The thin market argument would have to be stretched considerably to be applicable to all the audiovisuals that MIT offers.

Even a casual survey of catalogs from other educational institutions reveals that the thin market rationale for nonprofits entering the market is specious. The catalog of the Audio-Visual Center at Indiana University, for example, lists 6,388 titles of motion pictures in active use, ranging from "Ability—Testing" to "Zoos" and available for every age group and educational level. All of these films are in high demand, because those materials which have a low demand (i.e., the "thin market" films) are not even listed: "Many films for which there is little demand or where replacement materials are not available are retired to the reference library. The reference library currently consists of more than 2,200 titles which are available for use by writing the Audio-Visual Center."[29] Indiana University also acts as a distributor, listing more than 1,000 film sources—from the American Bankers Association to Zastava.[30]

It is debatable whether or not some of the films distributed by IU are educational. There is not much of a message, for example, in "The Monkey and the Organ Grinder," an 11-minute color film that "follows an organ grinder and his monkey as they spend the day entertaining shoppers and meeting people on the street. . . . Captures the feeling of loneliness the organ grinder experiences as he tells of his hard life and of the pleasure he receives from his monkey." This 1971 Encyclopaedia Britannica film purportedly deals with "animal legends and stories" and "social adjustment" for primary through high school students. Thirty-four of the films available from the Center show Indiana High School Athletic Association sporting events, such as championship wrestling, basketball, volleyball, football, and track.[31] The catalog of films distributed by the Educational Media Center at the University of Colorado is similar in content to that at Indiana University. Few of the 4,100 listings were produced at the university and one would be hardpressed to apply a public goods or thin-market rationale to films such as "Jack and the Beanstalk" or "Rumpelstiltskin."[32]

If nonprofit organizations only produced and distributed esoteric and highly specialized audiovisual instructional materials, private-sector firms would have no complaints about unfair competition. That they are concerned is direct evidence that nonprofits compete with them for sales. There is a great deal of duplication of products and services in the audiovisual and the microcomputer software industries. The competition seems to be especially intense in the vocational education market. Just how many different ways are there to show tire rotation?

Government has often encouraged nonprofits to compete with private firms by giving grants to institutions to make educational films and to purchase equipment that duplicates already existing facilities in the private sector. For instance, WGVC-TV, the western Michigan public television station, purchased its mobile unit with $600,000 in federal and state grants, even though there was little use for it. The station's program director admitted that "it takes about 10 people—half our staff—to run it. We just haven't been able to afford it."[33] No private firm would purchase equipment that it could not use effectively, but profitability is not a concern when investments are made with taxpayers' funds. Once grants are made available to nonprofit entities, the money must be spent. Unnecessary duplication of products and facilities occurs much less frequently in the private sector, where competition inevitably forces wasteful firms out of business.

Thus, the notion that nonprofits entered the audiovisual and computer software markets to provide services that the private sector neglected because there was insufficient demand is questionable at best. The cases of nonprofits producing highly specialized and esoteric material are the exception, and not the rule. A more likely interpretation of events is that some nonprofits started out to satisfy a perceived need that was not being met by for-profit organizations and, once in the market, they found it profitable to expand their offerings in competition with products and services already available in the private sector. All that is required for this scenario to be plausible is that economies of scale exist—that is, that unit costs decline as output rises. And, there are good reasons to believe that economies of scale are present in this industry. For example, printing costs do not double when the number of entries in a product catalog double, nor do promotional postage costs. Moreover, in a very thin market, the demand may be so limited that the costs associated with serving the market are prohibitive, even for a subsidized nonprofit. To realize the benefits of economies of scale and thereby lower costs, nonprofits may have found it necessary to expand their product line and services to break even or to attain an economically viable scale of operations.

The Extent of Unfair Competition

It is difficult to assess the extent of competition between CNEs and private firms, especially in the audiovisual and computer software field where there are a large number of small firms. Because data collection for this highly fragmented industry is not only costly but also difficult, the evidence developed about unfair competition is only suggestive of the scope and extent of the problem. With about 15,000 enterprises operating in the audiovisual industry and roughly 1,000 of them classified as educational institutions, nonprofits make up about 7 percent of the audiovisual industry. The major weakness with such aggregate figures is that competition may be more intense in some sectors of the industry than in others. For example, educational institutions may not be as active in the production and distribution of materials for entertainment as for instructional purposes, and CNEs do not typically engage in the manufacture, distribution, and sale of equipment.

Salvatore Parlato, a media coordination evaluator of films for the deaf, has conducted a detailed and enlightening analysis of the educational audiovisual marketplace. In 1980, he identified 289 organizations that sold or leased five or more educational films (16mm) or videotape programs. Altogether, these organizations offered 39,300 titles to the public. Of the 289 organizations, 31 (11 percent) were nonprofit foundations, societies, or professional associations; 18 (6 percent) were schools and universities; and 9 (3 percent) were religious groups. Parlato also reported that some of the organizations were museums, public television stations, and governmental and international agencies. Parlato supplied no numbers for this last group of nonprofits, but if it is assumed that it represented only one percent of the total, then nonprofits accounted for 21 percent of the total number of competitors in his sample. Parlato's data also show that the CNEs price their products aggressively, charging about 20 percent less for their films than did commercial firms—an average of $11.75 per minute compared to about $14.51 per minute. Moreover, among commercial distributors, videotape programs cost about 25 percent less than 16mm films; among nonprofits, they are about 33 percent less.[34]

These numbers are revealing, but they tell nothing about the intensity of the competition. A large, aggressive firm that operates on a national level and offers a wide variety of products and comprehensive services (e.g., training, consulting, equipment and facilities rental, and equipment repair) could have a much greater impact on private firms in the industry than a much greater number of small nonprofit distributors that serve only a local market. In Parlato's sample, 211 of the 289 organizations studied were relatively small operations, handling no more than 99 titles. Only 37 organizations listed 250 titles or more, and 120—more than 40 percent—had 24 or fewer titles. Unfortunately, Parlato did not cross-classify the data to show organizational size classified by type of operation, i.e., profit or nonprofit.

There is evidence, however, that some of these nonprofits, especially institutions of higher education, are large scale operations that offer thousands of film and videotape titles for sale and rent. To show that these examples are not atypical, brief profiles of 63 CNEs actively engaged in the instructional audiovisual or computer software industries were compiled (see Appendix A). In this small sample, organizations from each geographic region were included. All of the CNEs profiled received implicit subsidies through tax exemptions and most received taxpayer funds in the form of grants or subsidies. The sample is dominated by educational institutions (33) and by foundations, nonprofit corporations, and associations (31); only four are government agencies, although all of the state colleges and universities are directly affiliated with government and some of the nonprofit corporations were created by and are under governmental control. Thus, the distinction between public and private nonprofit entities is, at best, blurred.

As is evident from Appendix A, CNEs compete with private firms by producing and distributing their own audiovisual materials or computer software, producing products for others, distributing products created by other organizations, renting equipment and facilities, training, consulting, and by repairing equipment. All but 6 of the CNEs profiled produce and distribute their own materials; 11 produce materials for others to sell and 16 distribute the products of other organizations; 3 CNEs rent equipment and 2 rent facilities (e.g., recording studios); and 3 repair equipment. Six CNEs engage in training, 7 provide consulting services, and 7 CNEs purchase products and equipment on a cooperative basis. The CNEs in the sample are actively engaged in every phase of the audiovisual and computer software industry, except the manufacture of equipment.

Summary statistics can aid in understanding the intensity of competitive pressures between profit and nonprofit entities in this industry, but it is also useful to review the operations of two CNEs that operate on a national basis and have a major impact: the Minnesota Educational Computing Corporation and the National Audiovisual Center.

Minnesota Educational Computing Corporation. In 1973, the Minnesota legislature established the Minnesota Educational Computing Consortium (MECC) to provide educational computing facilities and services for the state. The consortium had four members: the State Department of Education (437 school districts), the Minnesota Community College System (18 campuses), the Minnesota State University System (7 campuses), and the University of Minnesota. In 1984, the legislature changed MECC into a public corporation directed by a nine-member board of directors appointed by the governor. According to MECC's 1985 Legislative Report,

> MECC is nationally and internationally recognized as a leader among educational computing support groups; is among the largest publishers of educational computer courseware; and is well-versed in all aspects of educational courseware design and development, including database management and information retrieval systems. Other services offered by MECC include training of educators, development and implementation of computer-based management information systems, and support for the acquisition and operation of microcomputers.[35]

When MECC was founded in the early 1970s, computers were very expensive (many cost millions of dollars), large in size, difficult to maintain, and beyond the capabilities of small colleges and universities and most school districts. Economies of scale are readily apparent in such situations. To provide computer services to distant users, MECC established the MECC Timeshare System, a large Control Data computer accessible to 400 users simultaneously through a telecommunications network that reached 1,200 timeshare terminals across the state. More than 300 point-to-point telephone lines and an equal number of "dial in" lines provided the connections to every public college campus in the state and to a majority of Minnesota's school districts. Users were billed only for their own equipment and for computer time.[36] MECC was responsible for the central computer and for developing software. This time-sharing arrangement provided powerful computational services at low cost and, at the same time, prevented the proliferation of incompatible equipment.

With the introduction of smaller, relatively inexpensive, and more reliable microcomputers in the late 1970s, the Timeshare System was maintained for applications requiring large-scale computational abilities, such as statistical packages, a database management system, and an electronic mail system. MECC's approach changed with the technology:

> In 1978, MECC established a precedent-setting statewide contract that allowed schools and colleges to purchase Apple II computers at reduced price. This contract was the driving force behind Minnesota's plunge into instructional microcomputing. In three year's time, nearly 3,000 Apple II systems have been purchased on that contract.
>
> In addition to training educators in how to use the Apple II, MECC set about to develop a collection of courseware for the classroom. This collection now encompasses nearly 50 diskettes containing several hundred programs.
>
> Over a dozen of these diskettes offer elementary school applications. Others include simulations in science and social studies, model accounting and payroll packages for business education, a complete set of drills for music theory fundamentals, utilities that help teachers create their own lessons, and programming aids that provide simplified routines for using the special graphics and sound capabilities of the computer.
>
> Each diskette is accompanied by a support booklet that gives the teacher learning objectives, program background, sample lesson plans, and student worksheets. It is this material that turns "software" (a program) into "courseware" that teachers will choose to integrate into their curriculums.[37]

In November 1982, *Newsweek* reported that "MECC's major asset is its stash of 700 computer programs, which range from physics lessons to the rules of volleyball."[38]

Microcomputer technology changed MECC from an organization that primarily provided centralized computer services to a developer and marketer of educational software and a cooperative purchaser of equipment. Through its mandate from the state, MECC became the preeminent source of computer services for hundreds of school districts and the state's large college and university system. By centralizing purchasing and offering large-scale procurements, MECC was able to acquire microcomputers and peripheral equipment directly from manufacturers at prices much lower than could be negotiated by small independent retailers who were effectively excluded from the educational hardware and software markets in Minnesota.

Once the programs for instructional use had been developed, MECC took the next "natural" step: to offer the programs to other educational establishments outside the state. Development costs could then be spread over many purchasers. The rapid expansion of "personal computers" also presented a lucrative market for MECC's software, as did the growing demand for software for administrative use in educational institutions. In its 1985 report to the Minnesota legislature, MECC proudly announced that its "entrepreneurial spirit" had already taken its products and services into all these markets.[39] MECC had committed itself to becoming a major force in the computer software industry for education:

> During the past year [1984–1985] MECC has implemented the process of analyzing appropriate product categories and distribution channels in order to most effectively distribute our products and services. The goal is to establish a significant revenue base outside of Minnesota and direct customers by adding markets and channels of distribution for MECC products and services. The strategy is to use all viable distribution channels in conjunction with sound techniques of market development and support.
>
> The markets for our products and services have been defined as three product categories. The first is targeted to sell MECC's school instructional products and services. There are over 275 products packaged to sell through school dealers. . . . The second market is for MECC's consumer products for the home computing user. MECC has 16 products in its Home Software Library. These products are packaged, documented and priced competitively to sell in retail stores. MECC's third market is for administrative productivity products for schools. There are 21 products involving 11 titles ranging from finance and payroll to health immunization record keeping.[40]

MECC not only expanded the scope of its products, but beginning in 1979 it also offered annual institutional membership to nonprofit educational institutions and agencies outside Minnesota: "The number of members served has grown substantially. During the 1984–85 service year, 153 agencies serving a clientele of over 4300 school districts have taken advantage of this unique opportunity. Memberships are held by at least one agency in 49 states, most Canadian provinces, Australia, Bermuda, and English-speaking schools throughout the world."[41]

Each institutional member pays an initial membership fee and an annual renewal fee, the amount paid depends on the number of schools in the district.

> Member school districts receive a variety of services and products, including a select group of MECC instructional products for the Apple II series of computers, copying rights to most MECC Apple products [at a nominal charge per disk copied], availability of copying rights to MECC IBM instructional products, complimentary registration to MECC's national conference, optional training services and discounted purchasing rights on all MECC products, including products for Commodore, Tandy, and Atari computers. These services also include telephone consultation and tailored in-service training sessions at member sites."[42]

In 1984, institutional memberships generated nearly $2.3 million for MECC, or about 34 percent of total revenues.[43]

To make its products more attractive to users outside Minnesota, MECC expanded the range of its services. Training sessions were offered to users on a consulting basis at their site and MECC held workshops at national conferences in conjunction with marketing efforts:

> In conjunction with efforts to market software across the country, MECC has provided training in other states on a consulting basis. Many of these sessions have been sponsored by MECC institutional members. The premier training event of the year was the MECC '84 national conference. . . . Over 2,000 educators, 40 percent of whom came from outside Minnesota, came to take advantage of the 100 presentations and 16 full workshops that were offered.[44]

In the 1984–1985 accounting year, MECC made 480 visits to school districts and held 60 short workshops, 200 extended workshops and classes, and 6 conferences. The annual conference generated almost $200,000 in revenue; instructional and administrative training and support produced about $225,000; and hardware installation and repair services contributed $529,000 to MECC's income.[45]

At the same time that its institutional members were contributing to MECC's support, this state-owned corporation was receiving revenues from governmental sources, such as the state university system, the Minnesota Department of Education, and the Bureau of Indian Affairs, as well as direct appropriations from the Minnesota legislature.[46] MECC's officers viewed taxpayers' support as an essential part of its "image" and its marketing strategy:

> MECC's ability to market product [sic] outside Minnesota is partially dependent upon our image as the major public educational computing organization in Minnesota. If the Minnesota legislature desires to fund courseware development projects . . . then making those funds available directly to MECC can result in two benefits. First, MECC will again contribute additional resources and its considerable experience to producing the best products for Minnesota, and two, MECC's reputation as Minnesota's public software producer will be maintained.[47]

Therefore, if the Minnesota legislature makes direct appropriations to MECC (rather than have MECC's funds flow through the state university system or the Board of Education's appropriation), both potential consumers and competitors will receive a clear signal that MECC has the government's imprimatur as the principal (if not sole) supplier of software and hardware to the state's educational institutions. The unstated intent is to discourage competition.

Even though MECC is formally an extension of the state government, it has quickly evolved into a commercial entity that has parlayed its virtual monopoly on state educational software and hardware markets into a dominant position in the national market. MECC's "entrepreneurial spirit" has been aided by the special privileges nonprofits receive from government; for example, there is no indication on the income statement that MECC paid any taxes. In fact, the Legislative Report specifically states that "MECC needs the ability to create subsidiaries in order to report revenues properly and *properly save federal tax payments.*"[48] Evidently, MECC officials were not only aware of the commercial nature of their activities, but they were also concerned about designing ways to protect the organization's revenues from taxation. In the 1985 Legislative Report, MECC did nothing to hide its competitive nature: "The MECC Board is presently limited in its management of compensation policies. This limitation should be removed in order to *allow MECC to compete in the very competitive markets of commercial software production and distribution.*"[49] Apparently, as a subdivision of the state government, civil service regulations placed restrictions on compensation policy, making it difficult for MECC to compete as effectively as it would have liked.

Like other CNEs that compete unfairly with private firms in the market for educational software and audiovisual learning aids, MECC implicitly claimed that private firms were not responsive to the schools it served; that is, the market was "too thin":

> A survey was conducted of Minnesota school needs for computing materials. The results indicated a high interest in database materials for social studies classrooms and writing tools for language arts classrooms. Working with the Minnesota Department of Education, MECC formulated a plan to build on these needs and expand them into an approach to the overall problem of preparing children for the information age. A review of commercial courseware showed only three of the proposed products existed in some form and that each of these were too expensive ($100 to $250 each) for the wide adoption in Minnesota school districts, so MECC set out to create this series.[50]

It is not surprising that few commercial products were available or that they were expensive. No private firm could possibly compete with MECC, which enjoyed the special privileges of CNEs, direct taxpayer subsidies, a favorable "image," and a captive market. Faced with this competition, private firms have been discouraged from developing innovative products. Most of the costs of developing new computer software are in writing and testing; the cost of duplication is purely nominal. For a producer to make a profit, the "up front" costs of a program must be recovered. If only a small number of copies are sold, the high fixed costs must be spread over a small number of units, so the price of each unit must be high. If a large number of units is sold, the price can be much lower. Again, economies of scale play an important role in the operation of the market, and MECC's captive customer base provides an important edge over any private competitor.

National Audiovisual Center. Private firms in the audiovisual industry face competition not only from nonprofits chartered by local and state governments but also from the federal government. The most blatant example of federal competition is the National Audiovisual Center (NAC), the central distributor of federally produced audiovisual programs. The NAC's *1986 Media Resource Catalog* contains a letter from Director John H. McLean addressed to the "Audiovisual

Buyer," in which he provides a overview of his organization's services and pricing policy:

> More than 2,700 of the National Audiovisual Center's newest and
> best titles have been specially selected for inclusion in this *1986
> Media Resource Catalog.* These video cassettes, films, and slide/
> sound productions discuss, explore, explain, and illuminate
> more than 400 different topics. Throughout this catalog, you'll
> find programs on diverse subjects such as history and anthropol-
> ogy, earth science and space science, safety and health at home
> and on the job, medicine and dentistry, and many more.
>
> Since 1969, the Center has given media users the opportunity
> to obtain fine quality programming at budget-stretching prices.
> This 16–year tradition holds true today. As you scan the pages
> of this catalog, you'll come across many video and film festival
> winners—*all available at not-for-profit prices.*
>
> If you've purchased from us before, we're sure you'll want to
> take advantage of our unique productions and pricing again. If
> you're considering your first purchase from us, you'll note how
> easy it is to build up your media library—*and keep expenses down.*
>
> Use these materials as curriculum enrichment tools, formal
> training packages, or just plain entertainment. There's some-
> thing truly for every need.[51]

There is little doubt left in a buyer's mind that NAC offers lower
prices on its audiovisual materials than are charged by private firms.
McLean has the luxury of not having to worry about profit and loss;
the costs of his operation are borne by U.S. taxpayers.

NAC's 1986 catalog covers subjects ranging from agriculture to
wounds, with audiovisual materials targeted at every level of audience—all of them produced by federal agencies or by contractors
under federal grants. Some of the offerings are more than curious.
For example, one 16mm film, "Dental Auxiliary Trigger Situations—
Interpersonal Relations," purportedly "discusses interpersonal problems in a dental practice [and] encourages serious thinking about
better understanding others, a personal commitment to react more
sensitively to others, and self-assessment in relation to the role of the
auxiliary as a member of a dental team." This film's content seems
demure in comparison with some of the other offerings, such as
"Female External Genitalia" and "Female Genital Examination—A
Humanistic Approach."[52] It is unlikely that a coherent argument

could be made that these (or most of the other listings) are public goods.

The 2,700 audiovisuals listed in NAC's 1986 catalog are merely the tip of the iceberg. The catalog announces:

> Through the Center's distribution programs, the public has access to more than 8,000 titles covering a wide range of subjects. Major subject concentrations in the Center's collection include history, medicine and dentistry and the allied health sciences, safety, aviation and space technology, vocational and management training, and the environmental sciences."[53]

No one, including NAC, knows how many films the federal government makes or sponsors each year; even those individuals in charge of the operations seem to operate in a fog. When CBS News made a "60 Minutes" segment ["Hollywood on the Potomac"] about the federal government's filmmaking activities, Mike Wallace and Maurice McDonald, chief of HEW's Audiovisual Department, had this exchange:

> *Mr. Wallace*: Do you know how many films you make?
> *Mr. McDonald*: No, I can't give you an exact answer.
> *Mr. Wallace*: Do you know how many films you have made in the last two years?
> *Mr. McDonald*: I haven't done a count on them.
> *Mr. Wallace*: Do you know where I would go to get that list? Is there a list?
> *Mr. McDonald*: There is no list.[54]

There is no question that the government is the largest producer of audiovisual materials in the nation, if not the world. In 1967, *Newsweek* reported: "In addition to operating several parks, printing firms, detective bureaus, dams, and armed forces, the United States Government runs the biggest bargain basement in the motion-picture world. More than 50,000 different educational films are on sale to the public. . . ."[55] Federal spending on audiovisual production and distribution each year runs into the hundreds of millions of dollars:

> According to a little-noticed report issued by the White House Office of Telecommunications in February, 1974, the [federal] government spent at least $375 million in 1972 to produce and distribute films, photographs, and an assortment of recorded programs and audio services. These programs covered a wide

range of subjects and were produced by government employees working out of at least 653 federal facilities scattered throughout the government.[56]

Except in those instances where national security considerations require that films be produced "in house," each of these facilities competes with private firms that produce audiovisual materials. But few federal productions, including those produced by the Department of Defense, meet this requirement. For example, "In the past two years [1970–1971] the Defense Department cranked out 12 films, all on the same subject: "How to Brush Your Teeth," and the Pentagon produced ten films on venereal disease during that period."[57]

The federal government's audiovisual activities are costly, they duplicate private sector facilities, and they contravene the stated policy of the federal government, as set out in OMB Circular A–76, that requires that goods and services be purchased from the private sector. When the federal government does contract out the production of films, the contracts are almost always given to nonprofit organizations, not to profit-seeking (and taxpaying) private firms (see Appendix B). Thus, the federal government directly competes with private firms when it produces and distributes audiovisuals itself, and it further penalizes private firms by directing grants and contracts to CNEs that also are in competition with private enterprises.

Conclusions

Private firms engaged in producing and distributing audiovisual materials and computer software for instructional purposes are subject to aggressive, intense, and unfair competition from a host of commercial nonprofit enterprises and from every level of government. The economic implications of this unfair competition may be stated simply: Existing private firms are threatened and new firms are discouraged from entering this industry. In view of the massive advantages enjoyed by CNEs and public enterprises relative to their private counterparts, it is reasonable to predict that the profit-seeking segment of this industry will continue to decline unless public policy is changed to alter the terms of competition.

Notes to Chapter 6

1. Senate Committee on Small Business, *Government Competition with Small Business, 1981 Hearings before the Subcommittee on Advocacy and the Future of Small Business*, 97th Cong., 1st Sess., 1981, p. 128.

2. Thomas W. Hope, "In the Matter of Money," *Instructional Innovator* (May 1981), p. 11.

3. Betty Decker, "Marketing Your Own Instructional Materials," *Instructional Innovator* (February 1982), p. 10.

4. Ibid., p. 11.

5. Ibid., p. 12.

6. William E. Geist, "Facing U.S. Cuts, Montclair Tries New Ways to Raise School Funds," *New York Times*, June 12, 1981.

7. Ibid.

8. Andrea Pedolsky, ed. *In-House Training and Development Programs* (Detroit, MI: Neal-Schuman Publishers, Inc., 1981), p. 268.

9. See the following articles in the *Grand Rapids Press*: "GVSC Reports $445,118 Given for Educational TV," April 1, 1971; "TV Station Heads Out," June 28, 1976; "Shortage of Local Programming is a Sizable Problem at Channel 35," April 22, 1979; "Federal Grant to Help TV35 Buy Minicams," September 27, 1979.

10. "PBS in Focus in West Michigan," *West Michigan* (June 1981), p. 38.

11. Toni Morris, "Cuts May Tune in Viewers to Needs of Public TV," *Grand Rapids Press*, March 10, 1981.

12. See the listing of unfair competitors in Appendix A.

13. *Publications 1982/83: Occupational Curriculum Laboratory* (Commerce: East Texas State University, 1982), inside front cover.

14. Ibid., p. 21.

15. "Out of the Woods. . . . Over the Bridge . . . Into Tomorrow With Bilingual Education" (Los Angeles: National Dissemination and Assessment Center, California State University, Los Angeles, 1980), pp. 1–2; letter accompanying brochure dated January 28, 1980, signed by Charles F. Leyba, Director.

16. Dale Cotton, "Oklahoma's Productivity Division," *Voc Ed* (May 1982), pp. 40–1.

17. Decker, "Marketing Your Own Instructional Materials," p. 12.

18. Dan Brook, "Providing for the Exchange of Software," *Voc Ed* (June 1982), p. 36.

19. Gordon Tullock, *Economics of Income Redistribution* (Boston: Kluwer-Nijhoff Publishing, 1983), p. 29.

20. Ibid., p. 96.

21. Brook, "Providing for the Exchange of Software."

22. Gerald Gleason, "Microcomputers in Education: The State of the Art," *Educational Technology* (March 1981), pp. 7–18, esp. pp. 11–12.

23. Dwain Thomas, "Review of 'Our Political System'," *Educational Technology* (April 1982), p. 49.

24. Gleason, "Microcomputers in Education," p. 12.

25. *Audio-Visual Resource Catalog, 1980–81* (Ithaca, NY: Cornell University, Media Services, 1980), p. 1.

26. Ibid., pp. 87, 123.

27. Marc Lane, *Legal Handbook for Nonprofit Organizations* (New York: AMA-COM, 1980), p. 273.

28. *MIT Video Short Courses for Continuing Education* (Cambridge: Massachusetts Institute of Technology, Center for Advanced Engineering, 1980), pp. 30, 52, 53.

29. *1980 Catalog Educational Motion Pictures* (Bloomington: Indiana University, Audio-Visual Center, Office for Learning Resources, 1980), p. 5.

30. Ibid., pp. 872–89.

31. Ibid., pp. 543, 413–16.

32. *Film Catalog, 1979–81* (Boulder: University of Colorado, Educational Media Center, 1979), pp. ii, 153, 231.

33. "Shortage of Local Programming is a Sizable Problem at Channel 35," *Grand Rapids Press*, April 22, 1979.

34. Salvatore J. Parlato, "40,000 Films Are Looking for a Home: A Profile of the Companies That Distribute 16mm and Video Educational Programs," *Instructional Innovator* (May 1981), pp. 20–21.

35. Minnesota Educational Computing Corporation, *MECC Legislative Report*, (St. Paul: MECC, March 1, 1985), p. 1.

36. Don G. Rawitsch, "The Minnesota Educational Computing Consortium," *VocEd* (April 1982), p. 43. Rawitsch was manager of user services at MECC when he wrote the article. See also Dale Schneiderhan and Shirley Griffing, "Instructional Software Development," *The School Administrator* (April 1982), pp. 14–15. Schneiderhan was executive director and Griffing was executive secretary of MECC when this article was written.

37. Don G. Rawitsch, "Minnesota's Statewide Push for Computer Literacy," *Instructional Innovator* (February 1982), p. 35.

38. Dennis Williams and Tracey Robinson, "Minnesota Leads the Way," *Newsweek*, November 22, 1982.

39. MECC, *Legislative Report*, p. 1.

40. Ibid., p. 7.

41. Ibid., p. 8.

42. Ibid.

43. Ibid., p. 13.

44. Ibid., p. 2.

45. Ibid., pp. 13, 14.

46. Ibid., p. 13.

47. Ibid., p. 6.

48. Ibid., p. 1, emphasis added.

49. Ibid., emphasis added.

50. Ibid., p. 5.

51. National Audiovisual Center, *1986 Media Resource Catalog from the National Audiovisual Center* (Capitol Heights, MD: NAC, 1986), inside front cover, emphasis added.

52. Ibid., pp. 91, 105. A counterpart film about male genitals is offered on p. 145.

53. Ibid., p. 1.

54. Quoted in Donald L. Lambro, *The Federal Rathole* (New Rochelle, NY: Arlington House Publishers, 1975), p. 34.

55. "50,000 Films for Sale," *Newsweek*, March 6, 1967.

56. Lambro, *The Federal Rathole*, pp. 29–30.

57. Haynes Johnson and Jack Fuller, "Federal Film-Making Hit," *Washington Post*, August 10, 1972.

Appendix A to Chapter 6

Summary of Activities of Selected Commercial Nonprofit Enterprises in the Market for Educational Audiovisual Materials and Computer Software

Aerospace Education Foundation, Washington, D.C. This nonprofit affiliate of the Air Force Association has as its purpose "the education of the public at large to a greater understanding of aerospace development." Its sales catalog, mailed at a nonprofit postal rate, lists 58 U.S. Air Force-developed course packages (sound/slide sets or videotapes) in automotive mechanics, communication arts, computer science, construction trades, education, electronics, environmental control, metal trades, paramedicine and health care, and miscellaneous—but not a single space-related title. Products are sold to "more than 850 schools, training centers, and colleges" at "cost of reproduction." Its catalog includes a "technical note on film quality—in some cases, the poor condition of the prints from which we were forced to make videotape transcriptions of films made top quality results impossible. . . . We think you will find, however, that despite these deficiencies, these transcriptions will be adequate." The Foundation is listed in *Video Source Book* and *EITV* magazine's November 1981 "Annual Directory of Program Sources."

Agency for Instructional Television, Bloomington, Indiana. This nonprofit American/Canadian organization, created in 1973, sells and rents 2,000 programs (broadcast videotapes, films, or video cassettes) in more than 100 series, most of which were produced with grant funds from state and local agencies. The agency has also produced 11 "consortium series," jointly developed and financed with groups of state and provincial agencies in which all 50 states and 7 provinces have participated. School systems within the service areas of participating agencies receive special broadcast/duplication rights and discounted prices. AIT allows unlimited duplication and broadcast for an annual

159

fee based on school population, or it charges one-time fees per duplication: 50 percent of purchase price for the first copy, 40 percent for the second, and 30 percent for each additional copy. A free "bonus" print or cassette is received if 10 or more are purchased during a year. Programs cover all subject areas for all grade levels and adults. The sales catalog is mailed at a nonprofit postal rate. AIT's predecessor organization, the National Instructional Television Center (NIT), was a nonprofit, "self-supporting" division of the Indiana University Foundation. For its first five years (1962–1967), NIT was funded by the U.S. Office of Education.

Alameda County Schools, California. The district produces and distributes a series of four video cassettes on micro-computers in the classroom, available for $50 each or $160 for all four. It is listed in *Video Source Book.*

American Association for Vocational Instructional Materials, Athens, Georgia. This nonprofit organization of state departments of vocational education and voc-ed schools at colleges and universities is affiliated with the University of Georgia. Its "purpose is to provide instructional materials." The association's catalog lists 32 vocational education course items, half of which include overhead transparencies, slides, filmstrips, and cassette tapes that are available for purchase only. The organization is listed in *Industrial Education* magazine's December 1981 "Annual Buying Directory" and exhibited at the American Vocational Association's December 1981 and December 1982 conferences.

American College Testing Program, Iowa City, Iowa. This nonprofit organization produces and distributes guidance-oriented programs for high school and college students. It is listed under "audiovisual soft-ware" in *VocEd* magazine's January/February 1982 "Directory of Suppliers" and advertises in *VocEd.*

University of Arizona, Tucson, Arizona. This state-supported school produces, sells, and rents videotapes and video cassettes in business, agriculture, home economics, mathematics, and science for college students and adults and offers production services for others. The school is listed in *Video Source Book* and *Audiovisual Market Place* and advertises in *American School Board Journal.*

Association for Continuing Education, Stanford, California. A nonprofit membership corporation founded by the government and industry groups, the association formed the Stanford Instructional Television Network, which offers courses over the network and recorded off-the-air for sale. Its catalog lists 32 video cassettes in administration, communication, electronics, technology, and mathematics for college students and adults. The brochure notes that "courses are also available for sale to non-members, as part of a plan to expand into other markets." The association is listed in *EITV* magazine's November 1981 "Annual Directory of Program Sources."

Brigham Young University, Media Marketing, Provo, Utah. A nonprofit, independent, religious school, BYU produces and sells audio and video cassettes, films, and sound filmstrips in all subject areas and for all grade levels and offers production services for others and distributes materials produced elsewhere. BYU is listed in *Video Source Book, Audiovisual Market Place*, and *EITV* magazine's November 1981 "Annual Directory of Program Sources."

University of California, Extension Media Center, Berkeley, California. This state-supported school sells and rents films, audio and videotapes, and cassettes on all subjects for adults and college students. UC is listed in *Video Source Book, Audiovisual Market Place*, and *Instructional Innovator* magazine's May 1981 "Directory of Suppliers."

California Polytechnic State University, San Luis Obispo, California. This state-supported school operates a Vocational Education Productions service through a university nonprofit corporation. The service produces and sells more than 200 items in agricultural education, including sound and silent filmstrips, audio cassettes, slides, and overhead transparencies. The order form requires adding state sales tax to purchase price. The school is listed in *Audiovisual Market Place* and *VocEd* magazine's January/February 1982 "Directory of Suppliers," and advertises in *VocEd*. CPSU receives grants funded under the Federal Vocational Education Act and is "operated on a self-support basis."

Center for Occupational Curriculum Development-see University of Texas.

Center for Southern Folklore, Memphis, Tennessee. This nonprofit association produces, sells, and rents films, audio and video cassettes, records, and slide/tape programs in folk music, art, literature, and lifestyles for all grade levels and adults. The center is supported by federal tax funds from the National Endowment for the Humanities.

Clemson University, Clemson, South Carolina. This state-supported school is testing microcomputer courseware in cooperation with the PICA foundation (see separate entry) for distribution to industrial training programs and industrial education classes.

Close Up Foundation, Arlington, Virginia. Close Up is a nonprofit association that promotes government studies and telecasts over the Cable-Satellite Public Affairs Network (CSPAN). It offers free off-air taping rights to individuals and schools using the materials for instructional purposes, and it produces, sells, and rents video cassettes for all others. The "core" of the Foundation's financial base is a congressionally established fellowship program. It is listed in *Instructional Innovator* magazine's May 1981 "Directory of Suppliers."

Clovis Unified School District, California. The district produces and sells financial/budgeting/accounting software packages, ranging in price from $15,000 to $35,000.

Coast Telecourses: The Coast Community Colleges, Fountain Valley, California. Telecourses is the marketing and distribution division of three district-supported community colleges (Coastline Community College, Orange Coast College, and Golden West College), which together own and operate a PBS television station. It advertises itself as "the nation's leading producer of high quality telecourses," which "offers more adult-level, total learning systems than any other producer/distributor in North America" and is "used at more than 1000 locations." Telecourses produces, sells, and leases video and audio tapes and cassettes and broadcasts tapes in all subjects for college students and adults. The catalog lists 18 course series, each available as a complete set, in modules, or as individual programs. It also offers production services for others and distributes materials produced elsewhere.

University of Colorado, Educational Media Center, Boulder, Colorado. This state-supported school offers for rent 5,700 films produced by 600 schools, associations, and corporations. The films cover all subjects for all grade levels and adults. Rental fees range from $7 to $21.50 (depending on running time) for nonprofits, but all "commercial organizations and individuals" are charged $25 per reel. The university also rents its TV facilities and equipment and offers complete video production and post-production services, script writing, and film and videotape distribution.

CONDUIT, Iowa City, Iowa. CONDUIT is a nonprofit organization formed by five regional computer centers (Computers at Oregon State, North Carolina Educational Computing Service, Dartmouth College, and the Universities of Iowa and Texas at Austin) to sell microcomputer software for Apple, TRS–80, PET, IBM, and Atari computers. The catalog lists over 100 different packages for high school and college students in 13 disciplines, including biology, chemistry, humanities, mathematics, physics, psychology, sociology, and statistics. Programs are written by college and university faculty members, who receive royalties. For most programs, after the consumer purchases an initial package, additional copies of the software are available for "a nominal fee," generally $10 each. "As a nonprofit organization we are unable to offer complimentary copies of our materials for review." CONDUIT is affiliated with the University of Iowa and was organized in 1971 with funds from the National Science Foundation; funds were also obtained from the (federal) Fund for the Improvement of Postsecondary Education.

Consumer's Union, Mount Vernon, New York. This nonprofit organization for the testing of consumer products derives its income from the sale of its magazine. It also produces, sells, and rents 16 filmstrips and 7 films on consumer education topics for grades 7–12 and adults. Cassettes are available for purchase only: "Films are not available for preview prior to rental." Consumer's Union is listed in *Video Source Book* and *Audiovisual Market Place*.

Cornell University, Audio-Visual Resource Center, Ithaca, New York. A private, nonprofit school, Cornell produces, sells, and rents 1,100 films, slide sets, and video and audio tapes in all subjects for all grade levels and adults. The Center also makes available materials produced by other schools, associations, and corporations. It is listed in *Video Source Book, Audiovisual Market Place,* and *EITV* magazine's November 1981 "Annual Directory of Program Sources."

Dallas County Community College District, Center for Telecommunications, Texas.

The Center produces and distributes nine telecourses for college students. It is listed in *Video Source Book* and *Instructional Innovator* magazine's May 1981 "Directory of Suppliers" and has exhibited at the Association for Educational Communications & Technology's convention.

Dallas Independent School District, Texas. This school district produces and sells microcomputer courseware for primary grades. See also Foundation for Quality Education, Inc.

Daughters of St. Paul, Boston, Massachusetts. This nonprofit religious association produces, sells, and rents slide sets, records, films and filmstrips, and audio and video cassettes in religious and communications subjects for all grade levels and adults. It is listed in *Video Source Book* and *Audiovisual Market Place*.

East Texas State University, Commerce, Texas. A state-supported school, East Texas produces and sells slides, transparencies, and audio cassettes in office and industrial education for high school, college, and special-needs students. Its catalog, mailed at a nonprofit postal rate, lists about 75 items available with A-V materials that are distributed through the school's Occupational Curriculum Laboratory, which is funded by the Texas Education Agency. The university also distributes materials produced by the Mid-America Vocational Curriculum Consortium (see separate entry) and exhibited at the American Vocational Association's December 1981 conference.

Education Development Center, Inc., Newton, Massachusetts. The center is a nonprofit corporation that sells and rents about 150 films, many of which were produced by other organizations or individuals. Also available are video cassettes for purchase only. Subject areas include women's issues, childhood education, health and medicine, science and technology, and social studies for high school and college students and adults. "EDC does not send out films for no-charge previews. Normal rental fees are charged for screening films. . . ." Each EDC project has its own funding and staff; some are funded by the U.S. Department of Education. "Because EDC is funded by the WEEA program within the [federal] Office of Education, these materials are sold at cost and are very reasonably priced." About 180 additional EDC-developed educational films are available through commercial distributors. EDC also offers production services for others.

Educational Resourses Foundation, Columbia, South Carolina. This nonprofit affiliate of the South Carolina Educational Television Network produces, sells, and rents films, video cassettes, audio tapes, and slide/tape programs for 25 courses in job skills, supervisory skills, secretarial training, economic education, and safety. "Many of the educational programs of the Foundation are produced in cooperation with South Carolina, regional, or national associations and educational organizations. . . . The Foundation . . . receives no federal or state funds." Income generated by the sale or rental of its resources provides the funds for continued service. The Foundation also distributes materials that are available from commercial distributors. South

Carolina purchasers are charged a state sales tax and are "eligible" for a 25 percent price discount. "ERF chooses to sell to libraries at normal retail prices realizing that libraries may charge fees for usage. ERF chooses to allow consultants to use our materials with their clients on a normal rental basis. Consultants may not purchase video components for long-term unrestricted use."

Essex County College, Newark, New Jersey. Essex is a district-supported school that rents video and audio recording facilities and equipment. It advertises itself as "New Jersey's secret studio. . . . Just 20 minutes from midtown Manhattan."

Foundation for Quality Education,Inc., Dallas, Texas. This defunct, nonprofit corporation was organized in 1977 to solicit contributions to and to market the educational products (including microcomputer courseware) of the Dallas Independent School District (see separate entry). The Foundation collapsed in 1979 amid financial irregularities. Materials are now marketed directly by the school district.

Great Plains National Instructional Television Library, Lincoln, Nebraska. A "service agency" of the state-supported University of Nebraska, this organization produces and distributes slides, films, videotapes, and cassettes, and it broadcasts programming for all grade levels and adults in all subject areas. It is listed in *Instructional Innovator* magazine's May 1981 "Directory of Suppliers."

Harvard University Press, Cambridge, Massachusetts. The press is the publishing arm of Harvard University, a private, nonprofit school. It produces and distributes slides, filmstrips, and audio cassettes in the humanities and social sciences for college students and adults and also distributes materials produced elsewhere. It makes its own materials available through commercial distributors. The press is listed in *Audiovisual Market Place* and *Instructional Innovator* magazine's May 1981 "Directory of Suppliers," and it advertises in *Instructional Innovator.*

Illinois Department of Administrative Services, Springfield, Illinois. This agency has contracted with Tandy Corporation for the direct supply of microcomputers to Illinois schools, thereby bypassing dealers and distributors.

University of Iowa, Audiovisual Center, Iowa City, Iowa. This state-supported school produces, sells, and rents transparencies, slides, films and filmstrips, audiotapes and cassettes, and videotapes and cassettes in all subject areas for all grade levels and adults. It also offers production services for others. The Center is listed in *Video Source Book* and *Audiovisual Market Place.* (See also CONDUIT.)

Maryland Center for Public Broadcasting, Owings Mills, Maryland. The Center sells and rents its own and other PBS stations' video cassettes. Its catalog lists about 100 programs and series categorized as drama and documentaries, performing arts, children's programs, how-to and consumer programs, and telecourses.

Massachussetts Institute of Technology, Cambridge, Massachusetts. This private, nonprofit school produces, sells, and rents films and video cassettes in science, engineering, mathematics, and management for college students and professionals. It is listed in *Video Source Book* and *Audiovisual Market Place.*

Miami-Dade Community College, Miami, Florida. A state- and locally-supported school, Miami-Dade produces and distributes telecourses for college students. It is listed in *Instructional Innovator* magazine's May 1981 "Directory of Suppliers" and exhibited at the Association for Educational Communications & Technology's 1982 convention.

University of Michigan, Michigan Media, Ann Arbor, Michigan. This state-supported school produces, sells, and rents slides, films and filmstrips, videotapes and cassettes, and audio tapes and cassettes in all subject areas for all grade levels and adults. It also offers production services for others. The school is listed in *Video Source Book* and *Audiovisual Market Place.*

Michigan State University, Instructional Media Center, East Lansing, Michigan. A state-supported school, MSU produces, sells, and rents 400 films, video cassettes, and slide/tape programs in all subject areas for college students. The Center is listed in *Video Source Book* and *EITV* magazine's November 1981 "Annual Directory of Program Sources."

Micro-Ideas, Glenview, Illinois. A project of six Illinois school districts, Micro-Ideas was funded in 1980–82 by federal grants but expects to become self-sustaining through membership fees. Membership is restricted to school districts within a 50–mile radius of Chicago that have student enrollments less than 25,000, and to colleges, museums, and libraries with no location restriction. Yearly dues (maximum for 1982–1983 school year is $10,000) entitle district members to automatic membership in the Minnesota Educational Computing Consortium (see separate entry) at no additional charge; access to "special collective bids" for microcomputer hardware and software; copies of selected software and participation in a software lending library of commercially produced, copyrighted programs valued at $20,000; in-service training valued at $6,750; technical assistance; professional consulting in educational applications; and software reviews and other publications.

University of Mid-America, Lincoln, Nebraska. This nonprofit corporation is governed and administered by a consortium of 11 midwestern, state-supported universities (Iowa, Iowa State, Kansas, Kansas State, Minnesota, Missouri, Nebraska, North Dakota, North Dakota State). It produces, sells, and leases films, video and audio cassettes, and broadcast tapes for 12 series in history, art, business, and social issues for college students and adults. It also offers production services and distributes materials produced elsewhere. The University is "funded principally by the National Institute of Education."

Mid-America Vocational Curriculum Consortium, Stillwater, Oklahoma. An organization of 10 state education departments (North Dakota, South Dakota, Nebraska, Colorado, Kansas, Missouri, Arkansas, Oklahoma, Texas, and Louisiana), the consortium produces and sells approximately 50 vocational education course packages, about half of which include transparencies or slide/tape programs. Listed in *Industrial Education* magazine's December 1981 "Annual Buying Directory," the consortium exhibited at the American Vocational Association's December 1981 and December 1982 conferences and has advertised in *VocEd*.

Minnesota Educational Computing Consortium, St. Paul, Minnesota. This consortium is a nonprofit organization created by the state of Minnesota in 1973 and comprised of the University of Minnesota, the state university system, the community college system, and the state department of education, which represents 430 school districts and 30 institutions of higher education. The consortium enters into statewide contracts for the purchase of microcomputers (Apple and Atari) by schools and colleges. The 25–person staff includes high school and college students, who produce and distribute microcomputer courseware (about 250 programs) in all subject areas for all grade levels. Minnesota residents can purchase courseware "for cost of reproduction." Minnesota school districts and colleges not only make low-cost purchases, but they may also duplicate courseware for educational use. Other states and out-of-state schools, school districts, and agencies may become MECC members (yearly dues required) and receive the same hardware discounts and software purchase and duplication privileges. According to *Newsweek*, MECC's out-of-state sales cover about 90 percent of Minnesota's costs. "It's the best deal since motherhood and apple pie," MECC's deputy executive director told *Newsweek*. MECC courseware is also available through eight commercial distributors. Finally, MECC offers consulting in the educational uses of microcomputers at a daily rate of $300 plus travel expenses. MECC publishes articles in the trade press.

Mississippi Department of Vocational/Technical Education, Jackson, Mississippi. This agency has developed a $100,000 mobile multimedia unit to produce industrial training slide sets and video and audio tapes on site.

University of Missouri, Instructional Materials Laboratory, Columbia, Missouri. A state-supported school, UM produces and sells about 500 course packages in vocational agriculture, business and office skills, cooperative education, marketing, home economics, industrial education, sex equity, and special needs for high school, college, and special-needs students. Most packages include transparencies, slides, filmstrips, and cassette tapes. The laboratory also distributes voc-ed materials produced by other schools and state agencies. Missouri educators may borrow materials on a free-loan basis. Residents are charged the state sales tax on purchases; out-of-state purchasers are charged a 6.5 percent "price accrual." IML's brochure notes that "for more than twelve years we have devoted our entire energy into producing instructional materials . . . at as low a cost as possible. This is possible because IML is nonprofit and because of a sincere interest in meeting vocational needs of students and instructors." The laboratory is listed in *Audiovisual Market Place*, and it exhibited at the American Vocational Association's December 1981 and December 1982 conferences.

Montclair Public School System, New Jersey. The Montclair school board announced in 1981 that it would begin offsetting federal funding cuts through the sale of products and services, including data processing, publishing, consulting, and school supplies. It also intends to bid on government contracts for educational materials and workshops. Ironically, the media center at nearby Montclair State College, a state-supported school, has an unwritten policy not to compete with commercial enterprise because "there are several A-V and TV vendors already in the area," according to Robert Ruezinsky, the center's director. The center honors all A-V requests (e.g., for slide production by college staff or for rental of studio time and equipment) from nonprofit organizations at no charge, but it denies all requests "of a commercial nature."

Mt. San Jacinto College, Beaumont, California. The college is a district-supported school that produces and sells about 300 films and video cassettes in business, health, and vocational education for college students and adults. It also offers materials available through commercial distributors.

National Association of Counties, Washington, D.C. This nonprofit organization offers "complete video services" for others, from conception through production and distribution. "We are able to serve our clients' videotape needs at much less cost than charged by most major commercial studios."

National Center for Research in Vocational Education-See Ohio State University.

National Council of Churches, New York, New York. A nonprofit federation of churches, the NCC sells about 55 films and video cassettes "for church and secular audiences," most of which were produced by commercial television networks. A few are available only to religious groups; all are priced at "actual costs incurred." Subject areas include religion, health, social science, and ethical/moral issues for high school and college students and adults. Products are also available for rental through EcuFilm (Nashville, Tennessee), in which NCC and other church groups participate. EcuFilm, an ecumenical film/video distribution service, "eliminates the variations in rental fees and policies among various distributors." NCC is listed in *Audiovisual Market Place* and *EITV* magazine's November 1981 "Annual Directory of Program Sources."

National Gallery of Art, Washington, D.C. The gallery, which is affiliated with the U.S. government, produces and distributes, on a free-loan basis, slides, films, and videotapes and cassettes in the arts and humanities for all grade levels and adults. It is listed in *Video Source Book, Audiovisual Market Place,* and *Instructional Innovator* magazine's May 1981 "Directory of Suppliers."

National Geographic Society, Educational Services, Washington, D.C. The society is a nonprofit organization which, through its Educational Services division, produces, sells, and rents 500 films and filmstrips, records, audio and video cassettes, and video tapes in all subject areas for all grade levels and adults. In general, the A-V materials produced for schools by Educational Services are unrelated to the Society's research expeditions.

National Public Radio, Washington, D.C. A nonprofit organization, NPR has produced and distributed more than 300 educational audio cassettes in all subject areas for high school and college students and adults. It is funded primarily by the nonprofit, congressionally established Corporation for Public Broadcasting. NPR is listed in *Instructional Innovator* magazine's May 1981 "Directory of Suppliers," and it exhibited at the Association for Educational Communications & Technology's 1982 convention. NPR advertises in *Instructional Innovator.*

Occupational Curriculum Laboratory-See East Texas State University.

Ohio University, Telecommunications Center, Athens, Ohio. This state-supported school produces, sells, and rents 40 videotapes and cassettes in art, communications, and child development for college students and adults. The center is listed in *Video Source Book* and *EITV* magazine's November 1981 "Annual Directory of Program Sources."

Ohio State University, National Center for Research in Vocational Education, Columbus, Ohio. In addition to producing and distributing mostly print materials in voc-ed, this nonprofit organization conducts federally funded "special projects," including technology adaptation, evaluation of career guidance counseling, community-based guidance training, and technical assistance and training for occupational skills. The center exhibited at the American Vocational Association's December 1981 conference.

Oklahoma Department of Vocational and Technical Education, Stillwater, Oklahoma. In a joint effort with the Associated General Contractors of America (a nonprofit), this state agency produces and sells about 150 vocational education course packages in agriculture, business and office skills, career development, marketing, health occupations, home economics, industrial education, and special programs for high school and college students and adults. Many packages include transparencies or slide/tape sets. The productivity division of this agency also offers voc-ed training services to Oklahoma schools and businesses. "The only cost to companies using this program . . . is for materials used." Listed in *VocEd* magazine's January/February 1982 "Directory of Suppliers," the center exhibited at the American Vocational Association's December 1981 conference and has advertised in *VocEd.*

PBS Video, Washington, D.C. This nonprofit organization sells 2,300 programs (as video cassettes) of public broadcasting stations covering all subject areas for all grade levels and adults.

Pennsylvania Department of Education, Harrisburg, Pennsylvania. Through its 28 regional service centers, the state rents and repairs A-V equipment. Now moving into microcomputers, the department is developing training materials (including slides, transparencies, and "sample" courseware) on the educational uses of microcomputers. Regional centers, which are training educators in all 505 school districts, offer hardware and software consulting and microcomputer repair services.

PICA (Printing Industry of the Carolinas) Foundation, Charlotte, North Carolina.

Together with Clemson University (see separate entry) and the South Carolina Department of Education, PICA has developed and distributed sound and slide programs for students in industrial arts and graphic communications. The foundation advertises that it has "850 users" and that its products have been "adopted by 4 state education departments." Listed in *VocEd* magazine's January/February 1982 "Directory of Suppliers," PICA exhibited at the American Vocational Association's December 1981 and December 1982 conferences and has advertised in *Industrial Education*.

Project Local, Westwood, Massachusetts. A nonprofit regional project for programmed instruction via microcomputers, Project Local offers training, consulting, and centralized purchasing to area school systems, which fund it.

Research for Better Schools, Philadelphia, Pennsylvania. This is a nonprofit, federally funded project in programmed instruction for basic skills, career development, and special education. The organization's "goal is large-scale coordination of new educational procedures, processes, and materials among local districts, intermediate service agencies, and state education departments."

Robbinsdale Area Schools, Minneapolis, Minnesota. This school district produces and sells, through commercial distributors, microcomputer courseware in mathematics and language arts for all grade levels.

State Fair Community College, Media Center, Sedalia, Missouri. A district-supported school, SFCC produces and sells 240 slide/tape sets and videotapes in vocational education for high school and college students and adults. Subjects include business, auto mechanics, building trades, electronics, and health occupations. The center is listed in *VocEd* magazine's January/February 1982 "Directory of Suppliers" and has advertised in *VocEd*.

Suburban Audio Visual Service, Burr Ridge, Illinois. Administered by the Suburban Library System, an organization of 74 public libraries, 12 academic libraries, and 19 special libraries in the Chicago suburbs, SAVS is funded by the state of Illinois. SAVS operates a lending library of 4,000 films and 7,500 records, produces talking-book records and cassettes for the blind and physically handicapped, and offers member libraries A-V equipment lending and repair, cooperative purchasing, feature-film rental, and hardware and software consulting.

University of Tennessee Medical School, Memphis, Tennessee. UT Medical School is a state-supported school that produces and distributes "for a nominal charge" on purchaser-supplied video cassette the film "Someone to Lean On: Your Job as a Support Person" (for husbands and others in the delivery room). The project was state-funded.

University of Texas, Center for Occupational Curriculum Development, Austin, Texas. UT-Austin is a state-supported school that produces and sells about 150 vocational education course packages, including transparencies or slide/tape sets. One slide/tape course, visual merchandising, was developed by

Sears, Roebuck and Co. and is the only course restricted for "sale to schools only." Other subjects include agriculture, health occupations, home economics, marketing, and industrial education. All Texas public schools receive a 20 percent discount off the catalog price. Texas residents must add 5 percent state and local sales taxes to the purchase price. "Complimentary and desk copies are not available since the Center operates on a cost-recovery basis." Its catalog, mailed under state indicia, describes the center as "a nonprofit, self-sustaining department" of the university. "Sales jumped 71 percent the first year" the Center advertised in the trade press (1970–1971). "No public funds are used for advertising. . . . We must rely on sales to keep our Center in operation."

Utah State University Foundation, Logan, Utah. This nonprofit corporation sells CHEC—Consumer & Home Economics Careers. It is available individually as 37 career modules or as a unit for use at the junior high school level. Each module includes audio cassettes. CHEC was developed over a four-year period by the Utah State Board of Education, the Utah State University, and eight Utah school districts. "All revenues will go . . . to cover costs at the . . . Foundation, with whatever is left over channeled back to Utah State University to allow the continuation of research and development activities." Sales kit includes "letters of recommendation" from other schools and "sample proposal forms" to be used for obtaining funding to purchase CHEC. It is listed in *VocEd* magazine's January/February 1982 "Directory of Suppliers" and has exhibited at the American Vocational Association's December 1981 and December 1982 conferences. The foundation has advertised in *VocEd*.

Vocational Education Productions-See California Polytechnic State University.

Vocational Research Institute, Philadelphia, Pennsylvania. A division of the Philadelphia Jewish Employment and Vocational Service (JEVS), VRI is a nonprofit, community-supported organization. JEVS, underwritten by the U.S. Department of Labor for more than a decade, produces and distributes three sets of work samples (including hardware and software) for vocational assessment. The first set, JEVS, designed for special-needs populations, is "now being used in more than six hundred facilities." The second, VITAS, designed for the disadvantaged, is the product of a three-year Department of Labor contract. The third, VIEWS, is designed for the mentally retarded. Listed in *VocEd* magazine's January/February 1982 "Directory of Suppliers," VRI exhibited at the American Vocational Association's December 1981 and December 1982 conferences and has advertised in *VocEd*.

Vocational Studies Center-See University of Wisconsin.

Wetacom, Washington, D.C. Wetacom is the taxable business subsidiary of WETA, a public television and radio broadcasting station. It offers "broadcast quality" teleconferencing (including program development) for which it draws on all the resources of the nonprofit parent: "With our own satellite and distribution service (270 public service stations nationally) we have the most economical service available in Washington, D.C. With our own studios,

highly trained technical and creative staff and 20 years of broadcast experience, we also think we are the best and most professional service around."

WGVC-TV, Allendale, Michigan. A public television station, WGVC-TV is
licensed to Grand Valley State Colleges, which sells video production services.

University of Wisconsin, Vocational Studies Center, Madison, Wisconsin. A state-
supported school, UW produces and sells, through the center, 50 microcomputer programs, films, and filmstrip/cassette sets for high school and college
students and adults in agriculture, career education, special needs, and
youth development. Some of the center's materials were produced by the
Wisconsin Foundation for Vocational, Technical, and Adult Education, Inc.
(see separate entry); some were state or federally funded. Wisconsin residents are charged a state sales tax. The center also offers technical assistance,
training, and consulting services to schools, state agencies, and businesses
in basic skills and vocational programming, microcomputer applications,
curriculum development, career counseling, and other areas. It is listed in
VocEd magazine's January/February 1982 "Directory of Suppliers." The center
exhibited at the American Vocational Association's December 1981 conference
and advertises in *VocEd*.

*Wisconsin Foundation for Vocational, Technical, and Adult Education, Inc., Mad-
ison, Wisconsin.* This nonprofit corporation produces and distributes two
video courses, each consisting of 30 videotapes, in electricity and marketing
for high school and college students. Listed in *VocEd* magazine's January/
February 1982 "Directory of Suppliers," the foundation exhibited at the
American Vocational Association's December 1981 and December 1982 conferences and has advertised in *Instructional Innovator*.

Appendix B to Chapter 6

Producers of Materials Distributed by the National Audiovisual Center, Excluding Departments and Agencies of the Federal Government

Arizona Center for Occupational Safety and Health
American Hospital Association
American Gastroenterological Association
American Rehabilitation Foundation
American Public Welfare Association
Association of Professors of Gynecology and Obstetrics
Baylor University
    College of Dentistry
Boston College
    Physics Department
California Department of Transportation
CBS Television Network
Chicago Dental Society
Children's Memorial Hospital
Connecticut State Department of Education
    Special Education Resource Center
Case Western Reserve University
    School of Medicine
Delaware Valley Regional Planning Commission-Philadelphia, PA
Emory University
    School of Dentistry
    Nell Hodgson Woodruff School of Nursing
Florida Department of Agriculture and Consumer Services
    Division of Forestry

Fox Valley Special Education Instructional Materials Center-Oshkosh, WI
Far West Laboratory for Educational Research Development
Georgia Heart Association
Georgia Department of Offender Rehabilitation-Atlanta, GA
George Washington University Medical Center
Montefiore Hospital and Medical Center
Indiana University
   School of Dentistry
Johns Hopkins University
McCulloch Corporation
Medical College of Georgia
McGill University-Montreal, Quebec, Canada
Midwest Regional Media Center for the Deaf
Medical University of South Carolina
   College of Dental Medicine
   Department of Endodontics
National Association for Industry-Education Cooperation
Smithsonian Institution
   National Air and Space Museum
   National Gallery of Art
North Atlantic Treaty Organization
New Mexico League of Women Voters
Northwestern University Dental School
University of Oregon
   Northwest Special Education Instructional Materials Center
Ohio Regional Medical Audiovisual Consortium
Ohio State University
   College of Dentistry
   College of Medicine
Pennsylvania Commission for Women
Planned Parenthood of Fresno, CA
React International, Inc.
Southern Regional Media Center for the Deaf
State University of New York at Buffalo
Temple University-Philadelphia, PA
Truman Centennial Committee
Texas Rehabilitation Commission
Texas Transportation Institute
University of Alaska
   Marine Advisory Program
University of Arkansas for Medical Sciences
University of California at Los Angeles
University of Cincinnati
   College of Medicine

Department of Biomedical Communications
University of Colorado
  Medical School
  Department of Anatomy
United Cerebral Palsy Association of Santa Clara County, CA
University of Denver
  Graduate School of Librarianship
  Center for Communication and Information Research
  Denver Research Institute
University of Illinois at the Medical College
  Abraham Lincoln School of Medicine
University of Illinois at the Medical Center
  College of Dentistry
  Department of Operative Dentistry
University of Iowa
  Department of Preventive Medicine and Environmental Health
  Institute of Agricultural Medicine and Environmental Health
University of Illinois
Washington State University
  Cooperative Extension
University of Texas at Austin
  School of Social Work
  Resource Center on Child Abuse and Neglect
University of Tennessee
  Division of Biomedical Communication Medical Units
University of Wisconsin
  Special Education Instructional Materials Center
WNVT-TV-Annandale, VA
Wayne State University
  School of Medicine

VII.

How Government Competes Unfairly With the Private Sector

In theory, the goods and services provided by federal, state, and local governments are public goods, but in reality governments at all levels compete unfairly with private businesses. State and local governments provide parks, campgrounds, marinas, amusement facilities, fitness facilities, audiovisual and computer software products, and hospital services, but this is only the tip of the iceberg. Governments in the U.S. produce literally thousands of goods and services in direct competition with private businesses.

Even more disturbing are the legislative and regulatory advantages granted to government enterprises. They enjoy all of the special privileges of commercial nonprofit enterprises, such as exemption from federal, state, and local income, sales, and property taxes and immunity from minimum wage, securities, bankruptcy, antitrust, and myriad other regulations. Government enterprises can also exercise the power of eminent domain and borrow at interest rates considerably below those paid by their taxpaying competitors (especially small firms) because of tax-exempt interest payments. Their capital and operating costs are subsidized by tax revenues, and, perhaps most importantly, they are often granted monopoly status by law. Thus, competition between private businesses and government enterprises is even more inequitable than competition between private firms and commercial nonprofit enterprises.

Even if consumers find private-sector substitutes for governmentally provided goods and services, they may still be forced to pay taxes to subsidize the government enterprise. Parents who send their children to private schools, for instance, must pay tuition and must also continue to pay property and other taxes to support public schools. Nevertheless, thousands of parents send their children to private schools, revealing dissatisfaction with public education. There is evidence that taxpayers are dissatisfied with many other governmental services as well.

Unfair Competition by Federal Government Enterprises

The federal government provides what many consider to be public goods, such as national defense and the justice system, but it also provides thousands of purely private goods and services. Former Senator S.I. Hayakawa (R-Ca.) stated in 1981: "Federal employees are currently operating over 11,000 commercial or industrial activities that the private sector also performs. . . ."[1] The Senator added: "Since the business of government is not to be in business, I ask myself why." The reason probably has something to do with the desire to supplement agency budgets with commercial profits. As seen in Table 7.1, federal agencies enter businesses as mundane as laundry work and as sophisticated as engineering and computer programming. All of the services listed in Table 7.1 are also provided by private firms.

TABLE 7.1
Examples of Commercial Occupations in the Federal Government
(as of October 31, 1981)

Occupation	Number of Employees
Painting and paperhanging	10,207
Industrial equipment operation	18,061
Food preparation and serving	22,680
Plumbing and pipefitting	18,640
Metal work	25,579
Warehousing and stockhandling	39,762
Laundry work	2,131
Guards	8,193
Computer operators	10,241
Computer specialist	30,617
Engineers and architects	154,210
Librarians and archivists	9,761
Supply clerks and technicians	31,501
Mail and file clerks	23,536
Electricians	13,096

Source: U.S. Office of Personnel Management.

Government Sponsored Enterprises. Over 70 years ago, the federal government entered the credit business by creating off-budget "government sponsored enterprises" (GSEs), including the Federal Home Loan Banks (FHLB), the Federal Home Loan Mortgage Corporation (FHLMC), the Federal National Mortgage Association (FNMA), the Student Loan Marketing Association (SLMA), and the Farm Credit System (FCS). According to the *Budget of the U.S. Government*, government sponsored enterprises "were created as government institutions, [but] all have been privately owned since 1969 and are not included in the . . . budget." Moreover, "since they were designed for the furtherance of government objectives . . . they . . . enjoy special benefits not received by other private financial intermediaries."[2]

GSE debt enjoys equal standing with U.S. Treasury debt as investments for most banks; GSEs are exempt from Securities and Exchange Commission and state banking regulation. Most of the enterprises also have a line of credit at the U.S. Treasury and their investors' interest income is exempt from state and local income taxes. The FHLB and the FCS do not pay any federal taxes on their earnings (see Table 7.2).

These special advantages have helped GSEs expand the amount of credit they can offer, primarily in housing, agriculture, and education. Consequently, this type of subsidized lending has grown more than three times faster than unsubsidized lending by private financial intermediaries. "Over the last five years [1980–1985], outstanding GSE debt grew by 142%, from $153 billion in 1980 to $370 billion in 1985. By comparison, loans outstanding to private businesses and corporations grew 45% over the same period."[3] Thus, GSE lending crowds out lending by private financial intermediaries, which in turn crowds out non-preferred private-sector individuals and businesses. "In general, sectors [of the economy] that do not benefit from the presence of a GSE will have less financing allocated to them, and the financing that is available will be more expensive because there is less of it."[4]

GSEs may be privately owned, but they are largely governmentally controlled. Many of the board members are presidential appointees, and various decisions often must be cleared by other governmental agencies and the Treasury Department. For example, the secretary of Housing and Urban Development must approve many FNMA decisions. In 1977, HUD secretary Patricia Harris noted the "mythical

TABLE 7.2

Competitive Advantages of Government-Sponsored Enterprises

Type of Benefit	FHLB	FHLMC	FNMA	FCS	SLMA
Line of credit at Treasury	Yes	Yes[1]	Yes	Yes	Yes
Exemption of corporate earnings from Federal income tax	Yes	No	No	Yes[2]	No
Exemption of interest income of investors from state and local income taxes	Yes	No	No	Yes	Yes
Eligibility for Federal Reserve open market purchases	Yes	Yes	Yes	Yes	Yes
Equal standing with Treasury debt as investments for most banks	Yes	Yes	Yes	Yes	Yes
Exemption from SEC registration and various state banking laws	Yes	Yes	Yes	Yes	Yes
Eligibility as collateral for public deposits	Yes	Yes	Yes	Yes	Yes

[1]Indirect line of credit through the FHLBs.
[2]Federal Land Banks, Federal Intermediate Credit Banks, and Federal Land Bank Associations.
Source: *Budget of the U.S. Government for Fiscal Year 1987*, Special Analysis F, "Federal Credit Programs," p. F-23.

nature" of "private" corporations such as GSEs by citing the following differences between FNMA and genuinely private businesses:

1. A large, ongoing and profitable business was turned over to the management and the holders of the equity interest in FNMA. By inheriting the assets and liabilities of the predecessor corporation, FNMA was assured that it would face no effective competition.

2. [FNMA] has the benefits of federal economic support through: authority to borrow up to 2–1/2 billion dollars from the U.S. Treasury; receiving the same preferential treatment for its securities as is accorded to the government-owned Ginne Mae [Government National Mortgage Association]; and use of Federal Reserve banks as fiscal agents.

3. [FNMA] is exempt from state taxes . . . as well as from Securities and Exchange Commission requirements, just as government entities are.[5]

Private mortgage lenders have protested the unfair competition from FNMA, which has "raised its investable funds under the protection of the Treasury at rates below the rates private investors paid for their funds."[6] These complaints appear to be justified. In 1980, for example, FNMA owned $56 billion in mortgages with an average life of over 14 years and an average yield of about 9.5 percent.[7] While betting on long-term rates to drop, FNMA relied heavily on short-term financing, accumulating $17 billion in short-term debt that had to be refinanced within a year. The agency borrowed about half of the $17 billion at 17 percent, with the remainder at about 9.7 percent. The entire $17 billion had to refinanced at about 17 percent, and FNMA lost $146 million in the first half of 1981. Despite these huge losses, the agency had no trouble rolling over its debt, which had been trading at less than a percentage point above short-term Treasury bills because of the federal government's implicit guarantee. Unlike private businesses, FNMA has the legal right to ask the U.S. Treasury to purchase as much as $2.5 billion of its debt to provide liquidity. FNMA (and other GSEs) are legally protected from such losses and, therefore, have weak incentives to avoid them.

Government sponsored enterprises are not the only vehicle through which the federal government competes with the private credit industry. During recent years, the federal government has directed more than half of all credit extended in the country through borrowing to finance the federal deficit, direct loans, guaranteed loans, and the activities of the off-budget Federal Financing Bank. In 1985, federal government agencies extended $64.4 billion in direct loans to subsidize economically inefficient but politically popular investments. The federal budget document reads: "Since Federal credit is subsidized, it can alter resource allocation . . . and . . . result in a loss in economic efficiency."[8] One example of this kind of subsidy is price support loans to farmers through the Commodity Credit Corporation. Others include the Farmers Home Administration, which lends money to farmers to purchase homes at subsidized rates; the Rural Electrification Administration, which subsidizes the owners and customers of power plants; military sales to foreign governments, which are supported by subsidized lending by the federal government; and the Export-Import Bank, which subsidizes American corporations that are in the exporting and importing business. In other words, large corporate farms, relatively wealthy rural landowners, large corporations, and foreign governments are the main beneficiaries of these lending programs. Thus, the programs are inequitable as well as inefficient.

The federal government also competes in the credit markets by guaranteeing loans that private creditors award to preferred borrowers. In 1984 the federal government guaranteed $55.5 billion in loans, most of them as subsidies to farmers, rural homeowners, students and their parents, homeowners, veterans, export and import businesses, and a handful (less than 1 percent) of small businesses.

Another federal financing vehicle is the off-budget Federal Financing Bank (FFB), which allocated $18.3 billion in credit in 1985. Various federal agencies, such as the Farmers Home Administration, the Rural Electrification Administration, the Student Loan Marketing Association, the Tennessee Valley Authority, the U.S. Postal Service, and others compete with private financial institutions through the FFB, an arm of the U.S. Treasury. The agencies can procure funds from the FFB that are off the books, and the agencies may then grant loans to their "preferred customers." The entire process is largely hidden from public view. Most of the FFB's off-budget subsidized loans went to farmers, foreign military purchasers, students, homeowners, exporters and importers, and the Tennessee Valley Authority. Private lenders simply cannot compete with government agencies that have the ability to tap the U.S. Treasury.

The Federal Publishing Business. Although much government printing consists of publishing congressional hearings, executive branch memoranda, IRS tax forms, and other tools of running the government, much of it is commercial and, therefore, competes unfairly with private printers. The Government Printing Office (GPO) is the largest federal publishing facility. According to the director of the GPO: "We have . . . 33 acres under our roof, 6,200 employees, of which over 5,000 . . . are in the main plants and well over 100 presses. . . . We are probably the largest . . . printer in the United States." There are also "more than 300 printing plants located in many government agencies."[9]

Even a cursory look at the GPO's monthly catalog of publications reveals that the federal government competes on a large scale with private publishing companies. Consider the following examples from the January 1987 catalog.[10] *The Backyard Mechanic* ($5.50) "can help you save money by doing simple auto repair and maintenance jobs yourself" and "discusses ignition systems and spark plugs and guides you through a tuneup, a brake relining, a brake system flushing and bleeding, a power-break check, . . . " etc. Oddly enough, the debt-ridden federal government claims expertise in financial management. In *Managing for Profits* ($5.50) readers are instructed in "production and marketing, purchasing and collections, financial management, taxation, insurance, and more." Also in the financial planning area, *Starting and Managing a Business of Your Own* ($1.75) offers tips on how to start and how to manage a business. *Insurance and Risk Management for Small Business* ($3.00) "provides basic information in selecting insurance and in reducing risk for the small businessman." The GPO also publishes advice to the individual investor in *A Guide to Individual Retirement Accounts*, which discusses "the various savings and investment vehicles available."

The federal government may be notorious for producing barely comprehensible laws, regulations, and forms, but it offers published advice on *How Plain English Works for Business* ($4.75): "twelve case studies describe how some business organizations have scored success by simplifying consumer documents."

One of the biggest areas of commercial book sales during the last few years has been health and fitness, including diet and exercise books. The federal government competes in this market with such publications as *Dietary Guidelines and Your Diet* ($4.50), which advises people to "maintain desirable weight; avoid too much fat; avoid too much sugar; and if you drink alcoholic beverages, do so in moderation." The federal government competes with the flourishing cookbook industry by publishing hundreds of cookbooks, including *Country Catfish* ($2.00), which "describes 18 ways to serve them" and exhorts that "Catfish are great—either plain or fancy." *Getting Fit Your Way* ($3.00) provides consumers with "a total physical fitness program" and also "contains information on weight control and how to stop smoking." Pregnant women concerned about their weight can purchase *Maternal Weight Gain and the Outcome of Pregnancy* for $1.75 to learn how smoking habits, age, and family income affect maternal weight gain. There is also *An Introduction to Running: One Step at a Time* ($2.75) for those desiring advice on "running style, warming up and cooling down, where to run, wearing apparel, and much more." For those who prefer walking to running there is *Walking for Exercise and Pleasure* ($1.00) which discusses "the importance of walking as a form of exercise." And the more energetic can learn how to build their own fitness trails in *Fitness Trail: Building, Signing, and Using the Trail* ($1.75). Children's health is a prominent part of any commercial bookstore, and the federal government competes in that area by publishing such books as *Your Child From 6 to 12* ($2.75), and *My Baby, Strong and Healthy* ($3.75) which gives directions on "making children's toys and games from household throwaways."

The GPO produces more than 18,000 publications, including all these books and thousands more that compete with commercial publishers. And they compete at a considerable advantage because of taxpayer subsidies and other benefits. Taxpayers pay for both the production of books and pamphlets and for the marketing as well. The GPO proudly boasts: "In addition to our mail order service, we [the GPO] maintain a nationwide network of Government bookstores."[11] All these subsidies enable the federal government to make a profit while charging prices that are lower than commercial publishers can ask. And the potential for profit is considerable. Some books, such as *Infant Care: Your Child from 1 to 6*, *Septic Tank Care*, and *Adult Physical Fitness*, have sold over a million copies.

In addition to underpricing commercial publishers, the federal government distributes countless "free" publications as a public relations strategy. For example, many federal agencies cooperate with the Consumer Information Center which publishes the quarterly *Consumer Information Catalogue* that describes over 200 brochures, pamphlets, and periodicals, many of which are free. Consumers can order up to 20 "free" items on such topics as "Money Management," "Travel and Hobbies," "Automobiles," and "Gardening."

Unfair Competition by State and Local Governments

State and local government enterprises provide few goods and services that are *not* private goods. At the local level of government the major category of expenditure is education, even though education is not a public good. Private schools existed long before public schools were established in the U.S., and they still proliferate despite the competitive disadvantages they face. At one time, there was a pretense that public schools provided a uniform education to everyone, but the great disparities that are apparent in the quality of public schools have abolished that myth. Supporters also argued that morality could be better taught in public schools, but many parents are concerned about the *lack* of morality taught in public schools, while others believe that teaching morality violates the constitutional separation of church and state.[12] Public education is also said to increase worker productivity through skill enhancement, but that, too, is questionable in light of the decades-long decline in educational achievement in primary and secondary education. Private schools, by contrast, have demonstrated superior quality education despite fewer financial resources.[13] Moreover, the mere fact that education may increase worker productivity does not justify governmental provision of education. In fact, the opposite may be closer to the truth. If one wishes to increase worker productivity through education, the appropriate direction should be in favor of private provision of education, not public provision, given the superior quality of private schools. Thus, the reason why local governments nearly monopolize the primary and secondary education industry is not likely to have much to do with market failure. Local governments have simply taken over a purely private activity.

Local governments provide dozens of other private goods and services. Appendix Table A7.1 lists a sample of 57 different services provided by both local governments and the private sector. As shown there, local governments are involved in many private activities, including garbage collection, tree trimming, transportation, day care, and housing. The mere existence of private sector firms in all these categories is direct evidence that they are inherently *not* public goods, but private goods. It would appear that there is no *economic* justification for governmental provision of *any* of these services. The most likely explanation for governmental provision of these services (and of public education) is the natural inclination among governmental bureaucracies to expand their domain by whatever means possible. Competing with private business is apparently an expeditious way of doing this, given that local governments have the taxing, spending, and regulatory power to do so. By using tax revenues to subsidize local government enterprises and imposing costly taxes and regulations on private sector competitors, local governments can easily dominate many industries.

State governments are also guilty of usurping the domain of the private sector. States spend vast amounts of money on education, highways, hospitals and health care, parks and recreation, liquor stores, and utilities—all private goods. There is no economic reason, for example, why state governments should monopolize liquor stores.

State governments are involved in dozens of other commercial enterprises. New York, for example, runs a transportation business, operates museums, constructs "industrial exhibits," operates sports arenas, builds parks and other recreational facilities, finances home mortgages, and many other activities. Other states do the same.

The Relative Inefficiency of Government Enterprises. As government enterprises crowd out private-sector businesses, costs are imposed not only on the businesses displaced but also on taxpayers. First, non-taxpaying businesses replace taxpaying businesses. Second, and more importantly, government enterprises are generally less efficiently run than private, competitive businesses and, therefore, need more resources to produce a given level of goods. Because these resources could have been used to produce other goods and services, the economy's productive capacity is reduced. Everyone is poorer than they would be had government left the provision of private goods and services to the private sector.

There are two important theoretical reasons why private firms should produce goods and services more efficiently than government enterprises. First, government enterprises generally serve a given political entity whose geographical boundaries may have been the result of historical accident rather than a conscious economic decision. Therefore, the size or scale of operation for government enterprises may not be optimal to achieve minimum cost.

In contrast to a public enterprise, private firms may adjust their scale of operations to exploit fully any economies of scale or to avoid any diseconomies that may be present. The government enterprise often serves all residents of the political jurisdiction, so that the scale of operation is determined by political considerations, not by economic criteria. If diseconomies exist, the political unit may be so large that an inefficient scale of operation is required. Alternatively, if economies of scale are such that unit costs decline as size increases, the jurisdiction may be too small to capture the economic benefits of optimal size. Even if a political jurisdiction is the ideal size for the production of a good or service, all goods and services provided by government enterprises are not subject to identical economies of scale.[14] Thus, the efficient provision of one service may necessitate the inefficient provision of another.

Even if optimal plant size were not a problem, the incentive structures between the two types of organizations are vastly different. Private firms must face the discipline imposed by the market mechanism. An inefficient firm runs the risk of incurring losses in the short run and being forced from the market by lower-cost competitors in the long run. Private-sector managers are worse off *personally* whenever their inefficiency causes profits to fall. They often own stock in the company, so that higher costs and lower profits reduce their own wealth. Lower profitability also reduces their opportunities for promotion and salary increases. Inefficient managers also face the possibility of losing their jobs because of a corporate takeover. Takeovers are a means by which inefficiently-run businesses are taken over by entrepreneurs who often fire most of the existing management and replace them with their own staff in the hope of increasing the firm's efficiency and raising profit levels. Private-sector managers, therefore, face the carrot of reward—increased salary, promotions, and personal advancement—for efficient performance and the stick of punishment— salary retrenchment, fewer professional opportunities, or being fired—for poor performance. These incentives do not necessarily guarantee efficiency, but they strongly encourage it.

The managers of government enterprises face neither the carrot of reward nor the stick of punishment. It is nearly impossible to fire government employees, no matter how poor their performance may be. As former Senator Charles Percy (R-Ill.) once said: "A manager in the executive branch of the federal government who finds it necessary to terminate an unproductive or noncontributing employee . . . must be prepared to spend 25 percent to 50 percent of his time for a period that may run . . . to 18 months. In many cases, managers have chosen to work around such a person or to promote the employee out of the office in order to quickly be rid of the problem."[15] In the public sector, incompetence is often rewarded, not punished; the only practical way to get rid of an incompetent employee may be to promote him!

Managers of government enterprises have, at best, minimal incentives for encouraging economic efficiency. Because there are no profit-and-loss statements in the public sector, managers do not benefit financially from cost reductions, nor do they bear the burden of cost increases.

Politicians also have something to do with relative inefficiency of government enterprises. In theory, elected politicians monitor the activities of government enterprises to ensure efficient production. In reality, it is difficult, impossible, or politically unwise for politicians to carry out rigorous oversight. One reason is that there is often no direct way to evaluate the output of governmentally provided services. When services are difficult or costly to measure, inputs such as the number of employees and the size of budget are used as surrogates for output. Politicians, therefore, are inclined to associate increases in inputs, e.g, budget size and number of employees, equipment, etc., with increases in output. There are reasons why politicians would encourage this growth. A high level of public employment facilitates a politician's survival in office by providing more opportunities for patronage. In addition, research has shown that because government employees are more intensely interested in the growth of government than the average citizen, they tend to be more politically active and to vote more frequently.[16] Thus, they are likely to exert a greater impact on governmental decision making than the average voter.

Finally, because government enterprises are often statutory monopolies, taxpayers would be distressed if service were interrupted due to a public employee strike. If the workers at a local supermarket go on strike, consumers can buy groceries elsewhere. But when the city trash collectors, schoolteachers, firefighters, or police officers go on strike, consumers must simply do without—often at the peril of public safety. Because voter displeasure can be deadly to politicians at election time, there is little incentive to stress cost-cutting measures (i.e., employee reduction) that might lead to public employee strikes or slowdowns. For all of these reasons government enterprises often employ more workers than they need.

Public vs. Private-Sector Production: The Evidence

A large body of empirical evidence supports the hypothesis that public-sector production is more costly than private-sector production. The evidence is so overwhelming that a "Bureaucratic Rule of Two" has been suggested: Whenever a service is provided by public rather than private enterprise, its unit cost will about double. The rule applies not only in the U.S., but also in Canada, Australia, Europe, and Asia.[17] Numerous studies reveal that taxpayers would pay considerably less for the same or better quality services if they were provided by private businesses (see Appendix Table A7.2). Many of the studies demonstrate that not only is private-sector provision less costly, it is also of higher quality. For example, the privately run United Parcel Service (UPS) handles twice as many parcels as the U.S. Postal Service; UPS is faster: a parcel sent by mail from Washington, D.C. to Los Angeles takes more than eight days— longer than a Pony Express trip from Missouri to California in 1861; the damage rate at UPS is one-fifth that of the Postal Service; UPS insures every parcel up to $100 without an extra charge; UPS keeps a record of each parcel; for a fee, UPS will pick up parcels from the sender; UPS makes three delivery attempts, compared with only one by the Postal Service. UPS also charges lower rates.

A study of public and private education (cited in Table A7.2) found that private schools generally offer higher quality education than public schools do, even though private schools spend about 50 percent less *per pupil*. There is some controversy surrounding these findings, but there is a growing recognition that they are probably correct. For instance, a recent Gallup poll found that more than half of American parents would send their children to private schools if they could afford it. Another survey found that black parents are more likely to send their children to private schools than white parents, even though they have to pay both private tuition and taxes to support public schools.[17] So dissatisfied are black parents with public education that they have established hundreds of their own private schools throughout the country.[19]

In the study of fire protection cited in Table A7.2, private companies supplied fire protection services at about half the cost of public-sector fire protection and were also much more innovative. They invented such devices as robotic fire-fighting equipment to minimize the possibility of injury to firefighters—equipment that would probably be opposed by public employee unions. They used higher-capacity hoses than their public sector counterparts, applied creative staffing patterns, and even used high-visibility paint on their fire trucks to reduce the likelihood of accidents. The profit motive is always a spur to such innovation, and these techniques have spread from one town in Arizona to other private-sector companies in Tennessee, Georgia, Florida, and elsewhere.

These examples illustrate the fundamental behavioral differences between private, competitive businesses and government enterprises. In 1944, economist Ludwig von Mises wrote:

> the terms *bureaucrat, bureaucratic,* and *bureaucracy* are clearly invectives. Nobody calls himself a bureaucrat or his own methods of management bureaucratic. These words are always applied with an opprobrious connotation. They always imply a disparaging criticism of persons, institutions, or procedures. . . . The abusive implication of the terms in question is not limited to America and other democratic countries. It is a universal phenomenon.[20]

Private-sector managers may have as much desire for "the quiet life" as public sector managers, but *competition* provides them with incentives to hold down costs. In the public sector such market pressures are largely absent. The only recourse that taxpayers have to costly and inefficiently-provided services is to either "vote with their feet"—move to another political jurisdiction—or replace incumbent politicians at election time. Neither of these actions, however, has effectively disciplined bureaucratic management in the public sector. Bureaucratic incentives and methods exist in all governments, and all politicians face the same incentives. As government enterprises crowd out private businesses, the inevitable result will be higher-cost and lower- quality provision of goods and services.

Unfair Competition and Political Corruption

Although many view white-collar crime as a serious social problem, there are laws and regulations designed to guard against it and hundreds of millions of dollars annually are spent each year on enforcement. The marketplace also punishes corporate crime. If the wrongdoing reduces stockholders' profits they will sell their shares and invest elsewhere. When stock prices decline a firm becomes a likely target for a takeover. After a successful takeover, corrupt managers lose their jobs. Lower profits also reduce the income and wealth of management directly, even without a takeover. A corporate scandal of large enough proportions can even lead to bankruptcy.

Market and legal restraints on corruption are largely absent in the public sector. In fact, those who are sometimes susceptible to corruption—politicians—are the ones who are responsible for enforcing the laws against it. Political corruption is apparently a very serious problem in one type of enterprise that competes vigorously (and unfairly) with private businesses—off-budget government enterprises (OBEs). OBEs are established largely by state and local governments as a means of evading constitutional or statutory limitations on taxing, spending, and borrowing. They are given legislative privileges that exceed even those of on-budget agencies, for example, special powers of eminent domain and exemption from civil service regulations. Thus, not only are OBEs detached from market pressures, they are also not subject to any significant *political* discipline. For this reason they have been breeding grounds not only for gross managerial inefficiency (recall the WPPSS and New York State off-budget spending debacles briefly mentioned in chapter 3), but also for political fraud and corruption.

Many episodes of political corruption within OBEs are documented in a recent book, *The Machinery of Greed*, written by investigative journalist Diana Henriques.[21] Among the forms of OBE corruption catalogued by Henriques are

the outright sale of jobs, the firing of whistle-blowers and cooperative government witnesses, and the use of authority payrolls
for the direct support of political consulting contracts or politically wired brokers, . . . [the use of] contracts to extort political
campaign contributions, to foster the welfare of [OBE] managers
themselves, and to enhance the values of selected politicians'
real estate. . . . Loans have been used to finance mob-controlled
construction projects. In one case, a totally fictitious public
authority was created in a complicated investment scam in which
bond investors unwittingly were to provide the funds for the
political payoffs. Abusers have inflated insurance premiums,
received kickbacks on motor fleet purchases, set up lush tax-
shelter deals, and sold useless equipment, supplies, or land to
public authorities.[22]

Some examples of such corruption include an engineering company that was "shaken down for a $100,000 political contribution . . .
in return for a contract" from a local utility authority in New Jersey;
the chairman of the Massachussetts Bay Transit Authority in Boston
was sentenced to a seven-to-ten-year jail term because of an extensive
kickback operation; and in "one of the largest public frauds on record
at the time" three Pennsylvania Turnpike Commission officers were
convicted of conspiring to steal $19.5 million in construction funds
by "transferring millions in turnpike funds [to] an engineering firm
headed by a . . . commissioner's nephew and his son."[23]

This kind of corruption is an inevitable consequence of a lack of
accountability. OBEs enjoy even greater legislative privileges than do
on-budget governmental enterprises, so they are likely to be even
more adept than on-budget government enterprises at crowding out
private businesses through unfair competition. As one writer concluded, OBEs "typify the modern practice of using public authorities
to perform work previously left to the private sector."[24] Unfortunately, as the private sector is replaced by off-budget government
enterprises, the effect is likely to be lower-quality and higher-cost
service as well as continued political fraud and corruption.

Conclusions

The direct expenditures of the federal government account for more
than one fourth of national income in the U.S. Although much of

that expenditure is for public goods, such as national defense and the federal justice system, federal employees are involved in over 11,000 private, commercial activities. As of 1987 there were at least nineteen wholly owned federal "corporations"[25] and numerous "quasi-governmental" credit agencies. The federal government is one of the largest electric power producers in the country, the largest insurer, the largest lender and borrower, the largest landlord (and tenant), the largest holder of grazing and timberland, a major grain owner, the largest shipowner, and probably the largest truck fleet operator, among other things. Given the inherently inferior quality and higher costs of governmental service provision, these enterprises could not have become as dominant as they are in a competitive marketplace. Governmental policies of unfair competition have given them artificial advantages with which they have driven many of their private-sector competitors from the market and deterred others from entering.

At the state and local levels, tens of thousands of off-budget government enterprises produce myriad goods and services that are often the domain of the private sector. There are also thousands of on-budget government enterprises that provide private goods and services ranging from airports to zoo maintenance. Considering that the U.S. is the world's principal exponent of private enterprise, this is a remarkable list. In the U.S., government has encroached on the domain of private enterprise on a massive scale through unfair competition by various types of government enterprises. The same bureaucratic incentives that have plagued nationalized industries in other countries are present in a large segment of the U.S. economy, especially at the state and local levels of government. It is ironic that countries all over the world— even communist dictatorships—are promoting private enterprise, while the U.S. continues to expand state ownership.[26] American taxpayers and consumers are picking up the bill, suffering the inevitable consequences of unfair competition: less efficient and more costly production of goods and services, lower quality, and, especially in the case of off-budget enterprises, political corruption.

Notes to Chapter 7

    1.   Sen. S.I. Hayakawa, Statement on "Government Competition With Small Business," *Hearings of U.S. Senate Committee on Small Business, Subcom-*

mittee on Advocacy (Washington: U.S. Government Printing Office, June 24, 1981), p. 1.

2. Executive Office of the President, *Budget of the U.S. Government for Fiscal Year 1987, "Special Analysis F,"* (Washington: U.S. Government Printing Office, 1986), p. F–22.

3. *Ibid.*

4. *Ibid.*

5. *Budget of the U.S. Government for Fiscal Year 1985, "Special Analysis F,"* (Washington: U.S. Government Printing Office, 1985), p. F–21.

6. Statement of Patricia Harris, *Hearings before the U.S. Senate Subcommittee on Housing and Urban Affairs*, 1968, pp. 1416–17, as cited in Lloyd Musolf, *Uncle Sam's Private, Profitseeking Corporations* (Lexington, MA: Lexington Books, 1983), p. 45.

7. A. Sloan, "Saving Fannie," *Forbes*, Oct. 26, 1981.

8. *Budget of the United States Government for Fiscal Year 1985*, p. 13. The following statistics are also taken from the U.S. Budget, various years. For a more detailed discussion of federal credit activities, see James T. Bennett and Thomas J. DiLorenzo, *Underground Government: The Off-Budget Public Sector* (Washington, D.C.: Cato Institute, 1983), chapter 7.

9. Danford L. Sawyer, Head of the U.S. Government Printing Office, *Hearings Before the House Appropriations Committee*, 97th Congress, 2nd Session, 1983, p. 14.

10. Copies may be obtained from Superintendent of Documents, U.S. Government Printing Office, Washington, D.C. 20402.

11. *U.S. Government Books* (Washington: GPO, Jan. 1987), inside front cover.

12. Jack High, "State Education: Have Economists Made A Case?" *Cato Journal* (Spring/Summer 1985): 305–24.

13. E.G. West, "Are American Schools Working?" Cato Institute *Policy Analysis*, August 3, 1983.

14. Werner Hirsch, *Urban Economic Analysis* (New York: McGraw-Hill, 1973).

15. Cited in Joel Havemann, "Can Carter Chop Through the Civil Service System?" *National Journal*, April 24, 1977, p. 619.

16. James Bennett and William Orzechowski, "The Voting Behavior of Bureaucrats: Some Empirical Evidence," *Public Choice* (1983): 271–84.

17. Thomas Borcherding, ed. *Budgets and Bureaucrats* (Chapel Hill, NC: Univ. of North Carolina Press, 1977); and Thomas Borcherding, Werner Pommerhene, and Friedrich Schnieder, "Comparing the Efficiency of Private and Public Production: The Evidence from Five Countries," *Zeitschrift fur Nationalokonomie* (1982): 127–56.

18. E.G. West, "Are American Schools Working?"

19. Joe Davidson, "Private Schools for Black Pupils are Flourishing," *Wall Street Journal*, April 15, 1987.

20. Ludwig von Mises, *Bureaucracy* (Westport, CT: Arlington House Publishers, 1944), p. 1.

21. Diana Henriques, *The Machinery of Greed: Public Authority Abuse and What to Do About It* (Lexington, MA: Lexington Books, 1986).

22. Diana Henriques, *The Machinery of Greed*, p. 37.

23. *Ibid.*

24. *Ibid.*, p. 52.

25. These include Federal Prison Industries, Commodity Credit Corporation, Tennessee Valley Authority, Federal Deposit Insurance Corp., Export-Import Bank of the U.S., Federal Crop Insurance Corporation, St. Lawrence Seaway Corp., Corporation for Public Broadcasting, Government National Mortgage Association, InterAmerican Foundation, Overseas Private Investment Corporation, U.S. Postal Service, Community Development Corporation, Board for International Broadcasting, Federal Financing Bank, Pennsylvania Avenue Development Corp., U.S. Railway Association, Pension Benefit Guaranty Corp., and the Legal Services Corp.

26. See, for example, Jim Hoagland, "Communist Leaders Administer A Dose of Capitalism," *Washington Post National Weekly Edition*, April 20, 1987; and "Vietnamese Present Rules to Liberalize Stagnant Economy," *Wall Street Journal*, April 20, 1987.

TABLE A7.1
Services Provided by Both Local Governments
and Private Businesses

Service	No. of Cities and Counties	% Using The Private Sector
Public Works/Transportation		
Residential solid waste collection	1,390	49
Commercial solid waste collection	1,143	58
Solid waste disposal	1,314	31
Street repair	1,640	26
Street/parking lot cleaning	1,483	9
Snow plowing/sanding	1,282	14
Traffic signal installation/maintenance	1,569	26
Meter maintenance/collection	767	5
Tree trimming/planting	1,454	31
Cemetery administration/maintenance	718	11
Inspection/code enforcement	1,588	6
Parking lot/garage operation	784	13
Bus system operation/maintenance	555	25
Paratransit system operation/maintenance	579	26
Airport operation	561	30
Public Utilities		
Utility meter reading	1,204	19
Utility billing	1,248	20
Street light operation	1,281	52
Public Safety		
Crime prevention/patrol	1,659	3
Police/fire communication	1,685	1
Fire prevention/suppression	1,520	1
Emergency medical service	1,361	16
Ambulance service	1,256	27
Traffic control/parking enforcement	1,502	1
Vehicle towing and storage	1,310	85
Health and Human Services		
Sanitary inspection	991	1
Insect/rodent control	1,059	13
Animal control	1,508	7
Animal shelter operation	1,262	14
Day care facility operation	441	35
Child welfare programs	567	6
Programs for elderly	1,190	5
Operation/management of public/elderly housing	611	12
Operation/management of hospitals	393	26
Public health programs	743	8

TABLE A7.1 (continued)

Service	No. of Cities and Counties	% Using the Private Sector
Drug/alcohol treatment programs	635	7
Operation of mental health/retardation programs/ facilities	508	7
Parks and Recreation		
Recreation services	1,458	6
Operation/maintenance of recreation facilities	1,539	8
Parks landscaping/maintenance	1,574	9
Operation of convention centers/auditoriums	452	8
Cultural and Arts Programs		
Operation of cultural/arts programs	707	9
Operation of libraries	1,189	1
Operation of museums	505	4
Support Functions		
Building/ground maintenance	1,669	19
Building security	1,499	7
Fleet management/vehicle maintenance		
Heavy equipment	1,642	31
Emergency vehicles	1,560	30
All other vehicles	1,622	28
Data processing	1,471	22
Legal services	1,605	48
Payroll	1,719	10
Tax bill processing	1,320	22
Tax assessing	1,098	6
Delinquent tax collection	1,254	10
Secretarial services	1,656	4
Personnel services	1,663	5
Labor relations	1,514	23
Public relations/information	1,547	7

Source: International City Management Assoc., *Municipal Yearbook 1983* (Washington, D.C.: ICMA, 1983), p. 215.

TABLE A7.2

Examples of Private/Public Sector Cost Comparison Studies

Author	Service Studied	Publication Source	Results
E. S. Savas	Refuse Collection	*Journal of Urban Analysis*, 1979	Private sector 29–37% less costly
L. DeAlessi	Electric Power	*Public Choice*, 1974	Private utilities have lower construction and operating costs, innovate more rapidly, offer more services
R. Ahlbrandt	Fire Protection	*Public Choice*, 1973	Private sector cost was only 47% of public sector cost
D. Davies	Airlines	*Journal of Law and Economics*, 1971	Private airlines in Australia operate more efficiently than public airlines
E. S. Savas	Postal Service	*Privatizing the Public Sector*, Chatham House, 1982	UPS handles twice as many parcels as U.S. Postal Service; UPS is faster; UPS rates are cheaper; UPS damage rate is one-fifth the U.S. Postal Services's; UPS makes 3 delivery attempts, Postal Service only one
C. Lindsay	Nursing Home Care	*Journal of Political Economy*, 1976	Veteran's Administration costs 83% higher than privately-provided care
W. Hsiao	Health Insurance Administration	*Inquiry*, 1978	Processing costs 35% greater for public firms
E. G. West	Primary and Secondary Education	Cato Institute *Policy Analysis*, 1983	Private schools spend 50% less, on average, than public schools; private schools usually provide higher quality education

TABLE A7.2 (continued)

Author	Service Studied	Publication Source	Results
U.S. General Accounting Office	Debt Collection	GAO Report FGMSD-78-434, Dec. 27, 1978	Federal government's debt collection is "expensive and slow" compared to commercial debt collectors
U.S. General Accounting Office	Ship Repair	GAO Report LCD-78-434, Dec. 27, 1978	On average, Navy ship repair costs are 17 times higher than commercial ship repair costs
J. T. Bennett and T. J. DiLorenzo	Weather Forecasting	Journal of Labor Research, 1983	Private sector cost only 28% of Federal government forecasters
U.S. General Accounting Office	Hydroelectric Power	GAO Report on "Increasing Productivity at Hydroelectric Plants," 1979	Cost/kilowatt hour $2.72 for private firms, $3.29 for Federal government
U.S. General Accounting Office	Day Care Centers	GAO "Report on National Day Care," 1979	Monthly cost/child $188 at Federal government day care centers; $102 at comparable private centers
J. T. Bennett and T. J. DiLorenzo	Military Base Support Services	Journal of Labor Research, 1983	Private contractors 15% less costly, on average than in-house provision
M. Crain and A. Zardkoohi	Water Supply	Journal of Law and Economics, 1978	Public agencies have higher operating costs than private firms
R. Poole	Policing Services	Cutting Back City Hall, Reason Press, 1976	Contracting out vehicle regulation enforcement, accident investigation, and noncrime calls for assistance to private firms cut costs of law enforcement

VIII.

Conclusions: What to Do About Unfair Competition?

The commercial nonprofit sector is an increasingly important part of the American economy. All levels of government provide thousands of private goods and services in competition with private enterprises, and the private commercial nonprofit sector is also large and rapidly growing. There are more than a million nonprofit organizations in the U.S., many of which are engaged in commercial enterprises. The private nonprofit sector alone employs one of every five service workers in the country and about 10 percent of all workers; this segment of the economy experienced an annual increase in employment of 3.7 percent from 1977 to 1982—a rate much faster than that recorded for all nonagricultural employees (2.0 percent). Nonprofit enterprises account for about 8 percent of GNP— more than is spent on either national defense or welfare, and comprise one of the fastest-growing sectors of the economy, with annual revenues in excess of $300 billion. In many large cities, private nonprofits employ more workers and spend more money than local governments.

The growth of the private nonprofit sector is a relatively recent phenomenon, because two thirds of existing nonprofits have been established since 1960. Many nonprofits were originally intended as private-sector appendages of federal spending programs, and have been largely funded by the federal government. Even though they are technically considered nonprofit organizations, many have entered into myriad commercial businesses over the past twenty years, profiting handsomely primarily because legislative privileges have enabled them to compete unfairly with private enterprises. The

199

commercial activities of the nonprofit sector are not new; they have accelerated in recent years as federal funding has declined and as nonprofits have found that commercial activities can be highly profitable.

This involvement of nonprofits in profit-making enterprises creates unfair competition that endangers future economic growth and competitive markets. The problem has become so serious that the 1986 White House Conference on Small Business judged unfair competition to be one of the three most important issues facing small business today. This issue clearly deserves the attention of policy makers, the general public, and all those who are interested in the future of private enterprise.

Why Worry About Unfair Competition?

Small businesses that are responsible for most of the new jobs in the U.S. economy are most adversely affected by unfair competition. In recent years, according to researchers at the Massachusetts Institute of Technology (MIT), "of all the . . . new jobs created . . . two thirds were created by firms with twenty or fewer employees, and about 80 percent were created by firms with 100 or fewer employees."[1] Even though small business ventures are risky and have relatively high failure rates, the MIT researchers found that small businesses "more than offset" the high failure rates with "their capacity to start up and expand dramatically. Larger businesses, in contrast, appear rather stagnant."[2] Larger firms, the researchers concluded, "are no longer the major providers of new jobs for Americans."[3] Moreover, businesses that create most of the new jobs "overwhelmingly tend to be providers of services"[4] rather than companies in manufacturing, agriculture, mining, and construction.

One of the reasons why small businesses find it so difficult to get established and to survive is unfair competition. Because commercial nonprofit enterprises are tax exempt, pay lower postal rates, and receive other subsidies, taxpaying businesses pay higher taxes than they would otherwise to make up for their "nonprofit" competitors' nonpayment of their fair share of taxes. Small businesses must also bear the costs of regulations that nonprofits need not comply with. Thus, unfair competition is crowding out of the market those organizations that are the principal source of new jobs in the economy, reducing the rate of economic growth and job creation.

Effects on Women, Minorities, and the Poor. Lower-income people have the most to lose when small businesses are crowded out of the marketplace. The small business sector is a particularly important avenue of employment for relatively unskilled workers—especially teenagers who are seeking their first jobs. Such jobs provide valuable, hard-to-find work experience that is indispensable to a successful working career. To the extent that entry level jobs are threatened by unfair competition, many employment opportunities will be lost. Thus, unfair competition places a disproportionately heavy burden on new entrants into the work force for whom these jobs often represent the only alternative to poverty. Disproportionately represented among this group are racial minorities which, because of racism, inferior educational opportunitites, and other factors, have been excluded from many economic opportunities.

Unfair competition also adversely affects another group of relatively new entrants into the work force—women. One of the most significant changes in the labor force over the past thirty years has been the increased participation by women, especially married women. Until relatively recently, female employment was concentrated in such areas as teaching, nursing, and clerical work because women chose careers that allowed them to move in and out of a job during their childbearing years. But more and more women have broken with these traditions in the post-World War II period, pursuing higher-paying careers in many other fields, particularly business. By entering such "nontraditional" fields, many women are choosing higher income over flexibility.

Despite their advances, women have had to face the age-old problem of breaking into the "old-boy" network, which is difficult to do in large corporate bureaucracies. But many women have overcome this problem by gaining entrepreneurial experience in a corporate setting and then moving into the small business sector, which is less bureaucratic. Researchers at the U.S. Chamber of Commerce have observed that women moved up in the business world "not only in larger corporations but also by the alternative routes of family businesses and enterprises they start up themselves."[5] Women now earn about one third of all business degrees, and about 28 percent of *all* businesses in the U.S. were owned by women in 1982, compared to only 7 percent in 1977.[6] More recent estimates from the U.S. Small Business Administration report that women now own about one third of the country's businesses, accounting for 3.4 million sole proprietorships that generated $56 billion in revenues in 1984.[7]

This is both good news and bad news for women. Women now have greater economic opportunities, but small businesses are the entities that are most adversely affected by unfair competition. Many of the advances that women and others have made in the small business sector have already been impaired by unfair competition, and further advances are likely to be slowed.

Productivity and Competitiveness. One of the major themes of this book is that nonprofit enterprises—private or governmental—are less efficient than private, competitive businesses (see chapters 3 and 7). This has serious economic implications for the productivity of the American economy; as the commercial nonprofit sector crowds out the private sector, overall productivity is diminished and less productive enterprises will be replacing more productive ones. This means that we must either use more resources to maintain the same quantity and quality of goods and services or face a decline in the quantity and quality of those goods and services.

When CNEs crowd out small businesses, there are also dire implications for the growth of personal income, which is primarily determined by the growth of worker productivity. With a rapidly-growing service sector, aggregregate income growth will increasingly depend upon productivity growth in the service sector. The service sector, however, has traditionally experienced sluggish productivity growth because it is labor intensive. In the capital-intensive manufacturing sector, capital investments in new plants or machinery are often quickly translated into substantial gains in output per worker. In more labor-intensive industries, however, productivity growth depends on increases in *human* capital—a better trained, educated, and experienced work force. It takes years, sometimes decades, to achieve significant improvements in the quality of the labor force, so that productivity growth in the service sector is necessarily slower.

As commercial nonprofit enterprises displace for-profit businesses, these productivity problems will be compounded. Because of the weak incentives for efficiency that exist in the nonprofit sector relative to the private sector, productivity growth is likely to be even slower in nonprofits. Productivity growth in the service sector—including both nonprofit and for-profit firms—is hampered by its labor intensity, and the predominance of nonprofit firms is likely to make matters worse. Because of the link between productivity and wages, American workers will inevitably become poorer.

The Rationales for Unfair Competition

Numerous rationales have been given for the subsidies and other legislative privileges granted to commercial nonprofit enterprises. But when there is unfair competition, the rationales are neither theoretically valid nor consistent with the evidence.

Thin Markets. Whenever the demand for a particular product is so small that a private firm cannot make a profit, nonprofits are supposedly granted special legislative privileges so that they can serve the market. But by definition, unfair competition occurs only when nonprofits compete with for-profit firms. If the thin-market rationale was valid, profitseeking firms would never have entered the industry in the first place. Moreover, nonprofits generally enter commercial activities where markets are very large and profitable, such as health care, fitness clubs, and audiovisual and computer software businesses.

Public Goods. One of the most common rationales used to justify the special privileges granted to nonprofits is that they provide public goods that commercial firms will not produce. It is true that many nonprofits do provide public goods and that tax exemptions and other subsidies help provide goods that benefit society. But the public goods rationale cannot be applied to the issue of unfair competition. Whenever there is unfair competition, by definition the goods and services provided are *private* goods; otherwise, for-profits would not supply them. U.S. governmental and commercial nonprofit enterprises provide literally thousands of *private* goods in competition with private enterprises, and one is hardpressed to discover *any* public goods or services provided by the commercial nonprofit sector.

Market Failure. One category of market failure—"contract failure"—is also used to justify special legislative privileges to commercial nonprofit enterprises. Specifically, whenever consumers find it difficult to judge a product's quality before purchasing it—as with health care, for instance—consumers are said to be at the mercy of suppliers. In such cases, profit-seeking firms will supposedly take advantage of consumer ignorance and increase their profits by offering lower-quality and higher-priced goods and services. Because of this tendency, nonprofits are widely held to be a more appropriate vehicle for the provision of certain types of services.

In theory, because the managers of nonprofits cannot *directly* claim any of the profits earned by their nonprofit enterprise, they have no incentive to reduce product quality or to raise prices. Instead, they are more inclined to reinvest the profits to provide even better quality services or to offer goods and services at lower prices. Many predict, therefore, that in industries where it is difficult for consumers to judge service quality nonprofits will provide better-quality and lower-priced services than proprietary firms. This argument stands reality on its head, as both economic reasoning and empirical evidence refute it.

Competitive pressures in private markets provide business firms with incentives to provide higher-quality and lower-priced services. By contrast, isolating nonprofit enterprises from competition through legislative privileges is likely to result in *lower-quality* and *higher-priced* services—just the opposite of the prediction made by the "market failure" theory. The evidence presented in this book supports this interpretation and contradicts the market failure theory. There is no convincing evidence, for example, that the quality of health care in nonprofit hospitals is superior to that in proprietaries (see chapter 4). In fact, the evidence suggests that proprietaries often provide *better* services than nonprofits. Nor is there any evidence that nonprofits are more cost conscious than proprietary hospitals. Again, the evidence points in the opposite direction: Proprietaries often provide lower-cost health care services of equivalent quality than nonprofits.

Perhaps the strongest evidence of the inherently inferior quality and higher costs of commercial nonprofit enterprises is found in chapter 7, which discusses government nonprofit enterprises. Numerous empirical studies have demonstrated how private, competitive markets are more conducive to lower-cost service provision than monopolistic governmental enterprises.

The fatal flaw in the "contract failure" or "consumer ignorance" rationale for unfair competition is the assumption that managers and employees of nonprofit enterprises do not personally benefit from the profits their nonprofits earn. While it is true that they cannot *directly* profit, they do profit indirectly, often at the expense of lower-quality and higher-cost services. Armed with legislative privileges and subsidies, and without the competitive pressures of private markets, they have wide discretion to promote their own personal careers and increase their personal wealth.

For example, as shown in chapter 4, there is evidence that the major beneficiaries of nonprofit hospitals are not consumers but the physicians who practice in them, the professional staffs who manage them, and the trustees who oversee them. Many individuals have profited handsomely from questionable real estate transactions, self dealing, and by charging exorbitant fees. Other examples of managerial profits from nonprofits were documented in chapter 5, which demonstrated that many YMCAs have become lavish private health clubs for affluent professionals. YMCA management and staff indirectly benefit from perquisites, hiring additional staff, and salaries financed with the profits of their "nonprofit" enterprise.

The clearest examples of the personal profits of nonprofit managers are found in the public sector. Government enterprises engaged in commercial activities have used their profits to further the political careers of the politicians who oversee them and to construct bureaucratic empires. There is also documentation of self dealing and even fraud and kickbacks as a way of personally profiting from public enterprises.

In sum, the idea that the managers of nonprofit organizations do not benefit from the profits of nonprofits is a myth. Further, because governmental policies of unfair competition isolate nonprofits from competitive pressures, nonprofit managers are even *more* likely than private-sector managers to benefit at the expense of their customers.

Promoting Equity. Subsidies and other special privileges enjoyed by commercial nonprofit enterprises are often defended on the grounds that CNEs help ensure a more equitable distribution of income and of services. CNEs are said to serve "our most vulnerable populations," groups that may not be profitable for private businesses to serve. They are, supposedly, largely charitable institutions that fill in gaps in service delivery left by profit-seeking firms. But the facts suggest that this is more a statement of an ideal than a description of reality. There is no evidence that the vast majority of commercial nonprofit enterprises generally serve the poor. While many nonprofits do have customers in the lower-income categories, many of them cater to a relatively affluent clientele, a practice called "cream skimming" when carried out by profit seeking businesses.

Although the terms "nonprofit" and "charity" are often used synonymously, only about 10 percent of nonprofits provide services to the poor or other groups in need. Many nonprofit institutions, such as Harvard University and local symphonies, primarily serve the middle class and the wealthy. There are hundreds of nonprofit "charities" engaged in commercial endeavors that are charitable in name only.

A strong case can be made that commercial nonprofit enterprises predominantly benefit the middle and upper classes, sometimes even at the expense of the poor. Many nonprofit hospitals, for example, devote few resources to serving the poor, even though that service is a principal justification for their tax exemption and governmental subsidies. Numerous law suits have been filed over the past twenty years claiming that *nonprofit* hospitals do not adequately serve the poor in accordance with the terms of the Hill-Burton Act, which subsidized the construction of many nonprofit hospitals. Nonprofit hospitals have routinely "turned away patients who could not pay, who did not have a private physician or who were on Medicaid. Critically ill patients were even refused admission to emergency rooms."[8] Many YMCAs have also largely abandoned their charitable role. One YMCA in downtown Philadelphia, for example, demolished a lower-income boarding house it once operated in order to construct a 15–story building with spas, racquetball courts, and swimming pools for its customers, who are primarily lawyers, architects, and local governmental employees. Oregon and Illinois courts have enforced federal tax laws that require an organization to have charitable activities as its "primary purpose" in order to be granted tax-exempt status and have withdrawn tax exemptions from YMCAs that have become essentially private businesses. The courts found that that only about 10 percent of the Y's revenues went toward charitable activities, and even much of that probably came from United Way contributions and other donations, not the profits earned on health club facilities.

Governmental enterprises rarely direct the bulk of their benefits to lower-income individuals, but instead tend to benefit the more affluent, who are generally more politically active than the poor. The federal government is engaged in literally thousands of commercial activities, and it is difficult to find more than a handful that benefit the poor. Not only is there no distinct advantage to the poor of governmental provision of these services, but lower-income individuals are made worse off because they must pay taxes to subsidize these enterprises. And to the extent that such governmental enterprises crowd out private businesses, the services are likely to be provided less efficiently and at higher cost. Thus, consumers are made worse off through higher prices, which ultimately impose a proportionately greater burden on lower-income groups than on the more affluent.

Accountability. Because nonprofits appoint community members to their boards of directors and solicit volunteers and donations locally, they are said to be more accountable to the public than are private businesses. It is claimed that nonprofits have an "ombudsman" effect that is absent in profit-seeking firms. But like the other rationales for the special privileges of commercial nonprofit enterprises, the accountability rationale is lacking on both theoretical and empirical grounds. The argument displays a fundamental misunderstanding of how our economic system works. Competitive pressures in product markets, labor markets, and markets for managerial control assure consumers that businesses will be reasonably responsive, regardless of who sits on an organization's board of directors. Because such competition is very weak in the nonprofit sector, if it exists at all, economic theory would predict that nonprofit enterprises are prone to be *less* accountable to the public than profit-seeking firms. The bankruptcy of the Washington Public Power Supply System (WPPSS) and the financial debacles created by off-budget governmental spending in the state of New York (see chapter 3), are extreme examples of the lack of accountability of nonprofit enterprises. The accountability rationale is also contradicted by the fact that governmental enterprises are generally less cost-effective and provide inferior quality services than competitive, profit-seeking firms. In addition, the numerous cases of fraud in government enterprises referred to in chapter 7 also makes the accountability rationale questionable.

Private CNEs are largely isolated from competitive pressures and, consequently, are less accountable than profit-seeking firms. In fact, CNEs are likely to be just as unaccountable, if not more so, than off-budget government enterprises, because they often are constrained by neither the economic nor the political marketplace. Eventually, government enterprise managers must face *some* political pressure to be accountable to taxpayers, however weak those pressures may be, but the managers of private CNEs never face an electorate. They are even more removed from public scrutiny than are government enterprises, even off-budget enterprises. Consequently, as discussed in chapter 4, many nonprofit hospitals seem to benefit primarily doctors, managers, and hospital trustees despite the prominent politicians and civic leaders on their boards of directors. Chapter 5 revealed how many YMCAs tailor their services to satisfy the preferences of their boards of directors, not necessarily the wishes and needs of the young people who are supposedly their main constituents.

It may be surprising to find that all of the rationales for special privileges granted to CNEs are contradicted by both theory and evidence. One might expect to find credence in *some* of them. We believe that the reason why the rationales are so contradictory is that some of them ignore fundamental economic principles, and others are not serious intellectual arguments, but weakly constructed justifications created to obtain legislative favors. All of the rationales ignore the fact that in a competitive environment the profit motive is a virture as long as personal property rights are protected by law. Those who support these rationales have never recognized that a profit motive exists in the nonprofit sector as well, but in a different form. There is no reason to believe that people sprout halos when managing a commercial nonprofit enterprise, nor that they grow horns when working in the for-profit sector. Perhaps the most overlooked point is that commercial nonprofit enterprises are arguably the *least* accountable of all forms of "business" enterprises because they lack either marketplace or political accountability. The one segment of the economy that is probably the *most* accountable to consumers, the small business sector, is increasingly crowded out of the market by some of the least accountable because of unfair competition.

What Should Be Done?

Although the rapid growth of the commercial nonprofit sector is relatively recent, the problem of unfair competition is not new. The federal government attempted to address the issue by passing the unrelated business income tax in 1950. The UBI tax was to limit unfair competition by nonprofits that had entered into commercial enterprises unrelated to their "charitable" purposes. According to a 1950 U.S. Senate report, "the problem at which the tax on unrelated business income is directed is primarily that of unfair competition."[9]

But the UBI tax is vaguely written and riddled with exceptions and loopholes, and as a result is not an effective control. More importantly, exemption from federal income taxation is not the only special privilege that commercial nonprofits enjoy. They are also exempt from state and local sales, property, and income taxes; they pay preferential postal rates; they receive special treatment from the federal government regarding unemployment insurance, minimum wages, securities regulation, bankruptcy, antitrust regulation, and copyright laws; and they are exempt from numerous state and local laws and regulations regarding franchises, inspections, and bonds. The Federal Trade Commission is prohibited from regulating the commercial activities of nonprofits, and many so-called consumer protection laws apply only to their for-profit competitors. Regulations impose heavy costs on for-profit firms, which works to the advantage of their commercial nonprofit competitors. Nonprofits also receive millions of dollars in subsidies from federal, state, and local governments, and they use tax-deductible charitable contributions from the United Way and other funds to help finance their business ventures. For any policy to deal effectively with unfair competition, it must address all of the means by which the competitive "playing field" is tilted in favor of commercial nonprofit enterprises. Even if the federal UBI tax was perfectly enforced it would still not solve the problem of unfair competition.

Competition *per se* by nonprofits is not the issue here; the issue is *unfair* competition. If competition by nonprofits was equitable and fair, both consumers and American industry would benefit. There is nothing wrong with nonprofits operating commercial businesses as long as they are subject to the same tax and regulatory environments as other commercial enterprises. There is even an argument to be made that unfair competition may not even benefit nonprofits. Many nonprofits have jeopardized their genuinely charitable functions by taking advantage of their legislative privileges to seek profits. By straying from their traditional and more charitable purposes, for example, several Oregon YMCAs lost their tax exemptions. Not only does unfair competition harm the owners, managers, and employees of profit-seeking firms and impose costs on consumers and taxpayers as well, but it also ultimately undermines the legitimate charitable functions of the nonprofit sector.

The Solution. The critical question is how to eliminate unfair competition without undermining the legitimate charitable and "public service" aspects of the nonprofit sector. The solution is straightforward: Nonprofits entering a commercial undertaking must form a for-profit subsidiary that must obey all the same laws and regulations that apply to for-profit enterprises. Again, it is not competition *per se* by nonprofits that is undesirable; it is *unfair* competition that is the issue here. An example is provided by Boston University's bookstore, which is a for-profit spinoff of the University. The bookstore probably still benefits from the university imprimatur, but its profit-seeking competitors are free to develop their own good reputations by offering high-quality products at competitive prices. By forming its own for-profit subsidiary, Boston University has all but eliminated the issue of unfair competition, at least as far as its bookstore sales are concerned.

There is no reason why government should discriminate against one form of commercial enterprise in favor of another. The "consumer protection" regulations that apply only to private, profit-seeking businesses but not to commercial nonprofit enterprises violate a basic democratic principle: that all individuals should all be treated equally under the law. If the regulations are socially beneficial and "in the public interest," then they should apply to *all* commercial enterprises, whether they are transparently labeled "nonprofit" or are for-profit enterprises. The regulations should be eliminated. They are basically unfair, and the fact that regulators are not willing to subject their own government agencies to them is damning evidence that they are *not* in the public interest.

There is much evidence that this latter alternative would be preferable. After surveying economic research on the effects of governmental regulation, Ronald Coase concluded:

> There have been more serious studies made of government regulation of industry in the last fifteen years or so, particularly in the United States, than in the whole preceding period. These studies have been both quantitative and nonquantitative. . . . The main lesson to be drawn from these studies is clear: they all tend to suggest that the regulation is either ineffective or that when it has a noticeable impact, on balance the effect is bad, so that consumers obtain a worse product or a higher-priced product or both as a result of the regulation. Indeed, this result is found so uniformly as to create a puzzle: one would expect to find, in all these studies, at least some government programs that do more harm than good.[10]

A case in point can be found in the physical fitness industry. Partly because of unfair competition by YMCAs and government-owned recreational facilities, many private health clubs have gone bankrupt in recent years. State and local governments have responded by imposing stricter regulations on private clubs (but not on nonprofit or government owned health clubs), giving governmental authorities a greater say in how the health club business is run. There is abundant evidence, however, that permitting governmental bureaucracies to have a hand in managing any type of business can only be bad for business. And what is bad for business ultimately costs the consumer. The costs imposed on private health clubs by regulation, for example, will be paid for through higher fees. Moreover, if more private clubs are crowded out of the market, the remaining CNEs will be able to exert a degree of monopoly power. This type of regulation is a misguided response to problems created in part by unfair competition. The appropriate response is not a regulatory crackdown on private clubs, but deregulating the regulators.

What Some States Have Already Done

At least forty-two state legislatures have passed resolutions recognizing unfair competition as a serious public policy problem. In 1981, the Arizona state legislature passed a law that went further than any other state in addressing this problem. Section 11 of the law states that

A state agency shall not engage in the manufacturing, processing, sale, offering for sale, rental, leasing, delivery, dispensing, distributing or advertising of goods or services to the public which are also offered by private enterprise unless clearly authorized by law excluding administrative and executive orders.[11]

Arizona state agencies are also prohibited from offering goods or services to the public for or through another state or local agency. Community colleges and state universities may not offer goods to the non-university community unless they provide an educational experience for students. State-funded educational institutions cannot enter competitive bidding for rendering goods and services unless there is a clear educational function. The law also establishes a Private Enterprise Review Commission that evaluates whether state agency functions are authorized by statue or prohibited by this act.

The Arizona law comes very close to implementing our proposed solution to the problem of unfair competition. How effective such legislation will be in Arizona and in other states that are considering similar legislation (including Louisiana, New York, Pennsylvania, California, and Washington) will depend on how well the law is enforced and on how many legal loopholes are permitted.

Some Taxing Issues of Fairness

It seems reasonable that nonprofits that operate commercial enterprises should "play by the same rules" as other businesses, but many nonprofits find the proposal objectionable. Some commercial nonprofits, for example, defend their special tax treatment and other special privileges on the grounds that they "earn" the privileges by serving a "public purpose." The "public purpose" rationale does not apply whenever there is unfair competition, however, since every private enterprise also serves a "public purpose," namely, providing the public with goods and services. It cannot be said that the private provision of goods and services does not fulfill a public purpose while the provision of *the exact same goods and services* by commercial nonprofit enterprises does. The public purpose rationale for the special legislative privileges of *commercial* nonprofits is not valid.

There is a subtle aspect of unfair competition that has not yet been discussed in detail. CNEs often claim that their special legislative privileges are justified on the grounds that the money they make is at least partly used to subsidize charitable activities. Even though competition may be admittedly unfair, they rationalize it on the grounds that the subsidies provide a public good. For example, a YMCA may sell memberships to affluent professionals, but divert some of the profits to provide services to lower-income youth. But if aiding lower-income youth or other worthy individuals is the objective of governmental policy, financing such programs through tax and regulatory policies that result in unfair competition is an inefficient and inequitable way of achieving those objectives. If the objective is to aid the poor, for instance, why not use general tax revenues, making the costs better known to consumers and taxpayers? Unfair competition hides the true cost of social policy. Furthermore, because it generates so many indirect and hidden costs, the costs may be much higher than direct income transfers or other more direct means of financing social policy.

It is not clear why most of the "taxes" to finance social programs should be paid, indirectly, by the the owners, managers, and employees of private enterprises which compete with commercial nonprofits. Tax and regulatory policies that place private enterprises at a competitive disadvantage are an implicit tax in that they reduce the income-earning opportunities of some individuals and transfer that income to the managers, trustees, employees, and clients of CNEs. Private business owners should not disproportionately pay for public goods that supposedly benefit all of society.

Unfair competition constitutes a discriminatory tax, and in the long run it is likely to reduce the government's ability to finance public goods by crowding private taxpaying businesses out of the market in favor of tax-exempt CNEs. Consequently, attempting to improve the welfare of the poor through policies of unfair competition is more likely to harm them than to help them.

A Concluding Thought

Even though much public policy in the U.S. is guided by the self-interest of politicians, bureaucrats, and special interest groups, a basic sense of fairness is still an important ingredient of public policy. For example, the overriding concern of the historic tax reform of 1986 was that the federal tax system was unjust. The tax-reform legislation was widely hailed as a victory against the "special interests" who had benefitted from the thousands of tax loopholes Congress had written into the tax code. Eliminating unfair competition would seem to be a natural extension of these efforts. There are no tax loopholes more blatant than the special exemptions granted to CNEs, which are just another one of the "special interests" benefitting from tax loopholes. While such loopholes comprise only one of the many legislative privileges CNEs enjoy, eliminating them would be a move in the direction of fair competition.

International trade policy is another area where fairness is an issue. Businessmen, union leaders, and members of Congress have complained that American businesses do not face a "level playing field" when competing in world markets. They charge that the field is slanted by the protectionist policies of foreign governments, which limit the access of American businesses to their markets, and by subsidies granted by foreign governments to their own industries. The foreign industries use the subsidies to compete unfairly in U.S. markets by "dumping" their products (much to the delight of American consumers) at "below-market" prices. American industry, it is said, can no longer compete in many of these markets, and members of Congress have proposed and enacted legislation intended to correct what they perceive as the unfairness of international competition.

American policymakers cannot credibly criticize unfair trade policies of foreign governments when their own policies create unfair *domestic* competition. Policies of unfair competition are responsible for a great deal of domestic "dumping" by commercial nonprofit enterprises. But the hidden subsidies that allow governmental and commercial nonprofit enterprises to underprice their profit-seeking competitors are ultimately paid for by American consumers, not foreign taxpayers. In short, by complaining about unfair international competition, American policymakers are throwing stones while doing business in a glass house. American policy makers should put their own competitive "house" in order before accusing our international trading partners of the same policy disorders.

Unfair competition is a pervasive and increasingly important economic phenomenon. We have only touched the surface of the relevant issues: A book could easily be written on each of the dozens of industries affected by unfair competition. We hope we have stimulated an interest in this timely and important public policy issue and have motivated others to consider the economic, political, and social implications of unfair competition.

Notes to Chapter 8

1. David L. Birch, "Who Creates Jobs?" *The Public Interest* (Fall 1981), p. 7.
2. Ibid.
3. Ibid., p. 8.
4. Ibid., p. 9.
5. Sharon Nelton and Karen Berney, "Women: The Second Wave," *Nation's Business*, May 1987.
6. Ibid., p. 23.
7. Ibid.
8. Michael S. Balter, "Broken Promise," *The Nation*, June 12, 1985.
9. Senate Report No. 2375, 81st Congress, 2nd Session, 1950, pp. 28–29.
10. Ronald Coase, "Economists and Public Policy," in *Large Corporations in a Changing Society*, ed. J.F. Weston (New York: New York University Press, 1975), p. 182.
11. Arizona House Bill 2148, Chapter 321, 1981 Arizona Revised Statutes.

About the Authors

James T. Bennett is an Eminent Scholar at George Mason University and holds the William P. Snavely Chair of Political Economy and Public Policy in the Department of Economics. He received his Ph.D. from Case Western Reserve University in 1970 and has specialized in research related to public policy issues, the economics of government and bureaucracy, and labor unions. He is editor of the *Journal of Labor Research* and has published more than 50 articles in such professional journals as the *American Economic Review, Review of Economics and Statistics, Policy Review, Public Choice,* and *Cato Journal.* His books include *The Political Economy of Federal Government Growth* (1980), *Better Government at Half the Price* (1981), *Deregulating Labor Relations* (1981), *Underground Government: The Off-Budget Public Sector* (1983), and *Destroying Democracy: How Government Funds Partisan Politics* (1985). He is an adjunct scholar of the Heritage Foundation, a member of the Mont Pelerin Society, and a member of the Philadelphia Society.

Thomas J. DiLorenzo is the Scott L. Probasco, Jr. Professor of Free Enterprise at the University of Tennessee at Chattanooga. He received his Ph.D. from Virginia Polytechnic Institute and State University in 1979. His research interests include public choice, public finance, industrial organization and public policy, and labor economics. He has published over 50 articles in such professional journals as the *American Economic Review, Economic Inquiry, Southern Economic Journal, Public Choice, Public Finance Quarterly, Policy Review,* and *International Review of Law and Economics.* His books include *Underground Government: The Off-Budget Public Sector* (1983), and *Destroying Democracy:*

How Government Funds Partisan Politics (1985). He is an adjunct scholar of the Cato Institute in Washington and an Adjunct Fellow of the Center for the Study of American Business at Washington University in St. Louis.